2400

W9-AYA-301

WITHDRAWN

Jonathan Edwards

Jonathan Edwards

AMERICA'S EVANGELICAL

PHILIP F. GURA

AN AMERICAN PORTRAIT

HILL AND WANG

A DIVISION OF FARRAR, STRAUS AND GIROUX

NEW YORK

Hill and Wang
A division of Farrar, Straus and Giroux
19 Union Square West, New York 10003

Copyright © 2005 by Philip F. Gura
All rights reserved
Distributed in Canada by Douglas & McIntyre Ltd.
Printed in the United States of America
First edition, 2005

Library of Congress Cataloging-in-Publication Data
Gura, Philip F., 1950–
    Jonathan Edwards : America's evangelical / Philip Gura. — 1st hardcover ed.
        p.   cm.
    Includes bibliographical references.
    ISBN-13: 978-0-8090-3031-6
    ISBN-10: 0-8090-3031-4 (hardcover : alk. paper)
    1. Edwards, Jonathan, 1703–1758.   2. Congregational churches — United
States — Clergy — Biography.   I. Title.

BX7260.E3G87 2005
285.8'092 — dc22

                                                                    2004008596

Designed by Jonathan D. Lippincott

www.fsgbooks.com

1 3 5 7 9 10 8 6 4 2

FOR DANIEL AARON,
MY "AMERICAN SCHOLAR"

He had an uncommon thirst for Knowledge, in the pursuit of which, he spared no Cost or Pains. . . . Tho' his Principles were *Calvinistic*, yet he called no Man, Father. He thought and judged for himself, and was truly very much of an Original.

—Samuel Hopkins, *Life and Character of the Late Reverend Mr. Jonathan Edwards* (1765)

Contents

Preface

This is a biography of an eighteenth-century American clergyman who by his own standards as well as those of his day had a disappointing—some might even say a failed—career. To be sure, for a decade Jonathan Edwards was well known for his leading a series of successful religious revivals. After these events had run their course, however, he found himself increasingly estranged from his church, so much so that he finally was dismissed from the pulpit. He then ministered to a small band of Native Americans in the wilds of western Massachusetts before being called to become Princeton's third president, a post he held for only a few months before his premature death. For the next half century his erudite theological treatises were kept alive by a small number of acolytes, but his thousands of pages of manuscripts could not find publishers. In 1800 most people would have concurred in Yale president Ezra Stiles's observation that Edwards's works soon would "pass into as transient notice perhaps scarce above oblivion." In the future, Stiles went on, the "rare character" who read Edwards would be looked upon as "singular and whimsical," and his works would constitute "the rubbish of libraries."[1]

Stiles's prophecy could not have been wider of its mark. By the

Civil War Edwards had become known throughout the United States and Europe as America's most famous and successful evangelical. His hortatory works circulated in scores of editions and reached hundreds of thousands of people through inexpensive reprints by the American Tract Society and other nondenominational religious organizations. His other theological treatises were found in multivolume editions of his collected works, and some of his more important manuscripts finally found publishers willing to trade on his immense reputation. So it continued through the late nineteenth and twentieth centuries: Asked to name the father of American revivalism, churchgoers of all denominations would as likely as not cite Jonathan Edwards. Today, just after the three hundredth anniversary of his birth, many of his works are kept in print by evangelical publishing houses, and since 1957 Yale University Press has labored assiduously to bring out a definitive edition of his writings. Jonathan Edwards indeed is America's evangelical. The fascination in writing his biography lies precisely in this disjunction between his ebbing reputation in the 1750s and his subsequent canonization, half a century later, into the chief exponent of American revivalism.

In 1854, in the preface to his biography of Edwards, the Reverend Samuel Miller felt compelled to speak to the nature of his project. In undertaking his assigned task, he "felt that he was venturing on the performance of a duty as arduous as it was honorable." When I began my biographical portrait of Edwards, I confess to a similar trepidation and sense of obligation as I considered how to present Edwards in my own way and for a new century. Miller had viewed his task as honorable because he sought "faithfully to exhibit one of the greatest of men, just as he was."[2] I would not have undertaken this work unless I believed that I could do the same.

Concomitantly, while as a biographer I must limn the context from which Edwards's ideas emerged, I do not treat my subject primarily as the purveyor of a religious system that many twenty-first-century readers immediately might find repellent. This is what Miller meant when he explained that in writing his book, he felt compelled "not to be the apologist of a party."[3] The Reverend David Sherman, another of Edwards's nineteenth-century biographers, similarly recognized the importance of presenting his subject on a broad canvas. "I know men have called [Edwards] a bigoted Calvinist," he wrote, but such critics had not taken his full measure. Rather, Sherman explained, Edwards was at home amid the "great questions of general truth, that in their labyrinthian windings puzzle the wits of the wise." Perry Miller, perhaps Edwards's most influential biographer, put it this way: "He was one of America's five or six major artists, who happened to work with ideas instead of with poems or novels."[4]

So, like Samuel Miller, I have tried faithfully to present the great man "just as he was." But throughout I have sought to communicate how what Edwards did and said in particular historical circumstances contributes to a deeper understanding not only of eighteenth-century British America but also of the religious life per se. As Sherman put it, Edwards "mounted above the special truths that busy most men, taking a flight loftier than the creed of a party or sect, into the sublime and glorious regions of catholic Christianity." He sought not "confirmations of a creed," Sherman continued, "but truth, in whatever field." I have thus sought to recover this Edwards, the one whom Moses Coit Tyler, in his 1879 pioneering study of colonial American writing, termed "the most original and acute thinker yet produced in America."[5] Around the same time, the Episcopalian divine Arthur Allen expressed a similar sentiment, remarking that Edwards "is always and everywhere interesting, whatever we may think of his theology."[6] Taking my cue from these biographers, who refused to treat their subject in a partisan manner, I unapologetically present Edwards as someone whose conceptions of man and the universe continue to challenge and enlighten us because of their universality.

Edwards's life, however, was not without its ironies, perhaps the most notable being that he did not have his greatest influence on subsequent generations in the way that he thought he would. He believed that posterity would remember him for his great theological treatises on sin, the will, true virtue, and other metaphysical topics that he had conceived even as a teenager and in which he believed he permanently put to rest any errant views of the subjects. Instead, his lasting influence came from his earlier writings, on the nature and meaning of personal religious experience, as they were republished and promulgated, beginning in the nineteenth century, for new generations. This does not suggest that the Edwards read appreciatively in the nineteenth and twentieth centuries is somehow a less sophisticated version of his towering eighteenth-century self. Rather, Edwards's profound analytical and lyrical gifts allowed him, even in work that he later regarded as marred by youthful enthusiasm and indiscretion, to write of spirituality in ways that transcended the time-bound controversies that had preoccupied him. But Edwards had to wait long for this other, larger readership that eventually placed him front and center in the history of American evangelicalism.

It is also important to remember that in emphasizing certain of Edwards's works over others, this large and catholic audience had only recovered an "Edwards" always there, even if one that his immediate literary executors and handpicked successors had chosen to deemphasize. By 1800 a large segment of American culture had realized the congruity of Edwards's life and work to their own experience and so adopted him as their spiritual godfather and his works as talismans for their own efforts to reform American society. Edwards's nineteenth-century readers liberated from his works concepts and vocabulary that forever changed their (and subsequent generations') understanding of spirituality and its manifestation in everyday life. That Edwards might not have approved of how posterity understood and used some of his ideas is not the issue. The marvel is that his work is so deep and broad that it can transform the understanding of personal religious experience across generations, denominations, and even cultures. This is the Edwards whom we must recover, he who was, as Harriet Beecher Stowe (herself the offspring of Edwardsean forebears) put it, "a man who united in himself the natures of both a poet and a metaphysician, and whose experiences and feelings were as much more intense than those of common men as Dante's or Milton's."[7] Like these artists' great poems, Edwards's works stand before us as grand ciphers that await each generation's explication of their truth.

In many ways, reading and thinking through Edwards is a lonely task, even as one knows that understood aright, Edwards demands that we leave the study lamp and walk in full sunlight, as he did in Northampton, Stockbridge, and Princeton. Although Edwards couched his vision in language that many today would find offensive or at least unpalatable, there is to it a generous acknowledgment of our common humanity. Edwards viewed all souls as irreducibly equal and capable of being touched by the "new simple idea" that subsequently transforms them into benevolent beings. History teaches us (as it taught Edwards) that such transformations are rare, but (again with Edwards) we must continue to believe that they are possible. Thus I do not write this book apologetically but rather in confidence that with the nature of true virtue set before us, we can only do more good in the world.

Philip F. Gura
Chapel Hill, North Carolina
2004

Jonathan Edwards

ONE

A Place in Time:
The Connecticut Valley
(1703)

GEOGRAPHY

In 1703 the Reverend Timothy Edwards and his wife, Esther, welcomed their sole male child, Jonathan, into a family that already included five girls and was to grow by five more.[1] For the previous nine years Timothy had ministered to Windsor Farms, the east parish of Windsor (later South Windsor), where he remained his entire career, which spanned another fifty-five years. One of the oldest towns in the colony of Connecticut, Windsor is situated where the Farmington River joins the great Connecticut River, New England's chief north-south waterway. This region, the Connecticut River valley, is one of the most storied in New England's history, in good measure because of Jonathan Edwards's long association with it.

For millennia the home of New England's native inhabitants, the Connecticut River valley by 1703 had been long settled by European colonists.[2] From its source in a ridge along the present-day United States–Canadian border, the Connecticut, or Long, River flows four hundred miles to the Long Island Sound at Saybrook. In the seventeenth century the river, a half mile wide along its lower reaches, was navigable as far north as Hartford, fifty miles above the Sound and a few miles south of Windsor. Farther north, rapids and falls, most notably at South Hadley, made travel by boat more treacherous and less appealing for trade. Despite such impediments, below the present-day Vermont border the river's banks were low and its current was manageable enough to encourage settlement. Of equal significance, to Native Americans and Europeans alike, the great river and its tributaries offered access to such distant regions as the Hudson River and Lake Champlain valleys.

The fertility of the alluvial meadows was as important to the early settlers as the river's navigability or its salmon and shad. During the spring thaw the Connecticut overflows its banks and deposits on its borders large quantities of fine, rich soil washed from its watershed. These constantly replenished alluvial lands are notably wide—as much as two miles across—as the river slows south of Agawam in Massachusetts to Windsor and Wethersfield in Connecticut, sites of the earliest settlement in the region. In such places the deep soil proved ideal for staple crops like wheat, rye, and corn, and the settlers frequently paid their colony and town taxes with the surpluses from their agricultural labor.

When Timothy Edwards's contemporaries spoke of the valley, however, they meant more than just the majestic river and its fertile interval lands. In the early nineteenth century Jonathan Edwards's grandson Timothy Dwight, who knew as much about the geography and history of New England as anyone, observed that for two hundred years the phrase *Connecticut Valley* had referred to a series of "expansions" where large tributaries like the Farmington, Agawam, Deerfield, Miller's, and White rivers met the Connecticut, made the terrain less rugged than in other parts of the region, and marked the location of clusters of towns and villages that defined the chief early settlements of the area.[3]

In 1703 the two most important of these subregions had at their centers communities pivotal to the social, intellectual, and religious development of the valley and of New England as a whole: Hartford in Connecticut and Northampton in what then was the Province of Massachusetts Bay. The larger, southern "expansion," where Jonathan

Edwards was born, began in the vicinity of present-day Middletown, Connecticut, continuing northward for fifty miles into Massachusetts, to Mount Holyoke and Mount Tom, near the South Hadley falls. This region encompassed Hartford, Wethersfield, Windsor, Suffield, and Springfield, among other communities. The other opening embraced Northampton, Hadley, and Hatfield and terminated on the north in Deerfield, at Mount Toby and Sugarloaf, from whose heights one viewed the Deerfield and Miller's rivers cutting through the rugged terrain to the east and west. Near Northampton, where Jonathan Edwards settled in 1727 as an assistant to his grandfather and made his indelible mark as a clergyman, the valley's breadth was close to twenty-five miles. Virtually contiguous and linked by the great river, these two parts of the valley marked separate spheres of influence. Even as most trade moved up- and downriver, politically Northampton had little to do with the colony of Connecticut. Rather, the upper valley's focus was Boston, 120 miles east and the capital of the province.

RELIGION

The Connecticut Valley was distinguished as much by its complex and volatile religious history as by its unique geography. Like their compatriots along the coast of New England, the vast majority of whom had ventured across the Atlantic to serve their religion, the valley's settlers were preoccupied with their faith. Most were English Puritans, heirs to the Protestant Reformation who had left England in the late 1620s and early 1630s rather than live with what they regarded as the incomplete reformation of the Church of England begun by Henry VIII (reigned 1509–1547). After the Catholic Church had refused to grant his divorce from Catharine of Aragon so that he could marry Anne Boleyn, Henry VIII severed the English church's relation to the papacy and installed the archbishop of Canterbury in the pope's stead, but he allowed the Church of England to retain many of Catholicism's trappings, both doctrinal and liturgical. Further change occurred during the reign of Edward VI (reigned 1547–1553), but his successor, Mary Tudor (reigned 1553–1558), a Catholic, severely repressed the reformers, executing many of the movement's leaders and forcing others to flee to Europe in what became known as the Marian exile.[4]

Elizabeth (reigned 1558–1603) restored Protestantism and accommodated reformers as much as she could without jeopardizing the support of those to some degree still attracted to Catholicism. By the end of her reign, however, increasing numbers of clergy and laity, influenced by those who had returned from Europe on Mary's death and who had been greatly influenced by their contact with Continental reformers, were seeking the church's full reorganization. In particular, they wished to abolish the use of clerical vestments and such symbols as the sign of the cross during services. They also objected to the continuing iconic stature of saints that had been canonized by the pope. Meeting resistance from the church hierarchy, they argued as well for a more decentralized church structure and a ministry that spoke more directly to the spiritual needs of the laity. In other words, these English reformers sought to purify the English church of all corruptions; hence their epithet, Puritans.

English Puritans also quarreled with their brethren in the Church of England on doctrinal matters, for their theology still reflected the Catholic emphasis on humanity's ability to repent and turn to God for forgiveness of their sins. On the contrary, Puritans adhered to the tenets of the Swiss reformer John Calvin, who in the early sixteenth century, along with the German clergyman Martin Luther, had fomented what became the Continent-wide challenge to Roman Catholicism.[5] Following Calvin, English Puritans worshiped an omnipotent and finally unknowable God who had irrevocably destined some individuals to heaven and others to hell, action justified because following Adam and Eve's primal transgression of God's law, all humanity was born into a state of sin. Christ's sacrifice on the cross, with his death the punishment for humankind's sins, satisfied divine justice, and now God saved whom he chose through his own freely proffered grace. God made known his intention toward the believer by radically transforming his or her heart, something that the individual recognized as a psychological experience marked by a turn from self-ishness to selflessness. To acquire such knowledge of the state of one's soul was to have experienced "saving faith" or "conversion," and Puritans devoted their lives to searching for signs of what they termed their election.[6]

The English Puritans believed that such individual experience was also intimately related to how one joined with others to practice religion and thus sought to reorganize their churches more in line with what they understood as the scriptural injunction for the "communion of the saints." Indeed, their migration to the New World was fueled in great measure by their conviction that membership in the church was not automatic. It did not come, for example, as a result of where one lived, as was the practice in the Church of England, where one's abode in a parish guaranteed membership in the local church. Rather, the Puritans regarded a church as a group of like-minded individuals volun-tarily "gathered" from the corruption of the world to pursue a more pure form of worship. The product of vigorous and unresolved de-bates in England over how such bodies were constituted, the Puritans, when they arrived in the New World, were agreed on little more than the imperative of removal from the utterly corrupt Church of En-gland. In New England they continued to argue many ecclesiastical matters but none more vigorously than how one became a member of their newly formed churches. Was mere assent to Christian doctrine acceptable, or should one have experienced the transforming power of God's grace, implying one's election?[7] Because church membership conveyed with it both religious and political status and privileges, it was central to a New Englander's sense of personal identity.

Many of the settlements in the Connecticut Valley originated in rancorous debates over just such issues.[8] In the late 1630s the region's first outpost, at Hartford, comprised colonists who had left Newtown (later Cambridge), Massachusetts, because of their disagreement with clergy and magistrates in the Massachusetts Bay Colony who had be-gun to require of prospective church members a personal narration of how God's grace had changed their lives. On this matter, Dorchester,

Massachusetts's minister John Warham and neighboring Newtown's Thomas Hooker disagreed with the emergent majority so strongly that they resigned their important pulpits and set out with their supporters for the Connecticut Valley across a hundred miles of wilderness. Believing such rules too restrictive, they required only public affirmation of sound doctrine as the requisite to church membership in the new towns they established, Windsor and Hartford, respectively.

Upriver in Northampton, settlement began even more problematically, for this community had delayed installing a minister until 1661, even though their choice, Eleazer Mather, had been preaching there for three years.[9] The largest number of this town's settlers also came from Dorchester, where Mather's father, Richard (who had succeeded John Warham), had had difficulty establishing a church in light of the colony's stringent new membership requirements. When he accepted Northampton's offer to be installed, Mather sought to bring some of his father's disgruntled parishioners with him, and as enticement he pressured the town to guarantee them choice property grants, a request that did not win him any friends among the established prominent landholders. Adding to the volatile mix, the town drew people from Hartford who had become dissatisfied with Hooker and others from Springfield, the commercial center of the upper valley, who viewed the new settlement primarily as an opportunity to further their economic ambitions. Predictably, in the decades immediately following the settlement of the northern part of the valley, disagreements arose primarily from the opposing views of church polity held by settlers from the various Connecticut and Massachusetts churches.[10]

THE HALF-WAY COVENANT

Clearly, there was need for a more authoritative statement on questions of church membership and its attendant privileges, which included participation in the sacraments of the Lord's Supper and of baptism of one's children. In the spring of 1662 the Massachusetts General Court took the unusual step of calling a synod, a meeting to which all churches were asked to send lay and clerical delegates, to sort out who should be given which benefits of membership. At one end of the spectrum were colonists who had acquired membership through what by then had become the predominant practice in the Massachusetts Bay Colony, by making a public profession of the way God, through his free grace, had changed their hearts to see and accept the truth of Christianity. Approved by the minister or a standing committee of church members, such an individual could vote in church affairs, partake of the two sacraments (the Lord's Supper and baptism) that the Puritans recognized, and could bring his or her children to the latter sacrament. Of equal significance, in Massachusetts, where the General Court limited the franchise to males who were church members, this status also conferred significant political privileges.

At the other end of the spectrum were those who, while members of local congregations by reason of where they lived, served what might be termed spiritual apprenticeships. Such Puritans, who had not yet had a change of heart that led to a genuine acceptance of Christianity, came under the church's watch and care but were prevented from voting in church affairs and participating in the sacraments. Because of their intellectual assent to Puritan doctrine, however, they were subject to clerical encouragement and censure. Always constituting a significant portion of any community, such individuals presumably hoped and prayed for God to allow them to accept uncritically the truths of Christianity.

But there was a complication. In the Massachusetts churches the children of church members were themselves guaranteed special consideration because of God's promise, in Genesis 17:10, to bless the seed of Abraham. Thus, as long as one parent was a full member of an established church, he or she could offer a child for baptism. The church nurtured these young people in the hope that as the offspring of those who believed that God indeed had conferred his grace on them and so strengthened their faith, they too would eventually know such favor and advance to full membership. But what rights and privileges did these probationary individuals have when they reached maturity *without* such an experience? Could *their* children be baptized?

After 1662 these children, of baptized but still unconverted church members, formed New England's new, third category of church membership, for at the synod a majority of the attendees voted to endorse these children's baptisms, even as they withheld any other prerogatives of membership.[11] Thus, like their unconverted parents, the "half-way" members could neither vote in church or civic affairs nor participate in the sacrament of Holy Communion. They occupied tenuous ground in New England society, constantly subjected to pressure to assume full membership.

Practical as this compromise appeared, to many it seemed a sleight of hand. The lack of unanimity among the delegates and of any legal mechanism to compel intractable clergy (or parishioners) to accept and institute the recommendations caused new fissures among the Massachusetts churches. Animosity was noticeable in the upper valley, where both Eleazer Mather and his neighbor John Russell of Hadley openly attacked what they regarded as this unscriptural extension of membership. Mather's resistance to the new policy caused no small consternation among his parishioners as well as among ministers in the eastern part of the Massachusetts Bay Colony (including his father, Richard) who sought agreement on the new measures to preserve their influence over the laity.

Mather already had antagonized Northampton's original settlers by his insistence on guarantees of land for his supporters among the Dorchester emigrants, and his difficulties only increased when after the town had requested his compliance with the halfway measures, he refused outright. For five years he held the line, but in 1668, with Mather weakened by what proved a fatal illness, the church voted not only to endorse the result of the synod but also to liberalize church membership by eliminating the need for any personal testimony and opening it to all morally upright inhabitants who assented to the chief points of Christian doctrine. In doing so, they followed the pattern already established in most churches downriver in Connecticut. Mather died before any new church members were added under these revised provisions, but he lived long enough to chastise his community in a series of sermons delivered in the summer of 1669.[12]

Across the river in Hadley matters were equally complicated, with Russell adamantly opposing the extension of membership privileges to the children of those who had been baptized but still did not believe that they had experienced God's grace. And Russell's voice counted, for at that moment he was the intellectual leader of the northern valley. Twenty years after the synod, he still bristled at what he regarded as its members' betrayal of New England's true principles. "It now stands them in hand, who were of the Synod of 62," he wrote Boston's Increase Mather, Eleazer's brother, "to looke to the maintaining of the churches from pollutions by unp[re]pared ones incroching upon full Communion in the Lord's Supper and voting [in church affairs]." Not coincidentally, in this same letter he also reported what he took as the logical conclusion of the synod's recommendations. Across the river in Northampton, Eleazer Mather's successor, Solomon Stoddard, had concurred in the congregation's wish to go beyond the synod's recommendations and welcomed to full communion any adult member of the community not openly a sinner.[13]

The lack of consensus in the synod's wake revealed the clergy's confusion about the scriptural bases of, as well as the practical rationalizations for, the new class of membership. When a minority of dissenters—well-respected men like the Reverend John Davenport of Boston's First Church, Increase and Eleazer Mather, and John Russell—resisted the compromise, the colonies witnessed the appalling sight of God's viceroys scratching and clawing at one another in ways never previously seen in New England. The Synod of 1662 thus created as many problems as it solved, some of which still dogged Jonathan Edwards almost a century later.

THE SHADOW OF SOLOMON STODDARD

When Timothy Edwards settled in Windsor in 1694, the valley had already seen forty years of religious bickering. To be sure, these disagreements reflected sharp divisions in New England's colonies, as their leaders sought to adapt the founding generation's ideas about church organization to new social conditions. With the arrival in Northampton in 1672 of Solomon Stoddard, however, matters took a new turn and set the course of the valley's religious history. After graduating from Harvard College in 1662, the year of the synod, Stoddard spent two years in Barbados before returning to New England to search for a suitable pulpit, which he eventually found in the valley.[14] Installed in Northampton, he promptly married his predecessor's widow, making him Increase Mather's cousin. He also began to cut a path through the ecclesiastical briar patch in which ministry and laity were caught, and he irrevocably molded the community his grandson Jonathan Edwards inherited.

Stoddard linked New England's often remarked spiritual malaise to the clergy's defense of what he regarded as an outdated and erroneous system of church government. In particular, he believed that the morass in which the colonists found themselves (most manifest in the extensive wrangling over church membership) had originated in his peers' misguided attempts to sustain religious fervor by methods no longer effective, particularly the concept of restricted church membership. In the first generation, when the New England Puritans' piety had burned brightly because it was fanned by hardship and persecution, many had experienced what they took to be the moving presence of God in their lives. They could speak convincingly of such matters, and church membership came easily, even under the stringent rules that the clergy had put in place. But by the 1670s, with the colonies economically well established and relatively safe from English interference, and piety not fueled in so dramatic a fashion as it had been among the first generation, Stoddard saw a need for a different, more inclusive definition of church membership.

In Northampton he discovered a congregation eager for him to move in this direction and especially to institute broadened criteria for the baptism of infants. In 1677, not satisfied that complicated distinctions among church members were at all scriptural (or expedient), he abruptly stopped entering into the church's record book members' particular status—that is, "full" or "half-way" memberships.

More radically, he soon allowed any member to participate in the Lord's Supper, regardless of whether he or she had offered an account of how God had worked to strengthen his or her faith, a requirement the Synod of 1662 had reaffirmed. By 1690 he had gone even further. Openly declaring that the Lord's Supper was an aid to conversion rather than just a sign of one's election, Stoddard argued that it should be administered to any who sought it as long as he or she was morally upright. To such individuals, he believed, meditation on the significance of the sacrament might bring home the truth of Christianity more convincingly and thus help a congregant know whether he or she had experienced conversion.

Three years prior to Edwards's birth, Stoddard sprang one more surprise. He stirred a vipers' nest with the publication in London of *The Doctrine of Instituted Churches*, a pamphlet so critical of New England's churches that supposedly no Boston printer would issue it. Herein he rejected the long-standing notion that New England should pattern itself on a New Testament model of churches of true believers gathered from the world. Instead, he reached back to the Old Testament to affirm the efficacy of the Instituted Church, an inclusive institution that offered the entire community the promises of the Gospel. Through regular exposure to preaching, discipline, and baptism and the Lord's Supper, any believer had reason to hope that God might work on his or her soul to strengthen faith. Stoddard's church, in other words, would not be divisive, as so many New England churches then seemed, but would open its doors to all who sought its ordinances.

In this pamphlet Stoddard lamented the chaotic situation in which New England's churches had found themselves in the wake of the Synod of 1662. Many parishioners, he wrote, now seemed "left at a loss whether there be any certain Rule to Guide" them or even if any certainty could be attained about such matters as baptismal privileges. Further, some were so confused by the incessant clerical bickering and ecclesiastical hairsplitting over these issues that they even willfully abstained from the Lord's Supper from fear of profaning the sacrament. Stoddard was convinced that most clergy misunderstood scripture when they argued for restrictive churches gathered from the world. "The Nature of the Church is the same under both Testaments," he wrote, but most colonists looked only to the New Testament churches as a guide because they had become so "exceeding Tenacious of the Traditions and Ancient Usages" of the New England churches, without considering that "a Corruption and Degeneracy" now prevailed in them.[15]

New England's problems thus stemmed from an embarrassing misunderstanding by the colony's founders, who in the eyes of their spiritual descendants could do no wrong. What the influential Mathers and other supporters of New England's established churches regarded as sacrosanct rules, Stoddard observed, were only "Blemishes and Errors" of the first generation of settlers, who in their zeal to establish a Puritan commonwealth on New England's shores mistook their own notions for timeless truth. Stoddard singled out for particular criticism the notion of requiring prospective church members to offer testimonies of God's confirmation of their faith. There was no such instruction in the New Testament, he wrote, and thus "We have no precept for it, we have no president [sic] for it. . . . There is no Syllable in the Word of God, intimating any such thing, neither is there any need of it." In this matter as in too many others, Stoddard observed, his contemporaries displayed an obsessive "Veneration for antiquity and adopt[ed] the sayings of the Ancient Fathers as Canonical." In place of this restrictive church membership, which made invidious distinctions among good Christians and gave so much power to those who attained membership, Stoddard encouraged a "National Church" in which all members of the community pledged to uphold Christian principles in exchange for God's promise of prosperity for them.[16]

The publication of Stoddard's radical tract was the first round in a vitriolic pamphlet war between him and Increase and Cotton Mather, the colony's two most prominent clergymen and now his relatives. In his rebuttals Stoddard pointed to his opponents' excessive and misplaced regard for the colony's first-generation leaders. In words that resonated for his grandson almost half a century later, Stoddard insisted that it was possibly "a fault and an aggravation of a fault, to depart from the ways of our Fathers," but it also might be "a vertue, and an eminent act of Obedience to depart from them in some things" if experience demanded it.[17] Hearing the shrill cries of the Mathers as paranoid attempts to reestablish a basis for their eroding authority, Stoddard reminded readers that "We may see cause to alter some practices of our Fathers, without despising of them, without priding ourselves in our own Wisdom, without Apostasy, without abusing the advantages that God has given us, without a spirit of compliance with corrupt men, without inclinations to Superstition, without making disturbance in the Church of God." Progress toward God's kingdom was assured by judicious examination of one's religious inheritance and redirection of faith, the better to align the church with the supreme logic of the Gospel plan. "Let our ancestors have as high a character as belongs to them," he concluded, but do not "look upon their principles as Oracles."[18] The true Christian Church was not to be realized through the worship of golden calves, even if they were called by the names of those who had founded the Puritan commonwealth.

By the time of Jonathan Edwards's birth Stoddard was the unchallenged intellectual leader of the valley, his ministry based on a refusal to venerate a past that did not serve the complexity of the present. His unique contribution to New England's development (not lost on his grandson, an assiduous reader of his works) was to tell the truth about the emperor's new clothes. He saw the New England churches as in constant evolution because of the demands of new social conditions. "Experience best fits men to teach others," he once declared, and experienced spiritual navigator that he had become, he understood how frequently a society might have to alter its course to account for the vagaries of time and chance above which no men, no matter how they practiced their religious beliefs, could rise.[19] Stoddard's legacy to his grandson thus comprised in part this willingness to challenge what others regarded as timeless wisdom.

Ironically, it also included a congregation that had come to regard Stoddard as little less than an oracle, like those against whom he inveighed.

THE EDWARDS FAMILY

The Edwards family had been in the New World since the 1630s, for Timothy's grandfather William Edwards had moved from England to the Massachusetts Bay Colony and then, around 1636, to Hartford, very likely with Thomas Hooker's contingent. There both he and his son Richard became successful merchants, moving from coopering (barrelmaking) to other business ventures. Richard's life was not easy, however, for he eventually took the highly unusual step of divorcing his first wife, Elizabeth Tuttle, after twenty-four years of marriage, during which her infidelity, coupled with an often remarked mental instability, severely tested his commitment to the marriage bond. The court that denied his first two petitions for the divorce granted his third, in 1691, and the next year he married Mary Talcott, who remained with him throughout the rest of his life.

Richard's son Timothy had successfully prepared for Harvard College with the Springfield minister Peletiah Glover and received both his A.B. and his M.A. in 1691, just as Stoddard was revising his notion of church membership. Three years later Timothy became the minister in the new east parish of Windsor, where he spent the remainder of his long life.[20] Windsor Farms, as the community then was known, stood across the Connecticut River from Windsor proper, and prior to Edwards's settlement its inhabitants had ferried themselves to the weekly church meetings in the larger town. Their decision to form a new church on their side of the river, however, was not greeted with unanimity; and when Timothy moved there, the precinct was still disorganized and had neither meetinghouse nor parsonage. By the time of Jonathan's birth, however, its hundred-odd families had begun to prosper spiritually as they already had economically; their rich alluvial meadows produced good crops of rye and Indian corn, which they sold downriver to Hartford and New Haven.

The house in which Jonathan was born was Richard Edwards's gift to his son when he assumed his new position. It was a plain two-story structure typical of the period, with the upper story jutting out slightly over the lower. A huge chimney, with openings into each of four rooms, bisected the whole dwelling. On the first floor were a combination of kitchen and sitting room and a parlor that also served as Timothy's schoolroom for his tutees. Upstairs were the family's bedrooms, with the younger children probably still sleeping with their parents; privacy was at a minimum, especially in a family of this size. At times the downstairs sitting room might also have housed some of the children. As the years passed, Timothy added vestibules and ells to provide more space.[21]

Here Timothy prepared his sermons and instructed the young men who came to him to prepare for the ministry. He was particularly well regarded as a scholar in the classical languages and in Hebrew, and at an early age his only son joined this tutorial, as did some of his older sisters. Jonathan's parents doted on him as the only male heir, and his five elder sisters (particularly Mary, with her penchant for theology) shared their own growing knowledge with him as he prepared for what everyone expected, a career in the ministry.[22] In this house, too, Timothy might have met with neighboring clergy to discuss and debate the ecclesiastical issues that animated the region. Although not a major participant in the church controversies that rocked the valley in the 1690s, Timothy, like many other younger clergymen, supported the recommendations of the Synod of 1662. But with a few others in the valley (notably, Westfield's Edward Taylor, posthumously to achieve fame as a poet), he resisted Stoddard's drive to open communion to all morally upright townspeople and continued to examine prospective candidates for membership. Although he occasionally quarreled with his flock (particularly about his salary), they respected his ecclesiastical positions.

Timothy's views on communion must have caused him some soul-searching, for in the same year that he was called to Windsor Farms he had married Solomon Stoddard's daughter Esther Warham Mather Stoddard, whom he had met while teaching school in Northampton. Esther's matrilineal pedigree was equally distinguished, for her mother was the granddaughter of John Warham, Windsor's first minister, and she had become Eleazer Mather's widow. She was remembered as "tall, dignified, and commanding in appearance, affable and gentle in her manner," and "a woman of distinguished strength of mind, of superior education, peculiarly fond of reading, and of ardent piety."[23] Like her daughters, Esther had finished her education in Boston. She also was hardy, living to ninety-eight. Marrying her, Timothy Edwards aligned himself with an extended family that controlled the economic, military, and religious life of the upper valley.

In this household there was always talk of religion and, in particular, of conversion, for with his father-in-law, Stoddard, Timothy Edwards shared a strong interest in and eventually a well-regarded success at evangelism. Yearning for times of religious revival when a heightened spiritual concern brought numbers of new members into the church, Timothy frequently preached on the need for God freely and generously to allow the sinner to accept the truths of Christianity. Indeed, by the early eighteenth century in the upper valley such sowing for spiritual harvest had become a local industry in which several other clergy, including Timothy Edwards's cousin William Williams, another of Stoddard's sons-in-law, participated.

Williams was an important contributor to the intellectual tenor of the upper valley. Graduating from Harvard a decade before Timothy Edwards, by 1686 he had settled in Hatfield, on the river just north of Northampton. After the death of his first wife in 1698, Williams married Christian Stoddard and thus joined the politically incestuous tangle of Connecticut River valley families, which now included his brother-in-law in Windsor.[24] Like Stoddard, Williams was a pragmatist unafraid to reconsider the constitution of the true church. In the early eighteenth century he did precisely that. Prompted by his observation that few took advantage of Stoddard's unorthodox ideas,

Williams argued in a 1707 published sermon that the clergy should try new tactics to bring townspeople into the churches. He stressed the importance of presenting the Gospel message to sinners and of providing a clear notion of the way God worked in conversion. Soon enough, he drew Stoddard to his point of view. Williams's affecting and uncompromising presentation of the great truths of the Christian religion complemented Stoddard's interest in how God worked to convince sinners to abandon any confidence in their own efforts toward salvation and so to trust in God's free grace to confirm their faith. Together these two men established a pattern of institutional response to spiritual awakening that Jonathan Edwards, trained by a father who equally valued conversion, found instructive and amenable.

EDWARDS AND THE VALLEY

At the time of Jonathan Edwards's birth, the Connecticut River valley had thus acquired a unique identity within New England, defined as much by the response of the region's intellectual leaders to ecclesiastical problems as by economic and social circumstances. To be sure, the valley's concerns were not all church-related, for frequently other matters impinged more viscerally than any controversies over baptism or communion. Since its settlement, for example, the region periodically faced threats from New England's Native inhabitants, incensed by the increasing usurpation of their ancestral lands. Such matters came to a head most memorably in Deerfield, just a few miles upriver from Northampton, in 1704, when Jonathan Edwards was only four months old. Without warning, the town was devastated by an Indian raid, and its minister, John Williams (William Williams's cousin and college classmate), and his family were carried off to Canada for ransom. Other encounters with Native Americans, no less frightening and violent, filled the region's early history.[25]

There were more mundane concerns, the lateness of a spring frost that delayed timely planting, say, or the severity of a winter that

closed the great river to traffic. There were worries about who represented one's interests in the General Court or whether there was an
adequate supply of legal tender to pay the militia. But for most early-
eighteenth-century New England settlers, religion remained the pre-
eminent concern. Theology was the undisputed queen of the sciences,
and the church the locus of one's personal and social existence. The
valley's inhabitants plowed, sowed, and reaped; traded surplus veg-
etables and grain downriver in exchange for imported staples; wrote
letters to their relatives in Boston or across the Atlantic; and, in what
news sheets they could secure, followed the course of warfare in Europe as Protestant Englishmen fought the French and other supporters of the Catholic Church. Above all, they contemplated the states of
their souls and, through assiduous study of the Bible, sought to understand the ways in which God worked out his plan in their very
lives.

The history of the Connecticut River valley is integral to the study
of Edwards, for the region's geography and institutions indelibly
marked him. Born into a region in good measure defined by its peculiar religious heritage and into an extended family counted among the
region's most powerful, with deep investments in the local and
colony-wide ecclesiastical debates, Edwards, whatever his genius, was
undeniably a product of his time and place.

TWO

Season of Youth

(1716–1727)

CHILDHOOD

Little is known about Edwards's early years. His playmates probably consisted of his six sisters, particularly Mary, two years older, and some of the eleven children of Captain Thomas Stoughton, who had married Timothy Edwards's sister, Abigail, and settled next door to the Edwardses. The Stoughton family eventually included no fewer than seven boys, some of whom must have offered Jonathan respite from sororal attention. Much of his time was taken by regular household chores, for during this period clergymen like Timothy Edwards, while provided with firewood by their congregations, still farmed their own land and otherwise prepared foodstuffs. There were opportunities for play, though, and from hints in Edwards's later writings, we know that he enjoyed the outdoors. The land to the east of his home, which sloped to a brook and then rose up a wooded hill, afforded frequent opportunities for Edwards's and his friends' outdoor games and explorations. Jonathan seemed particularly interested in the vast natural world that began right outside his door. When he was in his late teens, for example, he wrote a fascinating letter in which he described the phenomenon of "flying spiders" that he had observed in his childhood.[1]

A letter from Timothy Edwards to his wife, Esther, in the fall of 1711, when he was absent on military duty for the colony—he was chaplain to troops on an expedition against the French in Canada—provides a few more details of this early period of Jonathan's life, particularly the regimen that Timothy expected of his boy and girls. He asked his wife to make sure that Jonathan, then seven years old, continued his Latin lessons, reciting them to his sisters and in turn helping them "to Read as far as he hath Learnt," and also practiced his writing; Timothy had even left paper for that express purpose. He offered other instructions for the care of each child, imploring Esther to let her namesake and Betty "Take their Powders as Soon as the Dog Days are Over" and not to "Suckle Jerusha too long." Timothy also wanted his wife to make sure that their son "don't Learn to be rude & naught[y]," a topic he had previously discussed with her. He mentioned other homely but important details, including a new rope that needed to be put on the well pole. He closed by telling her that with his missive he included a note for forty shillings so that she would not "want mon[e]y in [his] Absence." If nothing else, this letter suggests that Timothy was a parent who, even with all his other duties, kept abreast of and greatly influenced his family's government.[2]

However else Jonathan spent his time in these years, from an early age religion was undeniably his major preoccupation. He opened an important window on this subject in his detailed "Personal Narrative," written in the 1740s.[3] Here Edwards dated his interest in spiritual matters to when he was around nine or ten years old, "a time of remarkable awakening" in his father's congregation. In that period of religious excitement, Edwards had been for months very concerned "about the things of religion, and [his] soul's salvation." He was moved to both private meditation and prayer and religious exercises with other children his own age (perhaps his cousins the Stoughtons). Seeking solitude for his religious exercises, he often resorted to "secret places" in the woods and with his schoolmates built, probably somewhere along the brook that ran below the Edwards home, "a booth in a swamp, in a very secret and retired place, for a place of prayer." Under the contagion of revival that swept his father's parish, Edwards's "affections seemed to be lively and easily moved." He wrote: "I seemed to be in my element, when engaged in religious duties."[4] His earliest extant letter, written to his sister Mary when he was twelve, reported the progress of this revival in his father's church, a time of "very Remarkable stirring and pouring out of the Spirit of God." Thirteen new members were added to the church roll. He also alluded to some of his sisters' suffering with the chicken pox, and he with a toothache, but his main concern was the renewed interest in religion among his father's flock.[5]

EDWARDS AT YALE COLLEGE

Given his interest in religion, it was only natural that in the fall of 1716, when he was thirteen, Jonathan Edwards left East Windsor for the Collegiate School of Connecticut (as Yale College was first called). He joined ten other boys, all between twelve and fourteen, the usual ages of students who commenced such study. Fifteen years earlier Connecticut clergymen, with the blessing of the Mathers and other Massachusetts colleagues disenchanted with Harvard College's drift away from an education based on Puritan tenets, had founded the new school. Intracolonial rivalries among the clergy and magistrates and a lack of funding, however, had prevented its sponsors from settling on a permanent location. At first the towns of Killingworth and Saybrook vied for its permanent settlement, but by the time that Edwards matriculated, the school also had a third branch, upriver at Wethersfield, where Elisha Williams, a member of the extended Stoddard-Williams family, served as rector. Here, only ten miles from his home, Edwards first traveled to continue the education begun under his father. After 1718, when a transatlantic gift from Elihu Yale assured the institution's stability, it moved to what became its permanent home, New Haven, and acquired the name of its chief benefactor.[6]

Through the Collegiate School, tiny as it was in its early years, the Connecticut clergy attempted to maintain their influence in the face of continuing conflict with and challenges from an emergent merchant class for which religion was only one of many concerns. This educational initiative dovetailed with others of similar purpose. In 1708, for example, at the initiative of Governor Gurdon Saltonstall (himself a clergyman), the ministry had endorsed what became known as the Saybrook Platform. This established both associations of churches in each of the colony's counties with oversight of local congregations and larger clerical groups whose responsibilities lay primarily in the examination and approval of ministerial candidates for churches in their jurisdiction. In addition, clergy were enjoined to meet annually for discussion of matters of mutual interest and concern. As had occurred in Massachusetts after the Synod of 1662, however, individual churches could accept these recommendations or not, even though their refusal to do so technically put them out of "communion" with the established churches. In East Windsor, for example, Timothy Edwards's congregation, protective of its own prerogatives, never approved the platform and thus set the stage for continual wrangling over his salary. For the most part, however, the colony's churches fell into line, and the example of the Saybrook Platform also spilled into the upper Connecticut Valley, where the Hampshire Association of ministers, led by Stoddard, assumed oversight of the churches in Hampshire County.[7]

The Connecticut clergy expected the leadership of the new Collegiate School to inculcate Puritan doctrine and promote the principles of the Saybrook Platform, and at first they were not disappointed. Both Edwards and his father welcomed this choice and the degree of stability it brought to what now was called Yale College. Rector Timothy Cutler, a well-respected Connecticut clergyman, oversaw a course of study that built on the foundation established in Timothy Edwards's home, and the young Edwards happily reported to his father that Cutler "keeps the school in excellent order, seems to increase in learning, and is loved and feared by all that are under him."[8] Cutler oversaw a rigorous program of study. When scholars applied for admission, for example, they had to show themselves "Expert in Latin and Greek Authors both Poetick and oratorial" and "ready in making Good Latin." Having satisfied the rector in this regard, the young men commenced their collegiate education the following September.

The days were long and full. Breakfast followed morning prayers, with classes through midday. An hour and a half of free time before afternoon classes followed dinner at noon, and later there were more prayers and Bible reading and explication. Supper came after early-evening recitations, with study hours from nine until eleven, when lights were put out. The regimen's deeply religious tenor suggested the institution's primary purpose, to prepare young men for the ministry.[9] First-year students, for example, typically spent Monday through Thursday studying Greek and Hebrew grammar, considered essential to their clerical training. In the sophomore year they also began work in logic, the two upper classes moving on as well to natural philosophy, mathematics, and metaphysics. All the students studied rhetoric, oratory, ethics, and theology, capstone courses to which all the others led. The texts were well established, standard at Harvard College as well as in English and other European universities where Protestantism reigned: Johann Wollebius's *Compendium Theologiae Christianae*, Williams Ames's *Cases of Conscience*, and the Westminster Assembly's catechism. In addition to working through these, students were often called on to dispute on different assigned topics, for practice in the logic that they pursued concurrently. The final examination for the B.A. was rigorous. A student had to convince the rector of his expertise "in Reading the Hebrew into Greek and into lattin and Grammatically Resolving said languages and in answering such questions in their systems of logic and in the principles of naturall philosophy and metaphysicks."[10] Edwards did so well that at his commencement in 1720 he gave the valedictory oration, in Latin.

Many students continued their education through the M.A., but this degree was based in large measure on two years' independent study and a public response on commencement afternoon to a *quaes-*

tio, a question in metaphysics or theology that the rector set. Delighted at the opportunity for further study in Yale's growing library, Edwards chose to stay on after his initial degree. He interrupted this period of intensive reading to preach to a Presbyterian congregation in New York City but, after eight months, returned to Yale for his M.A., awarded in 1723. The following year he again returned to New Haven, this time to assume the position of tutor, a post he held for two years.

"THE CONNECTICUT APOSTACIE"

Elihu Yale had provided for the college's financial security, but as Edwards worked toward his M.A., the infant college became intellectually traumatized. On Rector Cutler's watch, and presumably with at least his implicit consent, some of the faculty and students began to espouse so-called Arminian beliefs that circulated primarily through the books of a group of English clergymen who, beginning in the late seventeenth century, had overtly challenged Calvinist principles, particularly the doctrine of predestination, the belief that from creation God had established whether or not one was saved or damned. To the contrary, Arminianism, named for the Dutch Protestant theologian Jacobus Arminius (1560–1609), comprised the belief that men and women had it within their powers to choose, through the exercise of their free will, their eternal destinies. Many Protestants thought that such emphases smacked of the Catholic doctrine of salvation by good works rather than by faith alone, one of the principles over which the Protestant Reformation had been waged, and thus in 1619 Arminianism was condemned at the Synod of Dort. However, such beliefs, congruent with an early-eighteenth-century emphasis on the worth and dignity of man, grew in popularity in the Church of England and spread as well among freethinking latitudinarian clergy in other denominations who viewed the doctrine of man's inherent sinfulness as morally repugnant. Arminianism also gained new adherents among those who valued man's powers of reason and the remarkable new view of the physical universe, explicable in terms of empirical science, it allowed.[11]

This new emphasis on man's free will sent a shudder through most New England Calvinists. Its inroads at Harvard College and in the newly established Brattle Street Church in Boston had pushed some Massachusetts ministers to support the idea of a new college in Connecticut. Imagine Cotton Mather's horror, then, when in 1722 his friend Joseph Morgan, a minister in New Jersey with a son at the New Haven school, wrote that "some in Connecticut complain that Arminian Books are cryed up in Yale Colledge for Eloquence & Learning, & Calvinists cryed up for the contrary."[12] More astonishingly, Mather also learned that a chief proponent of such ideas was none other than Rector Cutler, who, with a handful of Yale tutors and students, had pored over Arminian works in the Yale library that were among a generous gift from the colony's London agent, Jeremiah Dummer.

This emergent group's main preoccupation was clerical ordination, for their reading had convinced them of the impropriety of a ministeral candidate's receiving it from his peers, as had become the norm in Connecticut. Cutler and the others believed that God's intention for this ceremony had been best preserved in the Church of England, in which bishops (church officials of higher rank) ordained new clergymen. Soon enough—this was probably why Morgan had written to Mather—the Yale group initiated with George Pigot, a representative in Connecticut of the Society for the Preservation of the Gospel, the missionary arm of the Church of England, conversations in which they expressed their wish for proper ordination. Pigot welcomed their interest and commitment, and the young men thereupon made plans to announce the results of their deliberations to the larger community.[13]

By mid-September 1722 the Yale rebels, who now included Cutler, tutor Daniel Brown, and Samuel Johnson, Jared Eliot, John Hart, Samuel Whittelsey, and James Wetmore, all clergymen in surrounding communities, were poised to act. At Yale's commencement, Rector Cutler dramatically ended his prayer with the words "*and let all the people say, amen*," a phrase directly from the Church of England's Book of Common Prayer. His extravagant gesture—he may as well have uttered an obscenity—announced the group's allegiance to the English church, and the next day, in writing, they made known their views to the college's trustees. Shortly thereafter they indicated their intention to seek ordination at the hands of an Anglican bishop. Ministers and laity across Massachusetts and Connecticut were aghast, and the phrase Increase Mather used to describe the events has stuck. It was nothing less than "the Connecticut Apostacie."[14]

Cutler, Johnson, and Brown sailed for London, where they were ordained the following spring, and the college trustees reacted by requiring of all its officers an examination in the soundness of their faith. Yale also had to replace Cutler, a task that dragged on for several years until Elisha Williams, previously a tutor at the Wethersfield branch of the college and now minister to Newington, Connecticut, accepted the position. Son of the highly regarded William Williams of Hatfield, Massachusetts, Elisha brought much-needed stability to an institution that many had regarded as New England's bulwark against further attacks on Christianity as it had been practiced by New England's original generation of saints.

Yale survived the great "Apostacie," but the religious ideas it announced were not readily suppressed. Moreover, some of the authors whose works Cutler and his cohort had used to reach their decision about ordination had broached other topics that, by the 1730s, proved even more threatening to the New England churches. As an undergraduate, the young Jonathan Edwards had begun to see firsthand the shattering effects of such unorthodox notions among his teachers and classmates. Like many of his fellow students and tutors, he had read the same authors who had inspired the apostasy and recognized the justness of some of their insights into the nature of man and the universe. Once he assumed his own pulpit he would have frequent opportunity to defend the principles of his faith. But still in his

teens when Cutler shocked Yale's commencement, he did not then realize that he would have to fight the specter of Arminianism until his
dying day.

NEW YORK CITY AND BOLTON, CONNECTICUT

During this turbulent period in the early 1720s Edwards prepared
further for a career in the ministry. His study for the M.A. culminated
in the late summer of 1723, when he returned to Yale to answer publicly his *quaestio* and, fittingly, defended the proposition that a sinner
is fully dependent on God for his salvation, a direct assault on the free
will the Anglican apostates so confidently embraced. In the previous
year he had spent eight months in New York City at a new Presbyterian church, which met at first in members' homes and then in a
building on Williams Street, between Liberty and Wall. Organized in
part by the family of one of his Yale classmates, its congregation was
tiny, having recently splintered off from the city's other Presbyterian
church over disagreement with its minister, James Anderson. Young
as he was, eighteen, Edwards found his work with the new church
greatly rewarding, and he later recalled that he had had a "most bitter
parting" with the family of John Smith (with whom he lived on
Queen Street), for he had "enjoyed so many sweet and pleasant days"
with them.[15] In this church Edwards preached his first sermons and
started the various notebooks that throughout his career served as
repositories of his thought.

New York City then already was a large, bustling community of
about seven thousand people, comprised primarily of merchants,
shopkeepers, and tradesmen, living on the island of Manhattan. Its
two thousand buildings, many of them made of brick and tiled roofs
(protection against the devastation of fires), stood along about a mile
of irregularly laid out streets paved with round pebbles. The city's
multiethnic labor force—New York, after all, had begun as a Dutch
colony—gravitated to the areas around the wharves, where ships

from all over the Atlantic rim brought and loaded cargo; Edwards's host, John Smith, was a leatherworker near these docks. The city's population worshiped at any of a score of churches, including two Episcopalian and two Dutch Reformed congregations. German Lutheran, Quaker, Moravian, and other fellowships also marked the thoroughfares.[16]

As much as Edwards enjoyed this experience, his father hoped his son would settle closer to home and so kept an eye open for positions in Connecticut. Shortly after Edwards's trip to New Haven for his M.A. degree, Timothy learned of such an opening, in a new church in Bolton, Connecticut, only fifteen miles from East Windsor. This congregation, composed of families that had moved from the Windsor area, was small, and Edwards had qualms about permanently accepting the pastorate, particularly since it was in a rural area so different from the excitement of New York City. He probably had hoped for a position in one of New Haven's churches or that a more permanent situation might open in New York, where he now counted many friends. No other position materialized, however, and he accepted Bolton's offer, leaving New York in the spring of 1723 to assume his new position the following November.

Jonathan was never keen about his work in Bolton. Moreover, his dissatisfaction led to conflicts with his new flock, though over precisely what is not clear. In his diary early in 1724, he reminded himself "not to spend too much time in thinking even of important and necessary worldly business," and a few weeks later he chastised himself that he had not been "as full and plain and downright, in my standing up for virtue and religion, when I have had fair occasion, before those who seemed to take no delight in such things," perhaps an allusion to a cool reception for his preaching.[17] In one of his extant sermons from this period, revealingly entitled "Living Peaceably with One Another," he addressed the problem directly from the pulpit. He urged "us of this congregation and this town [to] do what in us lies, as possible to live in peace with one another."[18] This irenic exhortation evidently had little effect. In May 1724, when Yale called him to serve as a tutor, he jumped at the chance, even though his acceptance derailed any immediate plans for the ministry.

Yale, still in disarray after Rector Cutler's defection, had not yet found a new leader. Edwards nevertheless found the opportunity attractive, for it returned him to the books that had already done so much to form his interests. But he had other duties beyond study, for Edwards was one of two tutors—Robert Treat joined him—who not only conducted classes but, before the appointment of a new rector, oversaw the institution's forty or so students. The schedule was grueling and took its toll on Edwards, who by September 1725 had fallen gravely ill and needed rest, a pattern that recurred whenever he was overworked. The arrival in 1726 of his cousin Elisha Williams as the school's new leader removed a large burden from Treat and him, but it took Edwards a while to resume his post as tutor. He recuperated at the home of a friend in New Haven; but three months passed before he could even travel to East Windsor, where he rested further at his parents' house. When mended, he returned to the college and served for two more years, until called to be the assistant to his esteemed grandfather Solomon Stoddard.

SPIRITUAL PROGRESS

Little is known of the young adult Edwards's physical appearance. He was tall and slender, probably about six feet in height, and not given to levity or the sorts of diversions that might have appealed to his contemporaries. If portraits from his mature years are any indication, his features were delicate, one biographer speaking of them as "of a feminine cast." During these years Edwards comes into sharpest relief via his own words, in a diary that he began late in 1722 and kept regularly into the period of his tutorship at Yale. At about the same time, he also began to frame a set of "Resolutions" that were to guide him in living the Christian life. Eager to pursue his intellectual interests, he also maintained a series of notebooks—on scripture, prophecy, natural philosophy, and other topics—that he continued to develop for virtually his entire life. These documents show us a young man who framed intellectual and spiritual questions that perenially preoccupied him.

Although in the 1720s Edwards began to write voluminously, his diary (kept primarily from 1722 to 1725) is unique, for never again did he record such probing assessments of his spiritual experiences as they occurred. What the diary makes clear is that in the years immediately following his graduation from Yale, Edwards's spiritual estate continuously preoccupied and unsettled him. Coupled with his contemporaneous "Resolutions," equally revelatory of his preoccupations, the diary shows Edwards yearning for spiritual security and struggling to control what he regarded as his untoward ambition for a suitable clerical position.

In its very first entry, for example, on December 18, 1722, Edwards fretted that he had not experienced "regeneration [that is, a sense that God had changed his heart to allow him to accept Christian doctrine], exactly in those steps, in which divines say it is generally wrought," an allusion to the kinds of preparatory admonitions that Thomas Shepard and other first-generation New England clergy had offered and that had been reinforced by Edwards's father in his home. He did not recognize a profound alteration in his religious life (he did "not feel the Christian graces sensibly enough," as he put it), and feared that what he hastily had identified as God's presence in his life was only what other, "wicked," men felt. Eight months later he was even more explicit. "The chief thing, that now makes me in any measure to question my good estate," he wrote as he prepared to receive his advanced degree in New Haven, "is my not having experienced conversion in these particular steps, wherein the people of New England and anciently Dissenters [that is, Puritans] in Old England, used to experience it."[19] Whatever his religious experience, he could not make sense of it by reference to the usual and accepted patterns.

Throughout 1723 such disillusionment was a constant refrain. "I find by experience," he wrote (in reference to his list of resolutions kept concurrently), that "do what I will, with never so many inventions, it is all nothing, and to no purpose at all," without a deeper sense that

God had helped him to accept the truths of Christianity. Aware of the self-deception with which churchgoers too easily masked their short-comings, he admitted that he sometimes thought that he had "a great deal more holiness" than in fact he did. Yet on other days he recognized how debilitating such self-denigration could be and rejoiced to find his piety "reviving." But ever suspicious of the state of his soul, Edwards frequently had to remind himself not to be despondent, for "'Tis a great dishonor to Christ, to be uneasy at [one's] worldly state and condition."[20]

His spiritual vacillations reached a critical point early in 1723, for on January 12 he recorded his solemn renewal of his baptismal covenant (his "self-dedication" he also termed it), initially made when he had joined the church. Since the late seventeenth century countless other New Englanders had similarly decided to reaffirm their faith.[21] Edwards promised that he would relinquish all reliance on his own power, accepting salvation by God's free grace alone. "I have been to God this morning," Edwards wrote, "and told him that I gave myself *wholly* to him." He continued: "I have given every power to him and have taken him for my whole portion and felicity, looking on nothing else as any part of my happiness." He further asked God to receive him as entirely his own, and the young man at the same time promised never "to act in any respect as my own." As Edwards later put it in his retrospective "Personal Narrative," he sought nothing less than to be "swallowed up" in the deity, to lose all sense of personal selfhood.[22]

A sense of his continuing failure to live just such a Christian life, as hard as he tried, was what had brought Edwards to this rededication. The diary thus painfully records a young man more often troubled than at ease, swinging between exaltation and depression. To his credit, Edwards recognized the tendency toward melancholy that such stringent self-examination brought on. "My spirits are down," he wrote in mid-January 1723, and "my resolutions have lost their strength." He added: "I differ today from yesterday, for I do not resolve anything today, half so strongly." He lamented his loss of vigor and his listlessness and was overwhelmed with melancholy. It got only worse. By the end of the week he was sunk so low that he was "almost discouraged from making any more resolutions." He asked: "Wherein have I been negligent in the past week?" And "How could I have done better, to help the dreadful, low estate in which I am sunk?"[23]

Such thoughts were not mere intellectual gymnastics but were initiated by very real external pressures, particularly the pressure to accept the call to the new parish in Bolton, a position his parents very much wanted him to assume. How telling, then, is Edwards's "Resolve," written in the late winter or early spring of 1723, in which he promised "never to allow the least measure of any fretting uneasiness at my father and mother." He continued: "Resolved, to suffer no effects of it, so much as in the least alteration of speech, or motion of my eye: and to be especially careful of it, with respect to any of our family."[24]

After his return to Connecticut that spring, again under Timothy Edwards's immediate influence and as he prepared to go to Bolton, Edwards remained disconsolate. Matters were tense between parents and son, for although Edwards had subdued a disposition "to chide and fret," he still recognized in himself an inclination "not agreeable to Christian sweetness of temper and conversation" and marked by either too much "dogmaticalness" and "egotism" or "a disposition to be telling of my own dislike and scorn." Revealingly, two days later he wrote that he understood what great obligations he was still under "to love and honor [his] parents." He also had good reason to believe, he reminded himself, that their counsel and education had been his "making." In July Edwards again recalled a child's duty to honor his parents and a month later, as he prepared to receive his M.A. at Yale, lamented that he had sinned "in not being careful enough to please my parents."[25]

Edwards's assumption of the tutorship in New Haven both rescued him from the position in Bolton and provided temporary respite from parental pressure. But the new job brought its own heavy demands. Unfortunately, Edwards's diary recorded only a few pages of this part of his experience and nothing explicit about Rector Cutler's proclamation of his Episcopal faith during the college commencement. The few diary entries he left indicated that as intellectually stimulating as his tutorship was, in terms of Edwards's spiritual state it marked a period of uncertainty and attendant melancholy. In the diary we see a young man who had internalized his search for grace through constant self-assessment and discipline and who believed that he had not yet assured his salvation. It also recorded someone defined primarily through his spiritual practice, for Edwards believed that complacency was a great impediment to the Christian life. Finally, given the ecstatic work of the spirit that he later associated with these years, the diary noted few moments of joy. Rather, its tone is diffident and sad, revealing a man often disappointed in himself and striving to be more than he thought he was. Among Edwards's last entries were those in which he reminded himself always to test the genuineness of his faith. He remained prudential, cautious, seeking ever-greater assurance of God's love for him.

In his "Personal Narrative," Edwards reported his earliest religious experiences and wrote that just prior to going to Yale, he believed that he had experienced spiritual transformation. But the fires of this awakening eventually guttered out, and, with them, Edwards's exuberance. Again he came to feel very "uneasy," at "the latter time of [his] being at college," when ill with what he called "pleurisy."[26] This bout of sickness pushed him to reconsider his spiritual estate and, in the retrospective of the "Personal Narrative," eventuated in what he finally regarded as unmistakably God's gift of grace that allowed him to accept without qualification all of Christianity's tenets. Importantly, as he recalled these crucial events, they bore little relation to the manner in which New Englanders hitherto had mapped religious conversion. His description of this experience, justly among the most famous of his writings, reveals instead how his deep reading in contemporary philosophy allowed him to redefine his understanding of the religious life.

Having made salvation the main business of his young life, one day (probably in the late winter or early spring of 1721, the year after his graduation from Yale) he found himself surprised that he now unreservedly accepted what he had so long resisted, the doctrine of God's utter sovereignty "in choosing whom he would to eternal life, and rejecting whom he pleased, leaving them eternally to perish, and be everlastingly tormented in hell." But as he reflected on his change of heart, he realized that he had not immediately recognized it as remarkable. Rather, he "never could give a account, how, or by what means" he was thus convinced, "not in the least imagining, in the time of it, nor a long time after, that there was any extraordinary influence of God's spirit in it." He continued: "Only that now I saw further, and my reason apprehended the justice and reasonableness of it." However this change of heart had occurred, there followed a "wonderful alteration" in Edwards's mind on this cardinal point of Christian doctrine. Rather than just having a conviction of its truth, he noted, he had a "delightful conviction," accompanied by a "sort of inward, sweet delight in God and divine things" that he had never experienced before.[27]

Novel too were the words in which, in 1740, he described this alteration. As Edwards's "sense of the glorious majesty and grace of God" increased, he remembered the appearance of everything as changed. There seemed "a calm, sweet cast, or appearance of divine glory, in almost everything." To him God's excellence appeared everywhere: "in the sun, moon and stars; in the clouds, and blue sky; in the grass, flowers, trees; in the water, and all nature." He now spent most of his time thinking about divine things and often walked alone "in the woods and solitary places, for meditation, soliloquy and prayer, and converse with God." The pleasure he took in these things was very different from anything he previously had experienced. His new feelings were of "a more inward, pure, soul-animating and refreshing nature" than anything he hitherto had known. Most important, he recognized that what he had earlier thought about religion had never reached his heart and thus had not arisen from "any sight of the divine excellency of the things of God; or any taste of the soul-satisfying, and life-giving good, there is in them."[28]

Edwards dated this remarkable change in attitude to the time between his graduation from Yale and his pastorate in New York, to the period, in other words, just before he began to keep his diary. Thus the spiritual turmoil that it recorded may have originated in his attempts to square his conversion with what, from childhood, he had been led to expect regarding its genuine form. This religious experience also helps explain why his time in New York meant so much, for there he lived in its afterglow, even as he struggled to understand it. While in the city, he recalled, he was sometimes greatly affected by "how late" in life he had begun to be truly religious. There too, in attempts to extend the joy he had experienced a few months earlier along the Connecticut River, he frequently retired to "a solitary place, on the bank of Hudson's River . . . for contemplation on divine things, and secret converse with God." He had "many sweet hours" in New York and much "sweet religious conversation" in the Smith family, with whom he boarded.[29]

In 1723 Edwards sailed from New York with heavy heart, keeping "sight of the city as long as [he] could," for his return to East Windsor might renew doubts about his vocation. But he also returned home with the knowledge of "an inward, sweet sense" of the work of redemption, "a calm, sweet abstraction of soul from all the concerns of this world." His religious experience had been so overwhelming that often he had "a kind of vision, or fixed ideas and imaginations, of being alone in the mountains, or some solitary wilderness, far from all mankind, sweetly conversing with Christ, and wrapped and swallowed up in God."[30] But what words could he use to explain such matters to his parents or the people among whom he settled?

INTELLECTUAL PILGRIMAGE

In the 1720s Edwards's life was marked not only by intense spirituality but also by great intellectual vigor, immersion in and cogitation over texts that permanently formed his conception of the religious life and provided him with a language to understand and express his spiritual experience. Further, this engagement with the life of the mind went hand in hand with his devotion to the cause of Christianity, for even in college he had begun to prepare himself to defend Calvinistic principles. This ambition manifested itself in a variety of ways: in his early sermons, in his catalogue of books and newspapers read, and in a variety of private compositions begun around the same time as his diary and "Resolutions." Among his extant manuscripts, for example, are volumes of topical notebooks. Some of these Edwards devoted to natural science, a subject that had enthralled him since his teenage years. Another, his "Miscellanies," comprises an immense collection of his thoughts on religion and philosophy. Others are labeled "Notes on Scripture," "Notes on the Apocalypse" (his thoughts on the millennial scheme), and philosophical observations on "The Mind." He added to these notebooks throughout his life.

Along with his earliest extant sermons (from the New York City and Bolton pastorates) these private writings indicate that by his early twenties Edwards had already identified his central intellectual interests. Moreover, he had discovered intellectual progenitors who provided his curiosity with spiritual purchase. Edwards, for example, understood that the new science, typified in the treatises of the polymath Isaac Newton but expressed more popularly in the works of those theologians who had influenced Timothy Cutler and the other Yale apostates, now posed the main challenge to Christianity.[31] If, as Newton and his followers suggested, the universe was best comprehended as an immense physical mechanism defined primarily by the perpetual movement of its constituent parts, what further place was there for God? To be sure, the utter complexity and beauty of this physical universal argued a first cause and sustaining power that could be conceived only in divine terms. But if the world was explicable scientifically, what did such concepts as redemption and damnation now mean? And most simply, if the universe was a self-sustaining machine, why should God intervene in it? Timothy Edwards's generation regarded the worlds of matter and spirit as intimately connected, a fact nowhere more terribly evident than in the crisis over witchcraft in Salem in 1692, when a belief in Satan's presence in the world had brought innocent people to the gallows. Edwards and his cohort, on the other hand, introduced at an early age to a mechanistic, scientific model of the universe, grappled with whether God still figured in human history and, if so, how.

Edwards was not alone in his struggle to reconcile faith with such new knowledge. But unlike the older Cotton Mather, who in *The Christian Philosopher* (1721) had awkwardly grafted bits and pieces of the new scientific thought onto traditional ways of describing God's role in creation, Edwards understood that the key to any reconciliation of science and religion lay in epistemology.[32] That is, John Locke, Newton, and their contemporaries had taught people to observe and understand the world differently, through empirical investigation. How did this affect one's understanding of the truths of Christianity? Burrowing into Yale's recently acquired collection of English books, Edwards began to formulate his answers.

Writers like Henry More and John Smith, who had resurrected Plato's idealist philosophy and ruled scholarship at Cambridge University at the turn of the eighteenth century, were particularly important to the young scholar.[33] Positing the notion that the physical universe was only the image or shadow of a greater spiritual reality and thus a communication of God himself, these Cambridge Platonists suggested to Edwards that rather than undermine Christianity, the scientific study of the natural world might actually make more visible the beauty and wisdom of God in disposing the universe as he had. When Edwards added to this his reading (probably around 1723 or 1724) in Locke, who posited that all human knowledge derives from sensory perceptions, he grasped how to speak to God's presence in the physical universe. To know the world scientifically, he believed, enabled men and women to know even more of God than they ever had.

Many passages in Edwards's manuscripts from this period explored questions raised by Smith and other philosophers and revealed the special vocabulary that he was developing to enable him to write on topics of interest and concern to contemporary thinkers. As early as 1721, in a lengthy entry in "Of Being," Edwards grappled with the philosopher Thomas Hobbes's proposition that Locke's empiricism led one to posit that the material world is the sum of existence, all that there is of reality.[34] With a logical acuity remarkable in someone so young, Edwards argued convincingly that the universe was sheer emanation of God's will (a topic he addressed definitively thirty years later in *The End for Which God Created the World*). Asking the reader to consider "nothing"—that is, what a world without light and motion would resemble—Edwards observes that "there would be neither white nor black, neither blue nor brown, bright nor shaded, pellucid nor opaque; no noise or sound, neither heat nor cold, neither fluid wet nor dry, hard nor soft, nor solidity, nor extension, nor figure, nor magnitude, nor proportion; nor body, nor spirit." What then becomes of the universe? he asked. Certainly, it can exist nowhere but "in the divine mind."[35] At any given moment, in other words, the universe exists purely as an exfoliation of God's will.

This deeply mystical understanding of the world captivated Edwards, and it led him in his early twenties to a remarkable insight. In his notes on "The Mind," he dwelled on "Excellencie" as one of the notions through which one can describe what God communicates through the natural universe. Beginning with geometric examples of right proportion, Edwards observed how all beauty consists "in similariness, or identity of relation." He continued: "This is an universal definition of excellency; the consent of being to being, or being's consent to entity."[36]

In a subsequent excursus on gravity, Edwards argued, as he had in "Of Being," that this basic law of matter suggested a central, abiding force that sustained the universe, that force being God, he "by whom all things consist." In a follow-up, Edwards proposed that love for all beings was best explained by, and perhaps identical to, the very same gravitational laws that held together the world of matter.[37] Here, as in so many places in his thought, the laws of physics mirrored the nature of divine being. Edwards had long trained himself to see in this way. In one of his early "Images of Divine Things" (no. 8), he noted, "We see that even in the material world God makes one part of it strangely to agree with another." Why, then, he continued, "is it not reasonable to suppose that he makes the whole as a shadow of the spiritual world?"[38] Anyone familiar with Plato's notions of identity, revived by his seventeenth-century Neoplatonist admirers, would answer this question in the affirmative. What gave Edwards's observations a different cast was how they reinforced his Calvinist worldview.

Another of Edwards's insights gleaned from his reading in contemporary English philosophy was directly related to his delight in the things of this world. Here More, Archbishop John Tillotson, and others had helped him refine his understanding of the place of the emotions (what Edwards called the affections) in the spiritual life. At ease in the world of nature, these thinkers regarded body and soul as integral, the very definition of the human creature. Thus they approved and encouraged preaching that raised one's emotional interest in salvation, as long as one remembered that, finally, only God wrought true conversion. Refusing to separate the logical "understanding" from the affections, these thinkers conceived humankind as complex psychological beings, thus opening a new space for the emotions in the religious life.[39] By the 1730s, when Edwards had to assess the significance of emotional displays of piety in religious awakenings, his exposure to such ideas had predisposed him to accept as genuine his parishioners' spiritual experiences.

This topic fascinated Edwards so much that in 1746 he devoted an entire book, *A Treatise Concerning the Religious Affections*, to it. But his interest in the affective aspects of religion had been visible even in his earliest accounts of his religious experiences. In the immediate aftermath of his newfound delight in God's sovereignty, he had found that holiness appeared to him "of a sweet, pleasant, charming, serene, calm, nature." It brought "an inexpressible purity, brightness, peacefulness and ravishment to the soul" and made it "like a field or garden of God, with all manner of pleasant flowers."[40] Here the mixture of the emotional and the spiritual is characteristic of Edwards's understanding of the religious life.

These early examples of quintessentially Edwardsean moments and locutions could be multiplied, but the lesson is clear. If Edwards the theologian did not spring full-grown from the college at New Haven, by 1726, when he had resigned his tutorship, he certainly had identified the topics that were to preoccupy him through his entire career. In his notebooks he confided the grandeur of his ambition. In his "Catalogue of Books," he recorded a wish to write nothing less than "A Rational Account of Christianity, or the Perfect Harmony Between the Doctrines of the Christian Religion and the Human Reason Manifested."[41] He also carefully planned how best to forward his reputation as a scholar. He reminded himself: "*Before I venture to publish in London, to make some experiment in my own country*," and thus "*to play at small games first, that I may gain some experience in writing*." Ambitious as he was, he cautioned himself to control any intellectual arrogance, for he wanted "not only to silence but to gain readers." He also recognized that no matter what fame he attained in New England, he always would be viewed as provincial. Thus the world would expect of him more "*modesty*" because of his circumstances— "*in America, young, etc.*"[42] By the early 1720s Edwards had thought long and hard about how to play to a transatlantic audience, so different from the farmers and merchants to whom he was to minister in New England's churches.

Within a decade Edwards's unique experience with revivalism made him bend his thought in new ways, but by his early twenties he had already deeply considered how the divine impinged on daily life. If God's work was indeed congruent with what the most advanced thinkers proposed about the physical universe and man's experience of it, the world was but an image or a shadow of the divine. In this sense, Edwards agreed with Archbishop Tillotson and other progressive English theologians: Christianity was "rational." To elaborate and defend this insight became his life's work.

LOVE AND MARRIAGE

During the early and mid-1720s Edwards furthered his relationship with Sarah Pierpont, a teenager whom he probably met in 1719 and whose brother James, Jr., two years Edwards's senior and also a tutor at Yale, he knew well. The daughter of a prominent orthodox minister instrumental in Yale's founding and the maternal great-granddaughter of Thomas Hooker of Hartford, Sarah was born to be the ideal helpmeet.

The details of this courtship are unknown, but his attention to the other sex was not yet attended with the romantic effusions that became characteristic later in the century. To Edwards and his father, as to most males in their culture, a wife was still considered, first and foremost, a suitable helpmeet and someone whose attraction consisted in her virtuous submission to husband and family. Further, Edwards, ever suspicious of the ways in which love for another was merely a version of self-love, was leery of too open a display of his feelings. It was, after all, only love for God that marked a truly virtuous person.[43]

That said, Sarah greatly impressed the young man. As the daughter of a prominent and pious family known to the Edwardses she seemed the ideal woman to support him in his earthly career as well as in his spiritual journey. An extant portrait shows her to be an attractive woman, as one of Edwards's early biographers put it, possessed of a "peculiar loveliness of expression" that derived from "intelligence, cheerfulness and benevolence."[44] So Edwards, despite his distrust of mere earthly affection, sometimes had recourse to the analogy between human love and the divine, arguing that the relation of wife to husband represented that of humanity to God. In a passage in his "Miscellanies" devoted to "Love to Christ," probably written at the time of his first interest in Sarah, he rapturously noted, "How greatly are we inclined to the other sex!" Nor, he added, does our love to God necessarily hinder this, for God "created the human nature to love fellow creatures, which he wisely has principally turned to the other sex." And even though Edwards addressed the larger point— that the "inclination which in us is turned to the other sex" in Christ was turned to the church—there is no mistaking the passage's relation to the young man's interest in Sarah Pierpont.[45]

So much had she won Edwards's attention that around 1723 he

wrote a beautiful apostrophe to her, worth quoting in its entirety: "They say," he wrote,

> that there is a young lady who is beloved of the almighty Be-ing, who made and rules the world, and that there are certain seasons when this great Being, in some way or other invisible, comes to her and fills her mind with exceeding sweet delight, and that she hardly cares for anything, except to meditate on him—that she expects after a while to be received up where he is, to be raised out of the world and caught up into heaven; be-ing assured that he loves her too well to let her remain at a dis-tance from him always. There she is to dwell with him, and to be ravished with his love, favor and delight, forever. There-fore, if you present all the world before her, with the richest of its treasures, she disregards it and cares not for it, and is un-mindful of any pain or affliction. She has a strange sweetness in her mind, and sweetness of temper, uncommon purity in her affections; is most just and praiseworthy in all her actions; and you could not persuade her to do anything wrongful or sinful, if you would give her all the world, lest she should of-fend this great Being. She is of a wonderful sweetness, calm-ness and universal benevolence of mind; especially after those times in which this great God has manifested himself to her mind. She will sometimes go about, singing sweetly, from place to [place]; and seems to be always full of joy and plea-sure; and no one knows for what. She loves to be alone, and to wander in the fields and on the mountains, and seems to have someone invisible always conversing with her.[46]

In addition to testifying to the degree of Edwards's affection, this pas-sage is remarkable for how he drew on the same vocabulary and lo-cutions that he used in his more theological and philosophical ruminations. It suggests that Edwards had developed a wholly differ-ent way of conceiving one's relation to the world, a mental apparatus that, when applied to the subsequent challenges posed by his career, indelibly marked his significance.

Edwards's position in New Haven allowed him to pursue the courtship, and early in 1725, when Sarah Pierpont was but fifteen, they became engaged and made plans to marry two years later. By 1726 the future they imagined together was upon them. The town of Northampton, where Edwards's grandfather Solomon Stoddard had labored for almost sixty years, sought to hire someone to assist its aged pastor.[47] Late in 1725 Israel Chauncy, the son of Hadley's minister and a recent Harvard graduate, filled the position on a temporary basis, and then, the following summer, Edwards was asked to consider it. From what the church committee knew of Edwards "by his preaching & conversation as also from his Character from other places," they were convinced he would do well in the job.[48] In late November Edwards was formally called to settle. He consented and the following February 15 was ordained in one of New England's most important churches. Thenceforth he was responsible for one of the two Sabbath sermons as well as a weekly evening offering. In July he and Sarah were married, uniting descendants of the most prominent clerical families in the Connecticut Valley. She assumed oversight of most of the family's temporal affairs and protected her husband's time and his health, paying particular attention to his diet. Their marriage was happy; people observed and admired the young couple for their "perfect harmony, and mutual love and esteem." He was fortunate to embark on his new journey with a woman who, as one biographer put it, "made their common dwelling the abode of order and neatness, of peace and comfort, of harmony and love, to all its inmates."[49]

In the autumn Edwards returned to the diary that he had neglected for years and again reflected on his spiritual estate. "Tis just about three years," he wrote, "that I have been for the most part in a low, sunk estate and condition, miserably senseless to what I used to be, about spiritual things." He continued: "Twas three years ago, the week before commencement; just about the same time this year, I began to be somewhat as I used to be."[50] This of course all changed with his marriage to someone whom he considered the paragon of true virtue and when he had the prospect finally of assuming a position that matched his clerical ambitions. But he still had much to learn as, over the next two years, he served an apprenticeship with the man considered nothing less than the "Pope" of the Connecticut Valley.[51]

[THREE]

Sowing for the Harvest:
Northampton
(1727–1734)

THE "PRIMATE"

When Edwards arrived in Northampton in 1726, Solomon Stoddard had ruled his church (and the upper valley) for fifty years. During his pastorate the community had doubled in size and significance, from one hundred to two hundred families, a prominence accentuated by Stoddard's openness to new ways of winning souls to Christ. Years later the Reverend Timothy Cutler conveyed something of what Edwards must have encountered when he worked with the patriarch. Stoddard, the Anglican convert noted, was undeniably "of a strong brain and thoughtful," but "Narrow and odd in his sentiments," Cutler continued. Northampton's champion was also "self-opinion'd, haughty, assuming, and impatient of Contradiction." Moreover, his "Stiffness"—that is, his stubbornness—was only increased by his "living remote from those he could improve by, or dared to oppose him" (presumably the Boston party of Increase and Cotton Mather and their supporters). But Cutler had to acknowledge what, despite such deficiencies of character, Stoddard had wrought. He was, Cutler said, "for many years the Oracle of the Country" and especially so in the valley, "where he lived long, had a numerous Family, and where a great number [of] the Ministers were related to Him by Bloud or affinity."[1]

An unnamed eulogist writing in the *Boston Weekly News-Letter* shortly after Stoddard's death in 1729 noted what struck most people: The Northampton minister was "well-vers'd in the religious Controversies" of his day. Like Cutler, this writer observed that even though this minister's "Station was in a remote Corner of the Land," his "Light and influence went out thro' the whole Country." Stoddard's presence, he concluded, was what gave Northampton "a Name and Reputation."[2] Benjamin Colman, one of Boston's most respected clergymen, concurred: Stoddard was a "*Prophet* and a *Father*, not only to the nei'bouring Churches and Pastors of his own County, but to those of the whole Land." He was, Colman noted, "very much our Primate."[3]

Much of the respect, grudging and otherwise, accorded Stoddard came from widespread knowledge of his debates with the Mathers over whether the sacrament of the Lord's Supper was an aid to or a reward for conversion. But beginning about 1710 and continuing up until his death, Stoddard also acquired a reputation as a highly successful evangelist who in the course of his ministerial career had had several noteworthy "harvests" of souls, occasions (specifically in 1679, 1683, 1696, 1712, and 1718) when greater numbers of people than usual evidenced a renewed interest in religious matters. As one parishioner put it, Stoddard had been favored with many times when "the Spirit of God so moved upon the hearts of his people, that it became almost a general cry of the place, 'What must I do to be saved?'"[4] By the time Edwards arrived in Northampton, Stoddard's success in this line was the envy of his contemporaries, and one of his works, *A Guide to Christ* (1714), became a touchstone for younger ministers who sought to emulate his pastoral skills. Northampton appreciated Stoddard's evangelical preaching, "chiefly suited to awaken Sinners, [to] direct Souls about the great work of Conversion, and to help Persons to judge of their spiritual State." [5]

Oddly, however, in his published works Stoddard rarely addressed his "harvests." To be sure, in such works as his *Guide to Christ* and *A Treatise Concerning Conversion* (1719) he treated how one brought more souls to Christianity, but only toward the end of a series of sermons, *The Efficacy and Fear of Hell* (1713), preached during his fourth harvest, did he broach the social significance of those occasions when "in a remarkable Manner," God "reviv[e]d Religion among his People." Hitherto Stoddard had regarded a religious awakening as an individual concern. But after 1712 he realized that an awakening, or harvest, also influenced the community as a whole. He began, in other words, to realize a revival's communal significance, as people felt "a common work of the Spirit on their Hearts."[6]

What did he mean? During times of spiritual harvest, he explained, parishioners often were so affected by their sinfulness that they reformed their "evil Manners" and engaged in religious duties with a new seriousness. Through such public displays of religious behavior, Stoddard observed, "a great Reformation is wrought," because people were disposed to lead morally upright lives and abided as much as they could by Christian tenets.[7] By witnessing or hearing of the spiritual experiences of their friends and neighbors, the unconverted assumed their social responsibilities more conscientiously. They also realized that despite their most sincere efforts, nothing they did could effect their own conversions. At that point, as they placed all hope of salvation on God's free grace alone, they were moved to the evangelical humiliation integral to the conversion experience.

In itself Stoddard's concern with the unawakened in his community was not extraordinary. Over the course of his ministry he had tried in various ways to bring more people under his watch and care, most strikingly in his sponsorship of a broadly defined Instituted Church and his belief that the Lord's Supper was a "converting" ordinance. After the harvest in 1712 he increasingly emphasized revivalism per se—that is, the encouragement of religious renewal as communal experience—as the most effective way to enlarge the church. With many of his contemporaries Stoddard shared the view that his age was degenerate, but he rejected the notion that this declension of piety stemmed from the progressive corruption of church principles. Rather than continue to bicker over church polity, Stoddard in his last two decades devoted himself to evangelical preaching; his aim was to bring the Word to as many people as possible.

Toward this end, in 1710, ever willing to rethink his principles,

Stoddard reversed himself on an important matter, a decision that may well have contributed two years later to his first significant harvest in more than fifteen years. Returning to a position he had first avowed in 1687 in his *Safety of Appearing at the Day of Judgment in the Righteousness of Christ*, he proclaimed the sacrament of communion preparatory to conversion rather than somehow effecting it. His career-long struggle to understand the role of the Lord's Supper suggests that he understood an unfortunate effect of the Half-Way Covenant. Rather than open churches to people who presented themselves for membership under the liberalized requirements, it actually inhibited the scrupulous from coming forward, isolating them from the church's watch and care. Declining church membership was the result. The Half-Way Covenant thus prevented some parishioners' participation in social and psychological rituals that provided an important sense of social identity and worth. "To this day," Stoddard wrote in 1708, "there be Four to One that do neglect the Lord's Supper." The reason was clear. Because conscience had "forbidden them to meddle" with the sacrament, members of the congregations felt as though they had "set upon thorns" and consequently "had a great deal of fear and disquietment of Spirit" over their worthiness to participate in so significant a ritual.[8]

Such distraught people were distracted from the sacrament's all-important symbolism. When they considered partaking of the sacrament, they did not think about what it commemorated, Christ's death, "but about their own dreadful venture in coming hither."[9] After 1710 Stoddard alleviated such insecurity and its attendant melancholy by opening wide the church's doors and inviting in all who lived morally upright lives and welcoming them to attend the Lord's Supper as part of their preparation for conversion. While the Mathers and their supporters maintained their right to judge the spiritual state of their parishioners, Stoddard prepared the soil for a new generation of revivalists. By emphasizing the experiential joys of conversion and insisting that no man could tell, absolutely, whether God had changed another person's life, Stoddard argued that all efforts should be made to help them prepare for Christ.

Edwards was well aware of Stoddard's theology and, whatever his thoughts about the legitimacy of his own conversion experience, was willing to walk the same path with his grandfather. Thus Edwards supported an open communion that went far beyond what the Synod of 1662 had counseled. He also became the youngest member of the Hampshire Association of Ministers, formed at Stoddard's instigation in 1714 on the model of the Saybrook Platform.[10] Members placed themselves under one another's watch and care on matters of doctrine and church policy and consulted with one another when there was a breach between clergy and laity in any member church. The association's semiannual sessions gave Edwards his first important lesson in the nature of clerical power and influence. He quickly learned that as much as the association supposedly created a deliberative body of equals, it was a highly politicized organization, one in which rank and privilege ruled, and at that moment Stoddard dominated it. Edwards was working on a daily basis beside an eighty-three-year-old minister whose charisma and political influence gave him virtually unchallenged authority. Stoddard's model of leadership was far different from any Edwards had thus far experienced and in clear contradistinction to the model he associated with his father, who was so often embroiled in petty disputes with his congregation that were not necessarily resolved in his favor.

UNCLE WILLIAMS

Stoddard was not Edwards's only role model. He also looked to other clergy in the Hampshire Association—John Williams of Deerfield, Isaac Chauncy of Hadley, Daniel Brewer of Springfield, and Nathaniel Collins of Enfield—with years of service to their credit. Most important of these, however, was his uncle (and Stoddard's son-in-law) William Williams, with whom the young minister now renewed and deepened his relationship. The Hatfield minister, himself the parent of several sons in the ministry (including Elisha, Yale's

rector), immediately contributed to the newcomer's tutorial in revivalism, for by 1726 Williams was second only to Stoddard in his
reputation as an evangelical preacher. Fifteen years into his pastorate,
Williams had made his own mark in the region and beyond, with such
success that the Boston minister Charles Chauncy, a younger contemporary and soon to be one of the central figures in New England's
religious history, thought him an even "greater man" than Stoddard.[11]

As early as 1693 Williams hurled himself into Hampshire County's
religious controversies with a treatise on church membership that
showed him clearly in Stoddard's camp.[12] But by 1717, with the publication of *The Great Salvation Revealed and Offered in the Gospel*, Williams
began to find his own voice. This work carried a preface by Benjamin
Colman, one of Boston's most respected ministers, and shortly after the
book's publication Williams rode to Boston, on a path the colony earlier had cleared for Stoddard's visits, to deliver *A Plea for God*, a classic
jeremiad of the period. Seven years later he had the honor of delivering
the sermon before the annual convention of the province's ministers.

Williams may even have influenced the shape of Stoddard's career.
For example, in his sermon *The Danger of Not Reforming Known Evils*
(1707), delivered just after his cousin John Williams had returned
from captivity among the Native Americans in Canada, Williams devoted several pages to neglect of the Lord's Supper. He danced
around the topic of whether the Supper was a converting ordinance
but suggested, cryptically, that within the valley people were "not so
well satisfied" about how it was administered. The divine injunction
to attend the Lord's Supper was "plain," Williams noted, yet "how
many are there who live from year to year in neglect of it" because
they pretend "a want of preparation for it and a fear of polluting it"?[13]
Was he referring to how his uncle's unorthodox ideas about the
Lord's Supper may have kept people from the communion table? Did
publication of this pamphlet signal Stoddard's increasing isolation on
this issue, so much so that within a few years he dropped his emphasis on the sacraments and focused instead on evangelism?

More important, in the decade prior to their young relative's arrival in Northampton, Stoddard and Williams struck complementary emphases. While in his published works Stoddard focused on preparation for conversion, Williams concentrated on persuading the clergy to preach sound doctrine in an affecting manner. In 1717 at his nephew Stephen Williams's ordination, Williams warned that when God sends "any into his Harvest, it is not to Loyter, but to Labour in it." A worthy minister's clerical labors never ceased, and he never could rest secure if his congregation needed chastisement or reformation: "[T]he Ignorant must be Informed, the Careless Quickened, the Erroneous Refuted, the Doubting Resolved, the Afflicted Comforted, Self-Deceivers Detected," and Satan's devices "laid open."[14] Here was a veritable prospectus for Edwards's own career.

Even more important, if young ministers like Edwards and Stephen Williams wished to bring souls to humility, and thus to Christ, their uncle counseled growth in "Wisdom, Prudence, and Experience." Paralleling Stoddard's advice in *A Guide to Christ*, Williams advised new clergymen "to Study Men, as well as Books," and above all to scrutinize their own hearts so that they would know "what is necessary to be spoken for Conviction, Direction, and Comfort of others." He pleaded for an experiential ministry that preached the Word "not as if a Man were telling a dull Story" but with "warmth and Earnestness of Spirit." The evangelist's work was fruitful only when he had an "Experimental Piety" and the "Presence of the Spirit in its Graces as well as its Gifts."[15]

Williams's exhortation to preach the Gospel uncompromisingly fell on sympathetic ears. Addressing the annual convention of ministers in Boston in the very year that Edwards became his neighbor, Williams explained to his auditors that they had to press the laws of the Gospel until all men saw the privileges of Christ's kingdom before them. More explicitly, ministers had to explain and state "solidly" the "great Truths relating to Men's Conversion and Reconciliation to God and [their] Comfort in Christ." In short, the minister had to preach experientially the "Great Salvation Revealed and Offered in the Gospel," the subject of Williams's major theological treatise.[16]

Williams filled the two hundred pages of this book with lessons from his thirty-year ministry in Hatfield. Most disturbing to him as he cast a backward glance over his career was the fact that although Christ had provided the means to salvation and offered it through the ministry, there were many people "nothing the better for it." Such people could not live without "Corn and Cattle, and Lands, or such worldly interests, conveniences, and honours" that others enjoyed, he lamented, but they could bear it well enough "to want spiritual and eternal mercies." Williams warned that if "to equal or outshine their Neighbours in Riches and Honours" was more important "than to have their Souls Adorn'd with Grace," New Englanders had every reason to expect such severe judgments as smallpox, earthquakes, and Indian wars. The only way to stay divine punishment was to embrace the Gospel, but it was, Williams caustically noted, "other News that men generally listen after." The only cries he heard were "What shall we eat, What shall we drink?" and not "What must we do to be saved?"[17]

More than any others in the Hampshire Association, Stoddard and Williams shaped and controlled the upper valley in the first decade of Edwards's ministry. By 1726 their powerful evangelism had become the talk of the province. Stoddard and Williams had reexamined the premises of their Christian labors and decided that to arouse men from their complacency they had to insist anew on the letter of Christian doctrine and present it effectively. Together, these two began to establish and promulgate patterns of institutional response to revivalism in their publications and through their contacts in the Hampshire Association. Most important, the two ministers encouraged an emotional response to preaching that could be channeled in constructive directions through a religious grammar that helped explain the revival experience. Their example was crucial to the young Edwards.

THE TOWN

Williams's observation that the present generation's besetting sin was inordinate attention to the world resonated powerfully in the Connecticut Valley—and even more so in Northampton—in 1726. He correctly singled out corn, cattle, and land as central to the region's interests, for as the town's population grew, access to fertile agricultural and grazing land became the chief pathway to wealth, which in turn devolved on those with the largest and choicest parcels, many of them descendants of the proprietors who first divided the common lands. Growing corn to fatten cattle for the burgeoning Boston market, the community's largest taxpayers demanded and received deference commensurate to their prominence in local and provincial politics.[18]

Stoddard's second son, John, was typical in this regard.[19] A Harvard graduate who had shown no interest in the ministry, he used his standing as one of the community's richest men to exploit many influential positions. His townsmen reelected him to the Massachusetts House of Representatives for virtually three decades, and royal governors appointed him to the Governor's Council, colonel of the Hampshire County militia regiment, and chief justice of the Inferior Court of Common Pleas. These posts effectively gave Stoddard control of the county's military and judiciary as well as a lucrative patronage system. Renowned for the luxury in which he lived, John Stoddard in the late 1720s exemplified the success of a new merchant and political class that vied for influence with the clergy.

Like his father, Colonel Stoddard brooked few challenges to his authority and had little trouble maintaining the support he had built over decades of public service. But this did not guarantee quiet in this western Zion. By the time John's nephew Jonathan Edwards arrived in Northampton, for example, social divisions within the town had become significantly exacerbated, in large part by the increasing scarcity of good land. Edwards himself provides the best glimpse into this bubbling cauldron, for in his retrospective account of the revivals that swept the region in the mid-1730s, he described at length what Northampton had been like at his arrival. At least for a generation, he suggested, increasing social instability had contributed to a potentially explosive situation.

After remarking on Solomon Stoddard's record of harvests, Edwards noted that during the two years he had worked with his grandfather before his death, most people appeared "very insensible of the things of religion, and engaged in other cares and pursuits," a description that fits with what his uncle Williams had observed in the region as a whole. More important, Edwards noted a long-standing "spirit of contention" between two parties in the town, always "prepared to oppose one another in all public affairs."[20]

Fifteen years later, in a letter to the Scots evangelist Thomas Gillespie in which Edwards tried to account for his own difficulties in Northampton, he elaborated the nature of this contention, remarking Northampton's fame for comprising people who were both "high-spirited" and "close, and of a difficult, turbulent temper." Moreover, even though the Stoddard family's extended patronage network had for the most part restrained the townspeople's rivalry, over the course of Solomon Stoddard's lengthy pastorate there had been "some mighty contests and controversies . . . managed with [such] great heat and violence" that the minister, "great as his authority was, knew not what to do with them." Indeed, during one ecclesiastical controversy, "the heat of the spirit was raised to such a height, that it came to hard blows"; a member of one group had assaulted and beat "unmercifully" the head of the opposing party.[21]

Some of these conflicts arose from the town's social structure. As Edwards told Gillespie, for a half century there had been "a sort of settled division of the people into two parties, somewhat like the Court and Country party in England." This division had its origins in the town's deeply stratified economic order. By 1700 the richest 10 percent of men controlled a quarter of the land, with the poorest 10 percent holding only 2 percent; and with little common land left, individuals at the lower end of the economic scale had little hope of bettering their station.[22] Thus Edwards accurately described the "Court" party as composed of those men "of chief authority and wealth, that have been great proprietors of their lands," and the other being those "who have been jealous of them, apt to envy them, and afraid of their having too much power and influence in town and church." Even in times of religious awakening, this division remained the "foundation of innumerable contentions among the people."[23]

Given Edwards's family connections to Northampton, he probably knew its history of ecclesiastical controversy, but he may not have
been aware of the social circumstances increasingly dividing the community. Moreover, when he arrived, the situation was not static, for
in the late 1720s Northampton had continued to grow in size and
significance. As the communal, agrarian ethos on which it had been
founded eroded, townspeople, replicating trends apparent in the
province as a whole, grew more and more concerned with their positions in an emergent market economy.[24] With loans now available
from colonial banks accepting land as collateral, men of a speculative
bent invested in more land and livestock while smaller landowners
could only look on. Credit was now a commodity like any other, and
the more of it one commanded, the more likely was one's success in
the new mercantile system. Many of the town's inhabitants now jock-
eyed for position in the complex provincial economy, their engagement in it marking them not as mere colonists but, rather, as provincials
seeking benefits in an ever-expanding commercial empire. However,
their young pastor soon enough forced another question on them:
Could one reconcile such self-centered behavior with Christianity?

ELIJAH'S MANTLE

Edwards did not long have the benefit of Stoddard's counsel. On
February 11, 1729, after sixty years in the same town and ministry,
the great man finally died, leaving his twenty-six-year-old grandson
to continue his work. Given Edwards's youth and inexperience, his
uncle Williams was asked to deliver Stoddard's funeral sermon. In
his moving address—in Boston, Benjamin Colman offered his own
eulogy—Williams compared Stoddard's death to "the felling of a
mighty spreading Tree in a Forest" that makes "all the trees about it to
shake" and in its absence leaves "a wide Breech [sic] where it stood,
which may be long where it is filled again."[25] Even as the assembled
crowd considered the young man whom they had chosen as Stoddard's successor, they knew that Williams was the most likely to fill

that breach, for no other valley clergyman commanded his prestige. Elijah's mantle had indeed fallen on Edwards, but he was still years from earning the respect it marked.

Not long afterward Edwards addressed Stoddard's passing in a sermon titled "Living Unconverted Under an Eminent Means of Grace." The young minister reminded his listeners how fortunate they had been under Stoddard's tutelage, but he also chastised them for their spiritual lethargy since Stoddard's last great harvests, almost fifteen years earlier. They who had so long had the luxury of Stoddard's powerful preaching, and previously had responded so well to it, now seemed "sermon proof." There were few places that had enjoyed "such eminent powerful means of grace," Edwards observed, yet all around him he saw "obduracy and blindness." God had sent Stoddard to Northampton because he had "an elect people here," Edwards reminded them, and the great man had gathered in many. Those who had resisted Stoddard's calls for reformation were now only greater provocation for God to unleash his wrath.[26] As his grandfather had done on so many occasions over the past sixty years, Edwards here indicted his flock's complacency.

The weight of the young man's new responsibilities quickly took its toll. In late April, emotionally and physically fatigued, he took a few weeks' rest in New Haven, but on his return he developed problems with his voice and could not resume a regular preaching schedule until July. When he returned to the pulpit in late summer, however, he seemed revived. Whatever the cause of his illness, it evidently did not affect Northampton's appreciation of his gifts, for by September his father had heard from a relative that the townspeople had "a great Love and respect" for his son and took "Great Content in his Ministry."[27] Edwards was ready to commence the first major phase of his career.

During this period he established routines that he kept for his entire life. He typically spent up to thirteen hours a day in his study but always punctuated this labor with some sort of recreation, usually walking or riding or, if the snow was too deep, chopping wood for half an hour or so. In the warmer seasons he commonly rode two or three miles "to some lonely grove," where he would dismount and walk for a while, sometimes jotting his thoughts on small pieces of paper that he would pin to his clothes for the ride home. He kept morning and evening prayers with his family and provided Bible instruction for his children. After the evening's prayer he often invited Sarah into his study to talk of family or religious matters, taking that opportunity for private prayer with her, "unless something extraordinary prevented" it. So that he could devote more time to the reading and writing through which he believed he could become most effective in his calling, he left the daily management of the household to his wife. By all accounts, she attended these matters expertly.[28]

The people of Northampton had to get used to a minister who could seem "stiff and unsociable" until one got to know him, for Edwards was "not a man of many words" and "somewhat reserved with strangers." Recurring to contemporary humoral psychology, his first biographer, Samuel Hopkins, noted that Edwards had "but a comparative small stock of animal life," by which he meant that Edwards was not physically imposing or hardy. "He had not strength of lungs to spare," Hopkins wrote, "that would be necessary in order to make him what would be called an affable, facetious gentleman." This characteristic affected his pastoral duties too, for Edwards was never comfortable visiting people's homes and making small talk. When his parishioners had spiritual concerns, he preferred to counsel them in his study.[29]

Edwards's pulpit manner reflected his constitution and habits. Nowhere was he described as an emotional preacher. His delivery was natural, one contemporary recalled, his voice not particularly loud. But he appeared in the pulpit "with such gravity" and spoke with such "distinctness, clearness and precision," in words "so full of ideas, set in such a plain and striking light," that he fully commanded his audience. He rarely moved his hands or looked up at the assembly, for like many of his contemporaries in the pulpit, he wrote out his sermons and read from his texts. In the heat of revivals he might be prompted to deviate from his notes, and when he did so, it was with "great propriety and fluency, and often with great pathos." On such occasions,

Hopkins remembered, Edwards's words were "attended with a more sensible good effect on his hearers, than all he had wrote." Such moments, however, were rare.[30]

As he gained confidence in the pulpit, Edwards evidenced a new-found willingness to grapple with what he was beginning to regard as some of his grandfather's errors in judgment, initial consideration of which may have contributed to his fatigue and illness earlier that year. By the early 1730s he had begun to suspect that some of the ill will that marked the community derived from some of his predecessor's unusual notions of church membership and its privileges. Indeed, entries in Edwards's "Miscellanies" and contemporaneous sermons that treated the Lord's Supper make it clear that he had started to rethink some of Stoddard's central premises even before his grandfather's death.[31] Edwards questioned whether Stoddard's was too generous an offer of the Lord's Supper.[32] He also reexamined the patriarch's willingness to regard uncritically a parishioner's emotional response to preaching as a genuine sign of conversion. At times, and particularly during the communal excitement of revivals, Edwards observed that "the imagination of the natural man" was more easily wrought upon "so as to imitate spiritual discoveries," more easily, in fact, than the heart could imitate "holy charity, and gracious inclinations, and a Christian spirit." In short, Satan might make a sinner think that he was converted when in truth he labored under sinful delusions.[33] Edwards counseled a more careful dissection of a convert's religious experience.

Edwards's difficulties with and refinements of Stoddard's thought were evident elsewhere. In his sermons in this period he often singled out the complacency of those who, because of their admission to the sacramental table under liberal membership rules, seemed uninterested in further cultivating their religion, an attitude that led to outright hypocrisy. In "Profitable Hearers of the Word," Edwards inveighed against those who pretended to holiness but really did not understand the Word of God. If a congregant's heart had really been changed, it would have irrevocably determined his "dispositions and

actions." Given what Edwards saw in Northampton, this clearly was
not happening on any large scale. No doubt thinking of those who,
knowing they were sinners, still partook of communion, he observed,
"There are many hypocrites that are of a very fair outside," people
who "do many things that are materially good, are very orderly and
regular as to anything that appears to the world, and are in many
things conscientious." But deceive themselves as they might, they
were "false Christians and mere pretenders to religion."[34]

Shortly after his grandfather's death Edwards revisited the topic
of spiritual complacency. In one sermon he took as his subject the
Arminian doctrines that had wreaked such havoc at Yale. His particular targets were those who outwardly disclaimed any "doctrine of
merit" in man's activities yet "secretly in their hearts" believed it. Dis-
avowing the "popish doctrine of merit," misguided Christians yet
thought that God "won't do fairly if he has no mercy upon them, seeing they have attended his rules for so long a time and have taken such
pains as they have done."[35]

In Northampton such spiritual complacency, and the self-
righteousness on which it was based, were linked to the people's ram-
pant backbiting, a consequence of the new economic order that had
emerged since the turn of the eighteenth century. Success in this new
world of capital and goods linking all parts of the Atlantic rim was
based on the principle of self-interest, which many contemporaries
now assumed was a positive trait, the foundation for all that was good
in human behavior. Edwards, however, lamented how coveting the
things of this world cut off people from their true interest, devotion
to God. In "The Dangers of Decline," preached in the spring of 1730,
Edwards decried the religious degeneration of the townspeople that
resulted from such an attitude. "What a general coldness and deadness is there about the things of religion!" he observed. "How different a face is there upon the country, with respect to religion, from
what there used to be," and given Northampton's spiritual heritage,
"How rare are instances of remarkable outpouring of the Spirit of
God in towns and congregations." How had this state of affairs come

to be? People were simply not interested in religion. Rather than talk about religion, they spoke incessantly "about their worldly business, about this and the other worldly design, about buying and selling." Or worse, they employed their tongues "in talking about their neighbor"; things of this world had become "the bone of contention."[36]

In August, in an attempt to shake Northampton from its spiritual lassitude, he visited these themes even more forcefully. "Envy," he explained in a sermon on that topic, "evermore arises from self-love and a want of loving our neighbor as ourselves." "Examine yourself," he directed each hearer, "whether or no you don't harbor within yourself an envious spirit towards any of your neighbors." Weren't people jealous of their neighbors' prosperity? "Don't it hurt your spirit and make you feel unpleasantly," he asked, "that they are under such advantages to get money; that they get it so easily and grow rich so fast?" Or that "such an one of your neighbors is advanced; he is put into offices; he grows great?"[37]

As Edwards admitted years later, larger, political divisions had sprung from such petty concerns. "There is generally much of this envious spirit," he noted, "and envious designs and actions, where there are parties in place." He explained, "If one party has the advantage of the other as to power and influence," the other will envy its members, and even more so when they could have their way in public affairs. Those that most fomented such factionalism were the "hottest with hatred, wrath, and strife, and envy" and acted only to enflame others. Tellingly, Edwards returned yet again to the communion ceremony in which so many obviously unconverted people took part. "So he that partakes of the Lord's Supper indulging of envy and malice in his heart," Edwards warned, "he eats and drinks judgment to himself."[38]

The lessons in this and other sermons were clear. Despite Stoddard's success as an evangelist, Edwards had inherited a church socially fractured and in spiritual decline. His grandfather's passing provided an opportunity to stir the community from its lethargy and redirect its spiritual interests. What Edwards did not anticipate, however, was the degree to which the town continued to revere Stoddard and view his principles as little less than canon law. To criticize him pointedly would be to jeopardize Edwards's own brief tenure.

"THE LATE LAMENTABLE SPRINGFIELD CONTENTION"

Edwards was temporarily diverted from his challenge to Stoddard's legacy by a controversy in Hampshire County over the appointment of a minister of purportedly Arminian tenets. As Edwards put it to his friend Benjamin Colman of Boston, despite Hampshire's growing social divisions, it had been "the freest part of the land from unhappy divisions and quarrels in our ecclesiastical and religious affairs," until "the late lamentable Springfield contention."[39]

The problem arose in 1734, with the First Precinct of Springfield's call to Robert Breck to serve as its minister. The church, having failed to hire any of the Yale graduates it sought, had settled on Breck, a graduate of Harvard College (1730). But some thought that the town was purchasing damaged goods, for Breck's career was already checkered. At Harvard, for example, he had been disciplined for serious misbehavior—the theft of books, one of his critics alleged. And in the Scotland District of Windham, Connecticut, where he had preached as a ministerial candidate before his call to Springfield, his interest in the thought of Thomas Chubb, who questioned the divinity of Christ, alarmed some parishioners and neighboring clergy.[40]

A majority of the Windham church gave Breck the benefit of the doubt and issued a formal call, but in view of the criticisms, he understandably decided to seek another position. The opportunity came when Springfield attempted to fill the post vacant since the death of longtime minister Daniel Brewer. Hearing of Breck's interest, members of the extended Williams family who ministered to a town near Windham alerted the Hampshire Association to the candidate's purportedly unorthodox views. Charged with certifying the orthodoxy of candidates for the ministry within the county, the association asked

Breck to obtain from clergy in the Windham area an attestation of the soundness of his faith. One of these ministers, Thomas Clap, of Windham's First Parish, long troubled by Breck's doctrinal views as well as his problematic record at Harvard, refused to endorse him.[41] Even though Breck tried to patch over matters, Clap adamantly refused to budge, and other clergy in the area joined him in refusing to attest to Breck's orthodoxy. In the autumn six members of the Hampshire Association, William Williams and Edwards among them, urged Springfield to reject the candidate. Three others, William Rand of Sunderland, Ebenezer Devotion of Suffield (Breck's uncle), and Isaac Chauncy of Hadley, disagreed with the association's recommendation.

However authoritative the association had seemed under Stoddard's rule, its role was only advisory. The Springfield church invoked its congregational prerogative and decided to press ahead with Breck's ordination. But when a disaffected minority brought the case before the association, a pitched battle ensued over a church's right to appoint its choice of a minister. Sidestepping the association, Breck secured the backing of eight clergy from outside the region. In October the Springfield church proceeded with the ordination, forming a council with Breck's three Hampshire County supporters and four other clergy from the Boston area. But the atmosphere had become so heated that before the ceremony could take place, some of Breck's detractors from the Windham area had him arrested for preaching heresy and returned him to Connecticut to answer the charges. Released on bond, he rode back to Springfield the next day and finally was ordained.

There ensued a three-year "pamphlet war" between the Hampshire Association and Breck's supporters, in which, at William Williams's urging, Edwards fired the final volley, his *Letter to the Author of the Pamphlet Called an Answer to the Hampshire Narrative* (1737). Breck's unorthodox religious views had been the opening volley in a battle now fought on ecclesiastical questions, specifically the authority of clerical associations to trump congregational prerogative. Edwards believed—and in this he had the support of a majority of the Hampshire Association as well as members of several other clerical associations in eastern Massachusetts—that ministers were accountable to their peers, who were best able to judge the soundness of one another's doctrine. On the other side, members of the Springfield church who supported Breck defended what they took as their right to private judgment in such matters.

The Breck affair came at a crucial time in Edwards's career, as he began to preach a series of doctrinal sermons critical of the very Arminian tenets Breck was charged with having embraced. Edwards regarded Breck's candidacy as another manifestation of the corruption that threatened the church because of the clergy's long-standing inattention to doctrine. To prevent further such catastrophes, parishioners had to be brought to a new awareness of the great truths of Christianity, a task at which Edwards began to labor assiduously. Within months the results of his commitment astonished the Christian world.

LANGUAGE AND VOICE

By the early 1730s Edwards had found his topic, the "great salvation revealed in the Gospel." Focusing on God's sovereignty, man's utter depravity, and the excellence of Christ, he devoted himself to awakening Northampton to its true spiritual condition. In this he was not unique, for other clergy, including a majority in the Hampshire Association, joined him in the defense of orthodox Calvinism. But the key in which he began to pipe his evangelical message set him off from his cohort, even as his distinctive notes prepared the way for his remarkable success as a preacher.

Edwards transformed his rhetoric so effectively because he regarded God's free grace as a divine illumination that irresistibly and irrevocably transformed one's experience of spiritual things. Long interested in this topic, he found in his early religious life, as captured in his "Personal Narrative," the experiences that directly yielded his mature theology.[42]

Edwards dated his conversion to his reconciliation to God's sovereignty, his realization that he could accept with full satisfaction what he had once objected to so strenuously. But he could never give an account of "how or by what means" he had become thus convinced, only now that his "reason apprehended the justice and reasonableness" of the doctrine and he "saw further." Edwards described this change as a wonderful alteration of mind that provided him with a "delightful conviction" of the truth of the doctrine of divine sovereignty and an "inward, sweet delight in God and divine things," a "new sense, quite different from anything that I ever experienced before." He continued, "The appearance of everything was altered," so much so that he spent virtually all his time in contemplation of the glory of God's presence in the world, in its people as well as its things.[43]

Scholars have long recognized that the language in which Edwards spoke of consciousness and cognition derived from his wide reading in contemporary philosophy, particularly in the works of the Cambridge Platonists John Smith, Anthony Ashley Cooper (the third Earl of Shaftesbury), and Francis Hutcheson among the "Moral Sense" philosophers; and John Locke and other empiricists.[44] In an early entry in his notebook "The Mind," Edwards tied Locke's understanding of consciousness to spiritual concerns; just as the philosopher had written that the "identity of person consisted in identity of consciousness," so too "identity of spirit" consisted in the same consciousness.[45] Now Edwards applied such propositions to his own spirituality. If grace was, in Locke's terms, "a new simple idea" and best described as spiritual effulgence or a "divine and supernatural light," then its effect on a human soul was incalculable as well as irresistible. Grace transformed all prior knowledge and affected all subsequent action.

In his earliest sermons and miscellanies, Edwards assimilated his spiritual experience to contemporary psychological theory. As early as 1723, reflecting on his own recent experience, he observed that the regenerate had a "certain intenseness and sensibleness" in their apprehension of divine things, "a certain seeing and feeling." It was "not the hearing of elegant descriptions of a beautiful face that can ever make a person have a sense of the sweetness and amiableness of the beauty" of it, and so it was in spiritual things. God gave to the elect, to "the immediate view of their minds," what others knew only by hearsay. The saint "sees things in a new appearance, in quite another view, than he ever saw before." He sees, Edwards wrote, "an excellency in God; he sees a sweet loveliness in Christ; he sees an amiableness in holiness and God's commandments; he sees an excellency in a Christian spirit and temper; he sees the wonderfulness of God's designs and a harmony in all his ways, a harmony, excellency and wondrousness in his Word."[46]

Such mystical thoughts preoccupied Edwards for the next decade. In an entry on "Faith, or Spiritual Knowledge" in his "Miscellanies," he explained how the mind truly apprehended what was "good or excellent," an understanding that occurred when a person was "sensible of the beauty and amiableness of the thing" and of his "pleasure and delight in the presence of the idea of it." This kind of "sensibleness," he wrote, carried in it "an act of will, or inclination, or spirit of the mind."[47] The implications were clear. One had to distinguish a "mere speculative and notional understanding" from one that "implies a sense of heart, or arises from it, wherein is exercised not merely the faculty of the understanding, but the other faculty of will, or inclination, or the heart."[48] True knowledge of spiritual things, even of mere natural things, could not but affect the heart and thus move the will. From here it was a short step to Edwards's realization that he had to renovate his religious vocabulary so that his people could understand all the cardinal points of Christian doctrine. To impress his listeners with the truth of the Gospel, Edwards fastened words to sensible things.

By 1733 he had several years of such powerful preaching behind him, and his reputation for it had begun to grow. In the summer of 1731, for example, after he had preached *God Glorified in Man's Dependence* (a sermon first delivered in Northampton the previous fall) to a clerical assembly in Boston, those in the audience were so taken that they urged and secured its publication, Edwards's first. If any in the colony doubted the young man's desire to preach uncompromisingly Christian doctrine, this effort, centered on the doctrine that "there is an absolute and universal dependence of the redeemed on God," set them straight.[49]

At this early juncture Edwards also invoked what had already become his shibboleths. Nowhere is his unique voice more evident than in *A Divine and Supernatural Light*, first delivered in Northampton in 1733 and published in Boston the next year.[50] Here he distilled a decade's cogitation on the experiential dimension of grace into a sermon on the transforming power of divine knowledge. Edwards's doctrine was as unexceptional as it was orthodox. "There is such a thing," he reported, "as a spiritual light, immediately imparted to the soul by God, of a different nature from any that is obtained by natural means." But through his new vocabulary he brought understanding of the doctrine to another dimension. God acts in the mind of one of the elect, Edwards claimed, "as an indwelling vital principle." To put it another way, God "unites himself with the mind of a saint, takes him for his temple, actuates and influences him as a new supernatural principle of life and action." But, Edwards went on, this spiritual light did not suggest any new "proposition to the mind"; it presented "no new thing of God, or Christ, or another world" but gave only "a due apprehension of those things that are taught in the Word of God."[51] Just as Edwards had seen "further" and so finally comprehended how right and natural the doctrine of divine sovereignty was, so too would the saint who similarly knew a divine and supernatural light.

At its core, this light provided "a true sense of the divine excellency of the things revealed in the Word of God, and a conviction of the truth and reality of them, thence arising." When someone was spiritually enlightened, he "truly apprehend[ed] and [saw] it, or ha[d] a sense of it." This experience consisted "in the sense of the heart," for when there was "a sense of the beauty, amiableness, and sweetness of a thing," the heart became "sensible of pleasure and delight in the presence of it." The divine and supernatural light, in other words, affected the "heart" and "effectually influence[d] the inclination, and change[d] the nature of the soul." As Locke had argued, just as any new sensory experience became irrevocably part of one's consciousness, inscribed on it so that all subsequent experience was understood in relation to it, so the experience of grace reoriented the heart of the saint and with it his inclination or will. This light, Edwards concluded, "as it reache[d] to the bottom of the heart," changed its nature and effectually disposed one to goodness. The fruit of conversion became "an universal holiness of life."[52]

Irresistible in its force, overwhelming in its effect, unlike anything a "natural" man knew, the divine and supernatural light that marked the presence of God in a believer was, however, not at all mysterious. It appeared and worked rationally, according to the laws that governed the scientifically verifiable universe. It was but a new, simple idea, a "true sense of the divine excellency" of the Gospel. In the 1730s Edwards began to work through other key points of Christian doctrine with just such novel insight, providing experiential and affective referents for topics that hitherto had fallen on deaf ears. Ever alert to the stirrings of grace that his grandfather Stoddard had worked so diligently to nurture, Edwards preached the unadulterated Gospel as he experienced it. Within a few years the results of his effort permanently altered America's religious history.

FOUR

The Chief Scene of These Wonders: Hampshire County

(1734-1739)

STIRRINGS

By the mid-1730s Edwards's doctrinal preaching had produced results. Writing to a friend in London late in the spring of 1735, the Reverend Timothy Cutler, now installed at King's Chapel, Boston, reported that "the Calvinistical scheme is in perfection about 100 miles from this place." There, in the Connecticut Valley, "Conversions are talked of, *ad nauseam usque*, [and] sixty in a place undergo the work at once." The colonists' behavior was truly remarkable to him. "Sadness and horror seize them, and hold them some days," he wrote, and then they feel an "inward joy" that often first shows itself "in laughing at the Meeting." Others are "sad for want of experiencing this work," which "takes up for the present the thoughts and talk of that Country." Everywhere "[t]he canting question trumped about is, *are you gone through*? i.e. Conversion."[1] Good Anglican that he was, Cutler found the whole matter disgusting, more evidence of the need for a stronger church presence in the colonies.

Since the past December the valley had experienced a remarkable religious outpouring. Subsequently known as the Little Awakening, this series of events originated in Edwards's congregation and spread rapidly to the surrounding communities. From the first, this religious excitement had a different dynamic from Stoddard's periodic harvests or the more local spiritual renewals fitfully reported after such events as the great New England earthquake of 1727 or outbreaks of diphtheria.[2] "Here was no storm, no earthquake, no inundation of water, no desolation by fire, no pestilence or other sweeping distemper, nor any cruel invasion by their Indian neighbors, that might force the inhabitants into a serious thoughtfulness," two English observers wrote. With "no such awful and threatening providence" attending the events, they could attribute them only to "the immediate hand of God."[3] As news of the revivals spread, Edwards found himself the center of attention in ways he could not have imagined a few months earlier.

How did all this come about? In the months before December 1734 Edwards had continued to preach on "the Calvinistical scheme," most notably on a "divine and supernatural light." But he also addressed more pastoral topics, some aimed specifically at the young people under his guidance who had grown increasingly concerned about their mortality. Instead of the usual neglect of religion that more and more characterized provincial youth, they flocked to Edwards for advice about their spiritual concerns. Surprised at this sudden unusual "flexibleness" in the young people's behavior, he began to single them out for injunction. He condemned their neglect of the Sabbath, particularly their use of it as an occasion for "diversion and mirth, taking of these times to get together in companies, and spending of them from time to time, as though they were time most fit and suitable of any times whatsoever to be devoted to divertisement."[4] What parental exhortations had been unable to do, Edwards finally accomplished. The young people began to comply with his counsel and use the Sabbath more profitably.

The youths' earlier intransigence had its origins in Northampton's lack of surplus land for those sons who wanted to set up housekeeping on their own. With no more common lands for dispersal after 1700 and even home lots increasingly scarce, the town's young men were forced to wait for their inheritances or anticipate smaller portions of land divided from generous parents' holdings. This placed young people, including women who wished to marry, in a period of prolonged dependence; hitherto by their late teens they might have assumed adult roles in the community. In this unsettled state, eager for independence but prevented by economic circumstances from attaining it, Northampton's youths were increasingly receptive to Edwards's preaching, because conversion and church membership offered another way to enter adult society (albeit without attendant economic independence).[5]

More immediately, Edwards's younger parishioners were impressed by recent tragedies. In April, in an outlying village, a young man "in the bloom of his youth" had been violently seized with pleurisy, become delirious, and died within two days. Edwards's preaching about this sudden death greatly moved the town's young people, and their concern was only heightened when, a short time later, a young married woman died. Deeply affected by Edwards's sermons before her illness, she had become "considerably exercised" about her salvation and as a consequence died "very full of comfort," warning others to heed their minister's counsel. These tragic events so "solemnized" the minds of the young people that in the early fall, at Edwards's suggestion, they agreed to spend some of their evenings "in social religion," dividing themselves into groups that met in various parts of the town.[6]

Edwards also continued his attempts to awaken the larger part of the community through his weekly sermons, delivered in what had become his characteristically understated way.[7] His audience had to attend to his words to feel their power, and with each passing week the increasing waves of revival suggested his effectiveness. In July he preached on a text from Jeremiah in which he warned against neglecting signs of God's impending judgment for obstinacy in sin. Not long after, he counseled his parishioners not to deceive themselves into thinking that they had experienced God's work on their souls when, instead, Satan had deceived them. A companion piece to *A Divine and Supernatural Light*, this particular sermon, "False Light and True," shows Edwards alert to the myriad ways people indulged their habitual selfishness and deluded themselves into thinking that they were destined for heaven.

At this point, Edwards recalled, people throughout the valley be-

gan to hear a "great noise . . . about Arminianism," an allusion to ac-
cusations being leveled at the Reverend William Rand of nearby Sunderland. According to the Reverend Stephen Williams of Longmeadow,
Rand had advanced "some new notions as to the doctrines of justification"—that is, to how a person recognized that God had singled
out him or her for salvation. Williams confided to his diary the fear
that if Rand were not quickly brought to see the error of his ways,
the "people's spirit [would be] exasperated and religion deeply
wounded."[8] Rand's words finally caused enough of a stir for the
Hampshire Association to get involved.[9] Pressured from within and
without his congregation to demonstrate his orthodoxy, Rand
quickly retracted his errors and for the moment won back the confidence of both his church and most of the neighboring clergy.[10]

Like other members of the association, Edwards was relieved at
his colleague's acknowledgment of his errors, but given his experience with the Yale apostates, he also regarded Rand's ill-advised pro-
nouncements as only the tip of an iceberg. To Edwards's surprise,
however, the public airing of this controversy seemed to renew
people's interest in spiritual matters. Many in "a Christless condition," he later noted, began to fear that God was about to withdraw
from the land and leave them "to heterodoxy and corrupt principles."
Others questioned doctrines to which they subscribed and had "a
kind of a trembling fear with their doubts, that they should be led
into bypaths to their eternal undoing." Then, Edwards observed,
there were "some things said publicly . . . concerning justification by
faith alone" that raised the spiritual temperature even more, an allusion to his powerful sermon on that very topic. Preached in the very
same month as the brouhaha over Rand, it proved a weighty coun-
terthrust to the Arminian threat.[11]

As would be the case in the Breck imbroglio, however, the Hampshire Association was divided on its opinion of Rand; some members
greatly reproached Edwards for making so much of the doctrine of
free grace from his pulpit, presumably because they did not want to
further enflame the passions the affair in Sunderland had ignited. But
Edwards's gambit worked, for this sermon, in which he defended the

notion that "We are justified only by faith in Christ, and not by any manner of virtue or goodness of our own," greatly moved all who heard it. Even as others attacked him for preaching the sermon, God's work wonderfully broke out in the town as souls began to "flock to Christ." The "noise" about Arminianism had put people's minds "into an unusual ruffle," and now he satisfied his congregation "with respect to the main thing in question, which they had been in trembling doubts and concern about." He implored them to be saved "in the way of the Gospel."[12]

Edwards never claimed any direct connection between his preaching and the religious awakening itself, for, a good Calvinist, he maintained that the latter came only by the grace of God. The minister was only his messenger, "deeply impressed with a sense of the danger of God's everlasting wrath" and so wishing "to treat with souls about their eternal salvation." When he subsequently published *Justification by Faith Alone*, he self-deprecatingly explained that the value of this and other sermons delivered during the revival had "arisen more from the frame in which [his people] heard them . . . than any real worth in them." Even so, he acknowledged the centrality of his preaching; he looked upon the recent events in the valley "as a remarkable testimony of God's approbation of the doctrine of justification by faith alone."[13] He also thought it important that he had not introduced any new doctrines but merely insisted on those that were orthodox and that he had stressed already to his community.[14] Increasingly confident in his manner of presenting the great truths of the Christian religion in his measured, rational way, Edwards now preached powerful, searching sermons that disposed people to think anew on eternal matters, an important step in their evangelical humiliation.

SOULS FLOCKING TO CHRIST

In late December, Edwards wrote, Northampton was transformed, for the spirit of God had "extraordinarily" set in. This began with the apparently authentic conversions of five or six people, one of whom was a young woman who had been one of the greatest "company-keepers"—that is, someone frequently with men—in the whole town. When word spread that God had given her a new heart, "truly broken and sanctified," the news affected young people all over town. Many went to talk with the convert, and her words greatly touched even those who had never shown any serious interest in religion.[15]

This interest in religious matters spread from the town's young people to those of all ages and stations in life. The conversation "in all companies and upon all occasions" was on religion. More remarkably, in a town continually indicted for its attention to secular matters, the world was now "a thing only by the bye." People carried out their usual tasks only as a duty, and many neglected quotidian concerns to spend time "in the immediate exercise of religion." Similarly, the petty backbiting that for years had characterized Northampton was now put aside. People ended their old quarrels, and "contention and intermeddling with other men's matters seem[ed] to be dead." Through the spring of 1735 the number of church members only increased. Northampton "never was so full of love, nor so full of joy," Edwards wrote, with all meetings, religious and secular, animated by the community's renewed Christian spirit.[16]

Subsequently, many visitors to Northampton (whether to see family, on business, or drawn by curiosity about the revivals) were "similarly wrought upon." Skeptics, quick to compare "what we call conversion to certain distempers," were surprised to find things beyond even what they had heard and told others that those who had not been to the town could not conceive of its state. Visitors carried back word of the remarkable events to their communities, where similar behavior often became prevalent, further fueling people's belief that this work was extraordinary. When Edwards quantified the results of the revival, he counted no fewer than thirty-two other communities up and down the Connecticut River, from Northfield, Massachusetts, to New Haven and Groton, Connecticut, that had been awakened. No one had seen anything like it. As Edwards concluded, God had "gone out of, and much beyond his usual and ordinary way."[17]

Just as what was transpiring in Northampton initiated a new interest in religion in other communities, so word of the swift and extraordinary propagation of comparable events elsewhere helped maintain the awakening in Edwards's church. "Continual news from town to town kept alive the talk of religion," he wrote, "and much awakened those that looked on themselves as still left behind, and made them the more earnest that they also might share in the great blessing that others had obtained." Within his church alone, the ramifications were great. Many more people—on one occasion, about a hundred—presented themselves at the bimonthly communion services. Although the precise number of new converts is difficult to gauge because there, as elsewhere in the valley, admissions standards were lax, during the five months of the revival Edwards calculated that more than three hundred people were "savingly brought home to Christ." Equally significant, they were of all ages, not just the youths whose conversions had initiated the revival but many middle-aged and beyond, "a thing heretofore rarely to be heard of," Edwards noted.[18]

Begun in the late winter of 1734–1735, the excitement was over by May, for the Spirit of God had gradually withdrawn from the region. Even more worrisome, the end of the revivals coincided with what Edwards presumed was the rising influence of the devil, for as more people were converted, "Satan seemed to be more let loose, and raged in a dreadful manner." June 1 marked the day when Edwards first unmistakably saw the evil hand, for that morning his own uncle Joseph Hawley took his life by slashing his throat. For some time Hawley had been concerned about his spiritual state, until he fell into a profound melancholy, which Satan took advantage of.[19]

Distressed that the revival had passed him by, Hawley could hardly sleep, and distraught for two months (even as the revival peaked), he seemed to lose his faculties. News of his death greatly affected the Northampton congregation. Indeed, it "struck them as it were with astonishment." The tragedy even affected those without melancholic tendencies and with no reasons to doubt their spiritual estate. It was as though they "had it urged upon 'em, as if somebody had spoke to 'em, 'Cut your own throat, now is a good opportunity: *now*, *NOW!* '[20] In a sermon preached shortly after this terrible event, Edwards wondered aloud if God had thus rebuked the town for its spiritual pride, "and as it were spit in our face, in that such a thing" should have happened among them.[21]

In his narrative of the awakening Edwards cited other examples of Satan's attempts to pull down the good work, notably two instances of people led into "strange enthusiastic delusions" that they had received direct communications from God. Such errant behavior began to make others (particularly those outside the county) doubt whether the work had indeed been divine or, rather, merely an aberration, the result of heightened emotions and hysteria. As word of such irregularities spread, so too did the suspicions. "To this day," Edwards wrote, "many retain a jealousy concerning it, and prejudice against it."[22]

Worldly concerns also worked to distract the valley's inhabitants from the revival. In August the region was abuzz because Governor Jonathan Belcher and some members of the General Court had traveled to Deerfield to negotiate with a group of Native Americans concerned over the province's expansion into their lands. Around the same time, the Breck controversy flared up and offered colonists the sad sight of clergy bitterly criticizing one another. In the latter situation, Edwards became deeply involved, even cosigning letters that the Hampshire Association sent to the Springfield church warning of Breck's unorthodox views. Because of ill health, however, he missed the commotion when Breck was arrested and then reappeared for his ordination by the rump council. Later the Northampton minister contributed a published defense of the association's actions.[23]

Closer to home, the construction of a new meetinghouse in Northampton initiated a controversy about how to seat people in its choicest pews, economic station replacing age as the standard criterion. A sermon he preached during this episode warned community members that their "mansion or abode in this world, however convenient and commodious it may be, is but as a seat that shall soon be taken down" when they passed to God's judgment seat.[24] The in-fighting over this matter took its toll on Edwards's health, so much so that he left the area for two months, spending at least part of that time in New York and New Jersey.[25] On his return, he found new conversions rare, and although he reminded his congregation of its special obligation to continue the remarkable reformation, by autumn it was only a memory.

A FAITHFUL NARRATIVE

As they ran their five-month course, the awakenings were not associated with Edwards so much as with the region itself. In his letter to Zachary Grey in London, written in the summer of 1735, Cutler never mentioned the Northampton minister. Nor did Eliphalet Adams, of New London, Connecticut, who, in a preface to a colleague's sermon, observed that recently God "hath been at work in divers towns, to awaken a concern in many about what they shall do to be saved, that this concern continues, that it spreads, and that persons are flocking into the churches as doves to their windows." Even Edwards's cousin Elisha Williams did not think that his relative's role merited particular mention. Writing to the English clergyman Isaac Watts after the revival's end, Williams only reported "a remarkable revival of religion in several parts of this country, in ten parishes in the county of Hampshire, in the Massachusetts province" and in nearly twenty in Connecticut.[26]

Edwards's authorship of *A Faithful Narrative of the Surprising Work of God in the Conversion of Many Hundreds of Souls* transformed him from just another provincial minister to one of the chief American spokespersons for transatlantic evangelism. Indeed, the complex textual history of this work, from its origins as part of a private letter to its eventual publication, first in London and then in Boston, two years later, as a substantial book, offers a case study of the significance of print culture in eighteenth-century British America. Because of an improving transportation system throughout the colonies and the proliferation of printers, the printed word, in weekly newspapers as well as in rapidly published pamphlets and books, now traveled at speeds unimagined a few decades earlier. People's knowledge of and relation to current events were transformed.[27] As much as any contemporary text, Edwards's *Faithful Narrative* marked the emergence of this new sphere of public discourse.

Those who sought information about the valley revivals often acquired it first through the letters of relatives and friends, and this was how people learned of what became Edwards's *Faithful Narrative*. In late April, Hatfield's minister William Williams had described the recent events in a letter to his friend Benjamin Colman, minister to Boston's Brattle Street Church. Impressed by the news, Colman asked the printers Kneeland and Green to include excerpts from the letter in their paper, the *New-England Weekly Journal*; as a result, on May 12, 1735, word of the Connecticut Valley revivals began to circulate more generally in New England.[28] Williams testified to events very different in nature and scope from Stoddard's well-known harvests, some of which he had witnessed firsthand. Colman, eager to know more and presumably because Williams had reported that the revivals had begun in Northampton, asked Edwards for his own account. Colman had known the young minister at least since 1731, when Edwards had traveled to Boston to preach *God Glorified in Man's Dependence* to the annual assembly of ministers. His performance suggested to Colman his fitness to provide a full account of what he had experienced in the town that was "the chief scene of these wonders."[29]

Edwards obliged in an eight-page letter that gave an account of the work's behavioral effects on Northampton and its rapid spread to different communities as well as a disclaimer of "the many odd and strange stories that have been carried about the country of this affair." Sensitive to reports of delusional behavior—one parishioner, for example, reported actually seeing "Christ shedding blood for sinners"—Edwards explained that those whose imaginations had run away with them had been "several times taught in public not to lay the weight of their hopes on such things." Sadly, on June 3 he had to add a postscript: news of his uncle Hawley's suicide and notice that the town had appointed a fast day because of this and "other appearances of Satan's rage."[30]

Colman was electrified by what he read. He quickly wrote an English friend, the clergyman John Guyse, who shared the news with his associate Watts, who then read parts of Colman's letter in one of his sermons (a common way to communicate such transatlantic news). In his next letter to Williams, Colman related the London clergy's interest and suggested that the Hatfield minister ask his nephew to work up a more detailed account. Williams conveyed the request to Edwards, who was obviously pleased with the attention people beyond the region were giving events in the valley. Because of his ill health, however, he did not complete his narrative until November.

Upon receipt of Edwards's lengthy manuscript Colman made "an accurate and judicious abridgement" that he appended to an edition of two of William Williams's sermons then going to press. The propriety of including Edwards's account, Colman explained in his brief preface to the redaction, was explained by Williams's having preached his sermons "at this time of extraordinary awakenings." More simply, Colman was eager to bring Edwards's narrative to a wider public in New England. In the wake of the initial newspaper notice of the revival, he explained, many had sought a more "particular account of the late wonderful work of God in some of the towns in the County of Hampshire." An advertisement at the end of the book promised that if "the taste here given" excited an interest in having the whole of Edwards's letter published, Kneeland and Green would take subscriptions at their printing office in Queen Street.[31]

Williams's four sermons, with the eighteen-page "Part of a large Letter from the Rev. Mr. *Jonathan Edwards* of *Northampton*, Giving an *Account* of the late *wonderful Work of* God in those *Parts*," appeared in mid-December 1736. Colman sent copies to Watts and Guyse, with a letter in which he granted permission for them to do as they pleased with the abridgment, "for the good of others." He also reported, cryptically, that Edwards was "not altogether pleased with the liberty" he had taken "of so general an extract." The Northampton minister had intended it to be published in full. Consequently, in respect to the disposition of Edwards's full manuscript, Colman wrote that should it not be printed in its entirety in Boston, he would forward it to them "with Edwards's leave." He added: "It will be yours to use as you may judge best for the service of souls."[32]

In late February 1737 Watts wrote Edwards that he and Guyse were delighted with what they had read but wanted the entire manuscript, for Colman's redaction omitted "many things" that they longed to know. Watts, exclaiming that he had not heard of anything like it "since the Reformation, nor perhaps since the days of the apostles," stated its publication was imperative. The two Englishmen assumed that the book would appear first in New England, with Edwards overseeing its production, and so subscribed five pounds to the proposed Boston edition. But because they fully intended to circulate the text in England, they also requested "as many copies in sheets" as would answer the booksellers' needs "and our desire to spread this narrative in the world."[33] In early April Watts reiterated their pledge, but neither the Boston edition nor the manuscript was forthcoming.

Fallout from Colman's initial publication of Edwards's narrative in his uncle Williams's book had caused the delay in the Boston edition. In May 1737, Edwards raised the issue directly, presumably in answer to a letter from Colman. Edwards had not been displeased, he explained, to find his own narrative in his uncle's book, for he looked upon that "as an honor too great" for him. Rather, the trouble lay with his relative, who had "never approved of its being put in his book."[34] Did Williams, now the valley's patriarch, object to the revival's being linked to his younger nephew rather than to himself? Or was he reluctant to endorse the narrative because he thought his nephew was too hasty and charitable in his judgments about some of the converts? Either could explain the roadblocks erected to its publication. When Timothy Cutler informed the bishop of London about the recent religious excitement in New England, he cited an informant from Hatfield who reported that Williams thought "Mr. Edwards had not been so full and forward in the matter" in publishing his narrative when it seemed to be "hurried on among us by an in[j]udicious Zeal."[35]

Despite the difficulty in getting the book published in Boston, Edwards told Colman that he would gladly forward it to Watts and Guyse for their "correction," for he noted (without any further explanation) that he was "sensible there are some things in it that would not be best to publish in *England*." He did not explicitly authorize them to print it, but by October, after Colman had sent the manuscript across the Atlantic, *A Faithful Narrative* was in sheets, ready for the London binders.[36]

In addition to providing the book with its permanent title, Watts and Guyse edited and emended the manuscript without Edwards's approval. They provided many marginal glosses, for example, some of which served as their own interpretation of Edwards's words. Further, they decided to omit many parts of it. Clues to what went missing are found in another letter to Colman written in late May. After apologizing for the egregious error of printing "New Hampshire" rather than "Hampshire County" on the title page, Watts explained that Guyse and he "were afraid to leave out very much," lest they be censured as Colman had been for his abridgment. But they still had found it necessary to alter the language so that they (and the book) would not be exposed "to much more contempt and ridicule." Further, given the "reproaches" that Guyse and he had sustained, "both in conversation and in newspapers," on account of their sponsorship of the narrative, Watts hoped that they would "receive no addition from New England."[37]

Watts alluded to Edwards's displeasure with their edition's errors and emendations. He pointedly asked Colman, however, to warn the young minister not "to make much talk of any mistakes he supposes we have made," for this would injure the *Narrative* by raising questions about its accuracy and general veracity. In addition, ministers in both England and Scotland, he explained, wanted further corroboration of the Hampshire County revivals, either though private letters or from the public testimony of some other New England minister "who was eye and ear witness to some of these numerous conversions."[38]

Edwards was troubled by how Watts and Guyse had come to print his account. They of course saw the justice of its first appearing in Boston. When Colman sent them the manuscript, they took it for granted that they could move ahead with plans to print it. They did not believe, Watts wrote to Colman, that they had "written or printed one word contrary to the meaning of orders we received." Nevertheless, the whole procedure troubled Edwards. Where the editors in his copy of the London edition explained how Colman had sent the manuscript to them—"to be communicated to the world under our care here in London, by Mr. Edwards' request"—he struck the last four words.[39]

In mid-October 1737 Watts and Guyse forwarded "as a present" one hundred books in sheets to New England to be divided between Colman and the author; also included were six bound in gilt, for the governor, the Harvard and Yale libraries, Colman and Edwards, and the one final copy earmarked (perhaps because of his sensitivity on the matter) for William Williams, "who preached the sermons." When Edwards received his copy, distraught at Watts and Guyse's abridgment and alteration of his "phrase and manner of expression," he carefully corrected the errors he found. Further, he said that by "not strictly observing the words of the original," they had, "through mistake, published some things diverse from fact."[40] The subsequent London edition of the same year and Edinburgh editions of 1737 and 1738 followed the text of the first edition, as did a 1738 edition translated into German and published in Magdeburg, which made Edwards's abridged and corrupt text available to Continental Pietists.[41] Not until he finally published the narrative in Boston later in 1738 could Edwards correct the errors that he had found in Watts and Guyse's edition. For this printing, he also secured from six ministers, all members of the Hampshire Association and including William Williams, an attestation of the veracity of his account, documents that Watts and Guyse included in their new edition of 1738.

EDWARDS AND THE SURPRISING CONVERSIONS

The significance of Edwards's *Faithful Narrative* is in part reflected in the resistance it met with from English and Scots evangelicals. What made his narrative at once so special yet problematic to those who, considering their own evangelism, should have welcomed Edwards's success and prayed for similar events in their own congregation? His English editors' preface provides some clues. First, Watts and Guyse pointed out that the Hampshire County revivals had involved a multitude of communities simultaneously, whereas previous awakenings— like Stoddard's harvests, say—had been associated with individual churches. Second, the dynamic of the events was remarkable. Rather than produce only external, moral reform, as had so often been the case with awakenings that followed formal covenant renewal ceremonies, in the Connecticut Valley God had deeply touched people's hearts. As Watts and Guyse put it, in a short space of time God had turned "a multitude of souls" from "formal, cold and careless profession" to "the lively exercise of every Christian grace, and the powerful practice of our holy religion." Finally, the English clergymen found it unusual that the awakenings seemed to have been initiated not by any external events (such as natural disasters, Indian attacks, or pestilence) but instead by "the immediate hand of God."[42] All this suggested that it was a genuine and important work of the Spirit.

Watts and Guyse also pointed out that Edwards's account offered a guide to what one might expect during times of special grace. Given Hampshire County's experience, wherever God worked for men's salvation one might expect to find "some discoveries of a sense of sin, of the danger of the wrath of God, of the all-sufficiency of his Son Jesus," all things that God had outlined in scripture. This process of conviction, humiliation, and acceptance of God's free grace informed virtually every example Edwards presented in his narrative. Watts and Guyse attributed this to Hampshire County inhabitants' nurture on "the common plain Protestant doctrine of the Reformation, without stretching towards the Antinomians [that is, those who believed that the Holy Spirit lived in and directed the saint] on the one side, or the Arminians on the other," precisely what Edwards offered them.[43] Such things convinced Watts and Guyse that through his work in New England, God intended yet greater things for Christianity.

Why, then, were some people's reactions to the events so negative, even before an account of them had appeared in print? His English agents realized that the problem lay in Edwards's language and emphases, the very things that made him unique among his contemporaries. "We must allow every writer his own way," the two observed, "and must allow him to choose what particular instances he would select, from the numerous cases which came before him." But while they gave him the benefit of the doubt in his description of the events, they wondered if his inexperience had blinded him to the significance of some of the problematic behavior he had encountered.[44]

In particular, the two clergymen singled out the amount of attention Edwards gave to Abigail Hutchinson and Phebe Bartlett "when he might have chosen others perhaps, of more significancy in the eye of the world." Edwards had featured these two—one a young woman, the other a four-year-old—so prominently because through them he sought "to give a clearer idea of the nature and manner of the operations of God's spirit"; he wished to show how it touched and transformed the heart.[45] But because of his insistence on the wholly affective nature of grace, rationalist critics of the awakenings, and even others predisposed to welcome the events, doubted these accounts. Different as these two people's experiences were, Edwards permanently linked them through his emphasis on the remarkable emotional transformation effected on each by the work of the Spirit in a short span of time.

Moved by other conversions in her neighborhood, for example, Hutchinson, long ill with what some would now term a version of anorexia nervosa, endured days of evangelical humiliation and despair before awakening one morning to an "easiness and calmness" of mind she had never before known. Her calm was "accompanied with a lively sense of the excellency of Christ, and his sufficiency to satisfy for the sins of the whole world." From this point, Edwards's account reads like what several years later he described in his "Personal Narrative." Hutchinson's mind "was swallowed up with a sense of the glory of God's truth and other perfections," and all day she felt "a constant sweetness." For several days together she had "a sweet sense of the excellency and loveliness of Christ in his meekness" and often expressed "a sense of the glory of God appearing in the trees, and growth of the fields, and other works of God's hands." Another time she described "how good and sweet it was to lie low before God," and the lower the better. More and more infirm as her illness became "seated much in her throat," such that she could take only liquid food, Hutchinson became an oracle for others still in the throes of conversion.[46]

Abigail Hutchinson died peacefully in late June 1735, as the revival wound down. Edwards was enough moved by her story to record it in painstaking detail, in part because her experience gave him a better understanding of his own spiritual struggles a few years earlier. Equally remarkable for different reasons was Phebe Bartlett, whose account he took primarily "from the mouths of her parents."[47] When Phebe was only a little over four years old, Edwards wrote, she had been greatly affected by the conversion of her eleven-year-old brother, whom she questioned about his religious experience. Moved by his words, she retired to her closet several times a day for secret prayer. After one particularly trying session, when she was terrified that she would die and go to hell, she suddenly stopped crying, smiled, and announced to her mother that the kingdom of heaven had come to her. Hitherto spiritually bereft, she exclaimed, "I can find God now!" Other children were fascinated by her experience, and as in Hutchinson's case, people came to listen to the child speak of her newfound happiness in God. Phebe also became particularly enamored of Edwards's preaching and missed him when he was absent, as he had been in the fall of 1735 because of his health. On his return to the pulpit she greatly rejoiced, shouting, "Mr. Edwards is come home! Mr. Edwards is come home!" Precocious far beyond her years, Phebe Bartlett typified Edwards's belief that grace could as easily transform a young child as the most intransigent adult sinner.

Edwards believed the experiences of Hutchinson and Bartlett were genuine, for in his general recounting of the awakenings he emphasized the same behavioral patterns he described at length in their narratives. First, individuals were awakened to "a sense of their miserable condition by nature" and so became aware of their dreadful, sinful state. Then followed a profound sense of the danger they were in of "perishing eternally," a stage that often left people despondent until they realized that they had nowhere to turn except to God. As Edwards had learned from the death of his uncle Hawley, this was a particularly dangerous state, for "some persons continue[d] wandering in such a labyrinth ten times as long as others" before they acknowledged their own insufficiency to effect salvation. Finally, to the fortunate few God brought a "conviction of their absolute dependence on his sovereign power and grace, and the universal necessity of a Mediator," a stage often followed by wonderful calmness. Although Edwards acknowledged "an endless variety in the particular manner and circumstances in which persons are wrought on," what he witnessed usually unfolded in this particular order.[48]

He also realized that in certifying such emotional behavior as the work of God, he opened himself to charges that his people had been swept away by mere "enthusiasm." Some critics, Edwards complained, even compared "what we called conversion to certain distempers." But he insisted that in what he had observed, such behavior, especially the converts' seeing things "with bodily eyes"—that is, their believing that they saw extraordinary things, like, say, a Christ bleeding for their sins—seemed to him "no more than what is to be expected in human nature in such circumstances, and what is the natural result of the strong exercise of mind, and impressions of the heart."[49] Moreover, members of his congregation who had participated in Stoddard's harvests convinced Edwards that "the work that has now been wrought on souls is evidently the same that was wrought in my venerable predecessor's day." Proof of the soundness of the town's behavior came when some Quakers, who had heard of the work of the Spirit there, visited the community, "hoping to find good waters to fish in," but left without anyone's taking their bait.[50]

Edwards wholeheartedly believed that in 1734 and 1735 he had witnessed a genuine work of God. He took seriously the cavils about "enthusiasm" and "distempers," but he had seen too much good come from, and too many lives changed by, the recent spiritual upheaval. He knew his critics thought him "very fond of making a great many converts, and of magnifying and aggrandizing the matter" to forward his own reputation as an evangelist. Further, he knew that some might think that for lack of better judgment, he took "every religious pang and enthusiastic conceit for saving conversion." Such concerns at first dissuaded him from publishing an account of the work, though many had requested it. But at the prodding of Colman and then of Watts and Guyse, he came to believe that he had to account for it. "Upon mature consideration," he wrote, he found it his duty "to declare this amazing work, as it appeared to [him], to be indeed divine, and to conceal no part of the glory of it."[51]

With the publication of *A Faithful Narrative*, Edwards mounted the stage on which he had always envisioned himself. Within a year of the book's appearance on both sides of the Atlantic, he drew the attention of an emergent cadre of similarly disposed evangelical clergy and, through them, of churchgoers who, like his parishioners in Northampton, yearned for spiritual awakening. In his *Faithful Narrative*, these people had a vivid example of what happened when such yearnings were answered. When the Spirit stirred them, even ever so slightly, they could return to its pages for inspiration and guidance.

In his account of the Hampshire County revivals Edwards introduced and began to legitimize a new grammar and sociology of religious revival. He presented Gospel truth in new and powerful ways based on what he had learned, through the natural sciences as well as Scripture, of the nature of man and of God. His preaching was profoundly effective, for people of all ages and from all walks of life began to think and talk about the spiritual dimensions of their lives in novel ways. As the Northampton hat maker Ebenezer Hunt testified to his diary, during the awakenings he had indeed learned "something about spiritual light," including the fact that it was "far different" from what he "had conceived it to be."[52]

Equally important, by approving the behavior that he had witnessed as the genuine work of the Spirit, Edwards gave people new ways to approach their spirituality in their everyday lives, a practice based in a subjective, intuitive interpretation of religious experience. His description of the progressive emotional states through which converts passed soon became the litmus test for other Christians who were "getting through" to salvation. Hereafter revivals were judged not merely by a community's reaffirmation of its church covenant or its degree of moral reformation but by the affective and volitional dimensions of the individual converts' spiritual experiences. In the conversion of an ill and impressionable young woman and a mere child, he had recognized the same movements of the Spirit that he had witnessed everywhere else. Watts and Guyse's concern that Edwards had been injudicious in highlighting these two cases did nothing to change his mind, and with each reprinting of the book, readers internalized the remarkable stories of Abigail Hutchinson, Phebe Bartlett, and other Northampton converts, making them their implicit role models.

PRAYING FOR RAIN

When Edwards returned to Northampton late in November 1737, refreshed from his trip to New York and New Jersey, he sought to relight the revival's fire, virtually extinguished after Hawley's suicide. For several months after that horrible event religion nevertheless had remained the main subject of conversation. The truly converted had had "an abiding change wrought on them" and were now alive to "a new sense of things, new apprehensions and views of God, of the divine attributes, and Jesus Christ, and the great things of the Gospel." They enjoyed a "new sense of the truth of them," Edwards wrote, and these truths affected them "in a new manner." He may have erred in his judgment of who precisely had been transformed, but "in the main," there had been "a great and marvellous work of conversion and sanctification" among his people that he sought to continue.[53]

But the aftermath of the revival also brought great disappoint-

ment, for having witnessed and, in some cases, undergone such marvelous work, his people again seemed dead to his offer of the Gospel.
In the spring of 1737, Edwards wrote Colman that his people displayed "an over-carefulness about, and eagerness after the possessions
of this life."[54] In a sermon the following fall he took pains to remind
his listeners that God had "most evidently and wonderfully manifested himself" among them of late. "Remember how helpless you
was [sic], and God helped you," he implored. "Remember how you
cried to the Lord, and he unsnared and delivered you."[55]

What better proof of this than the fortuitous event earlier that
year? Seated in their old meetinghouse, its foundation weakened by
the frost heaves and spring freshets of years past, Edwards's parishioners were shocked when the gallery collapsed, tumbling scores of
people onto others below. The meetinghouse was filled "with dolor-
ous shrieking and crying," Edwards reported, "and nothing else was
expected than to find many people dead, and dashed to pieces." Yet
God so cared for his people that not one was killed, nor was even one
person's bones broken. It seemed unreasonable, Edwards continued,
to ascribe this deliverance to anything but "the care of providence in
disposing the motions of every stick of timber, and the precise place
of safety where everyone should sit and fall." This was sufficient argument, he concluded, "of a divine providence over the lives of men."
Others agreed. After he reported the events to Colman, they were
published in the *Boston Gazette*.[56]

Edwards viewed this calamity as a warning to a people who had
again strayed from the truth. Would God continue so to preserve
them if they fell away yet further? To assure the orthodoxy of his congregation's faith, Edwards in his sermons continued to hammer at
them. Among the most poignant of his postrevival efforts was "A City
on a Hill," a text that clergy had regularly invoked since Governor
John Winthrop had famously used it in 1630 in his "Modell of Christian Charitie" to remind New Englanders of their pivotal role in the
history of redemption. Edwards preached on the operative text
(Matthew 5:14) in the summer of 1736, shortly after Watts and

Guyse had shown interest in his narrative. He explained that the inhabitants of a city so recently marked by God's extraordinary presence were obliged to live in an exemplary manner, for the entire world viewed their failure or success as an index of Christianity's fortunes.

When Edwards looked about him, however, he saw a people who brought dishonor on their solemn charge. He reminded them of how because of the awakenings, their fame had been "spread abroad everywhere," with people inquiring "what manner the work was carried on," "what effect it has upon those that are the subjects of it," and "how they behave themselves." He also reminded them of how from the revival's commencement, Satan had attempted to pull down their work. Such revilement had continued to the present when, in the wake of Hawley's death and revelations that a few converts had been led away by "enthusiasticall impressions and imaginations," critics doubted that the revivals had been a work of God. To make matters worse, Satan had used the Breck controversy to cast more of "an odium" upon the county and to "raise a kind of mobbish rage and fury" against its ministry, especially those who had "chiefly stood in the defense of those truths of the gospel" on which the late revivals had been based.[57]

Edwards also pointed out that people had forgotten the language through which they should comprehend vital religion. All memory of the powerful work of God's spirit that they had witnessed seemed to have been erased "out of their minds." A great part of the country, he continued, had gotten "into another way of thinking of things of religion, looking chiefly at morality and a sober life" as the way to salvation.[58] If believers "read" their religion through that vocabulary, he warned, Northampton's city on a hill would become merely a byword for hypocrisy.

Explicit too in this and other sermons was Edwards's insistence that his parishioners live up to their destiny by modeling exemplary behavior—to adorn, as he put it, "our profession by our practice." He exclaimed, "No town in America [is] so like a city on a hill," for it had been in Northampton that God had "in so great a degree, betrusted the honor of religion."[59] But alas, here too the town failed miserably.

In May 1737 Edwards again had to inveigh against contention and "party spirit," the "old iniquity of this town," he called it. "It has been remarkably a contentious town . . . for this thirty year," he reminded his congregation and "people have not known how to manage scarce any public business without siding and dividing themselves into parties."[60] Once again they behaved as they had in Stoddard's era. Men nurtured grudges and ill temper and showed "a great deal of secret contriving and caballing." For twenty years and more there had been men in town whose spirits were always "[on] edge, and their mouths open in evil speaking, in fierce and clamorous talk, and backbitings and evil surmisings." Such people would change, Edwards concluded, only when "God takes their hearts in hand, and makes 'em much better men than ever yet they be."[61]

In those years of spiritual drought, Edwards made other attempts to revive his congregation's interest in spiritual matters. In 1738 he saw through press his *Discourses on Various Important Subjects*, a collection of five sermons, four of which he had delivered during the revival. In his preface he explained that he had been urged to this task by his townspeople, who hoped the publication of the discourses might "renew the same effect of them what was wrought in the hearing, and revive the memory of that great work of God." He singled out his treatise on justification, noting that "certain reverend gentlemen, my fathers"—presumably members of the Hampshire Association who had stood with Edwards against Breck and Arminianism—had encouraged its inclusion in the volume.[62]

In the late 1730s Edwards began to preach more systematic, serial sermons on doctrinal topics, efforts that he clearly regarded as potential publications. Late in 1737, for example, he preached a nineteen-sermon sequence on Matthew 25:1–12, the parable of the ten virgins, in which he distinguished between true and counterfeit grace. The next April he followed this effort with a twenty-one-sermon series on 1 Corinthians 13, in which he argued that Christian behavior was the most reliable assurance of one's gracious state. Finally, in March 1739, he started a thirty-unit sequence on Isaiah 51:8, which became *A History of the Work of Redemption*. Powerful examples of Edwards's synthetic mind, these sermons were part of the great project he had assigned himself in the early 1720s, to prepare "A Rational Account of the Principles and Main Doctrines of the Christian Religion."[63]

Despite these projects, by the late 1730s Edwards was living with the bitter disappointment that attended the end of the Connecticut Valley revivals. In 1735 he had ridden the crest of a spiritual tide so powerful that he thought only God could have directed it. But by 1738, when his *Faithful Narrative* was finally published in Boston, his church looked much as it had before the remarkable events. What had happened to make God withdraw? Could Edwards have erred in his management and assessment of the awakenings? Might Watts and Guyse have been right in questioning some of the language and emphases of his narrative? "I don't know," Edwards admitted to his congregation in the spring of 1737, "but I have trusted too much in men, and put too much consideration in the goodness and piety of the town."[64]

Even as he wondered aloud, though, if in his encouragement of the Hampshire County revivals he had made serious errors in judgment, his *Faithful Narrative* was poised to assume a new life that would keep the events of 1734 and 1735, and Edwards himself, at the center of transatlantic religious debate. The book began to perform its office beginning in 1739, with the arrival in America of the great English evangelist George Whitefield.

[FIVE]

A Great Deal of Noise About Religion

(1740–1743)

TRANSATLANTIC STIRRINGS

Edwards had reason to hope that his labor in the valley had not been in vain, for in his travels he heard of other, similar revivals of religion. In New Jersey the Reverend William Tennent, a Presbyterian, spoke of a large awakening under Tennent's brother Gilbert, another overseen by John Cross, and yet a third witnessed by Theodorus Frelinghuysen of the Dutch Reformed Church, all in the area around Freehold. More important, William Tennent and others assured Edwards that the Hampshire awakenings had encouraged their own efforts.[1] Similarly, from one end of Long Island to the other, the godly "talked much" of the excitement in the valley and asked Edwards about it. Clergy in the middle colonies even alluded to the Connecticut Valley events from their pulpits as part of their revival efforts.[2] As early as June 29, 1735, Gilbert Tennent sought to jar his parishioners by announcing that since people were "coming to Christ in Flocks in New England," his congregants should heed his words and not be left behind.[3] Simultaneously, an emergent evangelical movement in England gained strength, eventuating not only in a strong Pietistic strain within the Church of England but also in the emergence of the "Methodist" movement under John Wesley.[4] By the end of the decade evangelists from both Anglican and Methodist camps had witnessed their own remarkable revivals and measured their success against what had occurred in Hampshire County.

In England, John Wesley was central to the promulgation of this evangelism.[5] Wesley was a product of Oxford University, where the Arminian divinity of William Law, Jeremy Taylor, and others had influenced devout young Anglicans, and his horizon was greatly expanded after he traveled to the colony of Georgia in 1735 to help the Society for the Propagation of the Gospel in its efforts to convert Native Americans. There he met Moravian missionaries engaged in the same work who emphasized the importance of the conversion experience and belief in a personal relation to Christ. Returning to England, Wesley sought to reconcile his Oxford Anglicanism with the intense Moravian Pietism. In May 1738 he experienced personal conversion and began to develop a theology based in both Law's belief in moral perfectionism and the Moravians' emphasis on salvation by faith. A few months later Wesley discovered Edwards's *Faithful Narrative*. "Surely this is the Lord's doing," he wrote in his journal of the American revivals, "and it is marvelous in our eyes."[6] From that point, Wesley and his brother, Charles, were committed evangelists who encouraged community-wide religious revivals on the scale that Edwards had experienced.

George Whitefield was the most important Anglican convert to the evangelical cause.[7] Under John Wesley's tutelage he questioned the Arminian thrust of his colleagues' piety and, like Wesley, emphasized the centrality of the "New Birth" to religious experience. He began preaching in 1736, and within a year newspapers were noting his sermons' power and pungency. Like Wesley, he traveled to Georgia and upon his return to England raised money for an orphanage that he wished to start in that colony. Officially ordained as a priest, Whitefield became the main target for Anglican critics of the Methodist movement who resented his and others' condemnation of their preaching as dead and dry and their lack of emphasis on the emotional experience of the "New Birth." A writer in Boston's antirevival paper, the *Evening-Post*, epitomized the opposition to Whitefield, whom he termed "the *first Itinerant*, the grand Instrument of these Disorders, the great *Master-Builder* in the *Babel of Confusion* which has been erecting in the four preceding years."[8]

Despite his detractors, however, Whitefield's undeniable oratorical power—folk tradition has it that he could make an audience laugh or cry by the way he pronounced the word *Mesopotamia*—brought him large crowds and excited fellow English evangelists.[9] Further, unlike his mentor, Wesley, who based his success on the careful nurture of converts through a hierarchical church organization, Whitefield reveled in preaching to any and all and essentially invented itinerancy as a revival tool. Indeed, with many traditional venues closed to him because of what other clergy perceived as his eccentricity, Whitefield preached often in the open air, an equally radical innovation. By 1737 the editor of the *Virginia Gazette* thought him newsworthy enough to bring him to the attention of an American readership.[10]

Wesley, Whitefield, and, eventually, sympathetic nonconformists like Isaac Watts and John Guyse believed that they were witnessing a unique stirring of God's spirit. Through their emphases on regeneration and justification by faith they challenged the spiritual languor and smugness that had long characterized the Church of England. With news of the Connecticut Valley revivals, the English evangelicals believed that God was beginning to work in ways that presaged the final triumph of Christ's legions. It was a heady time, and clergy had to seize the initiative.

THE "PEDLAR IN DIVINITIE"

When Whitefield announced his intention to return to the colonies in the autumn of 1739, to bring his message to an even wider audience, the excitement was palpable. Alerted to his (and, to a lesser degree, Wesley's) evangelical triumphs in England and to Pietist revivals on the Continent under Count Nikolaus Zinzendorf, colonists from

New Hampshire to Georgia yearned for Whitefield to generate similar excitement on their shores.[11] When he finally arrived, newspapers detailed his every move, and to build anticipation for his American tour, he made certain that his sermons and journals, already published to good effect in England, were widely available to whet people's interest. He even employed an agent, William Seward, who accompanied him and made sure American newspapers ran accounts of his previous triumphs and excerpts from his journals. The result was a well-orchestrated publicity campaign that ensured large crowds, whether fully sympathetic to Whitefield's message or not, and that earned him and other revivalists the epithet "Pedlars in Divinitie."[12]

This revivalism was of a different tenor and scale from that which the Connecticut Valley had experienced a few years earlier. Now as clergy and laity alike sought and provided information about Whitefield and his colleagues' remarkable work, a veritable cascade of language accompanied the spiritual awakenings.[13] Consider the pro-revivalist Jonathan Parsons's description of how he had learned of Whitefield's American visit. In a lengthy account of a revival in his church in Lyme, Connecticut, Parsons observed that God had made use of "frequent Accounts" of Whitefield to focus attention on the religious excitement sweeping neighboring towns and colonies. Soon after the Anglican clergyman had arrived in Boston, Parsons's friend Benjamin Colman had sent him a description of the evangelist's "Zeal and Success in his daily Administrations among them," examples Colman communicated to his church.

His interest in Whitefield and the new revivals awakened, Parsons next heard of a great concern about religion in Hartford, "which stirr'd [him] up to take Pains" to discover more about it. He talked with numerous people who knew of the revivals, some of whom told him they had seen "very surprising Effects of some Cause," and he eventually wrote "several letters to *Gentlemen* in that town, whom [*sic*] [he] thought were *judicious* and *prudent*, desiring particular Accounts of the most interesting Facts observable among them." Parsons received some replies, but seeking "further light if it was to be had," he visited

Hartford to speak personally with the individuals involved. These "Pains I tho't it necessary to take," he explained, because Whitefield's crusade stirred his belief that a great work of God was unfolding before his eyes. Because of Parsons's assiduity, within a few weeks he had been furnished with "a considerable History of the work from many Places, attested by credible witnesses." Before long his congregation, periodically informed of what was occurring elsewhere, felt the waves of revival wash over them.[14]

Interest in Whitefield's visits was not restricted to the clergy. In his spiritual narrative, Nathan Cole, a Farmington, Connecticut, husbandman, strikingly recorded his first encounter with the itinerant clergyman. "Now it pleased God to send Mr. Whitefield into this land," Cole wrote, "and I longed to see and hear him." One day Cole heard that Whitefield had come to New York and New Jersey, where multitudes flocked after him, "under great concern for their Souls." Next Cole heard that Whitefield was on Long Island, then at Boston and Northampton. "Then on a sudden," he recalled, "in the morning about 8 or 9," a messenger announced that Whitefield was to preach that very day in neighboring Middletown. "I was in my field at work," Cole wrote. "I dropt my tool that I held in my hand and ran home to my wife[,] telling her to make ready quickly to go and hear Mr. Whitefield preach." After a hectic journey along the Connecticut River with hundreds of other people rushing to Middletown on foot and on horseback, Cole arrived in time to hear Whitefield's sermon, an event that marked the beginning of his spiritual rebirth. As Cole put it laconically, "I was born Feb 15th 1711 and born again Octo 1741."[15]

As Cole's story indicates, few escaped knowledge of Whitefield's tour, publicized as it was by the complex communications network centered in the expanding printing trade. Having landed in Philadelphia in October 1739, the evangelist worked his way southward to Savannah, Georgia, where he had been officially assigned a pastorate. After two months he traveled to Charleston, South Carolina, then commenced a tour northward, again preaching in the middle colonies. After a few more months in Savannah, he headed for New

England, where he arrived on March 15 and remained for seven weeks. His sermons drew immense crowds, particularly in Philadelphia and Boston, with newspapers reporting upwards of twenty thousand people in attendance on several occasions.

Whitefield's publicist made sure that sympathetic ministers in major cities received copies of his sermons and journals well in advance of his arrival. In the Boston area Colman became the young revivalist's strong promoter. Still excited by the recent events in the Connecticut Valley, Colman hoped that the news from both England and the other colonies promised a more general outpouring of God's grace. Attracted to Whitefield's ecumenical spirit—people of all denominations warmed to his message—as well as to his insistence on preaching sound doctrine, Colman recognized the emergence of a new kind of revivalism, one based not in the awakening of discrete communities (as Edwards's had been) but rather in the virtually simultaneous conversion of thousands of individuals in disparate places, united by itinerant preaching on almost a daily basis.

Edwards too was moved by what he had heard of Whitefield's evangelism and in the late winter of 1740 wrote him in Savannah to invite him to Northampton. This was no mere courtesy, for Edwards still struggled to reawaken piety in his community. From what he had learned of Whitefield from Colman and others, Edwards thought that the English clergyman might catalyze his people's reformation. Moreover, in the spring of 1739 Edwards had begun a lengthy sermon series (subsequently published as *A History of the Work of Redemption*) in which he presented evidence of God's revealed will through the course of recorded history. What he heard of events in the other colonies and England struck him as congruent with the ways God always had worked to reveal his divine dispensation.

Also, Edwards was much troubled by his diminished energy as well as his ineffectiveness; his delicate constitution was prone to exhaustion on account of his demanding (though self-imposed) work schedule. In late May 1738 he wrote Colman that he was "in a poor state of health" and asked his Boston friend to pray that God would strengthen and renew him so that he could continue "to perform to his acceptance and his people's profit."[16] A year later matters had not improved. With Whitefield already in the colonies, Timothy Cutler wrote Edmund Gibson, the bishop of London, that Edwards was "very much emaciated, and impair'd in his Health." Cutler added: "It is doubtful to me whether He will attain to the Age of 40."[17] For some time the Northampton minister remained debilitated, in part because of his anxiety over failing to maintain the revival. As late as the summer of 1741 he wrote his friend Moses Lyman that his letter had to be brief because of both his "prodigious fullness of business" and his "great infirmity of body."[18]

Edwards's invitation to Whitefield in 1740 was effusive and be-spoke his sincere belief that the visitor might effect what he had failed to do among his townspeople. Yet he worried that Whitefield would have less success in the Connecticut Valley than elsewhere. As he put it, "we who have dwelt in a land distinguished with light, and have long enjoyed the gospel, and have been glutted with it, and have de-spised it, are I fear more hardened than most of those places" that Whitefield already had visited. On the other hand, Edwards was con-fident that if anyone could revive the flame, it was Whitefield. If his health would only permit it, Edwards told Whitefield, he hoped to see the kinds of results that had followed the evangelist's preaching elsewhere. He closed on a practical note, asking Whitefield and his as-sistant, Seward, to stay at his own home.[19]

Despite the encouragement of Colman, Edwards, and others, however, Whitefield did not return to New England until much later that year. As Edwards waited, he sought news both of Whitefield's work and of the growing international scope of the revivals. In early June, he asked Josiah Willard, the secretary of the province and some-one who regularly provided news about the progress of evangelical re-ligion, for more details of Whitefield's "labor and success." Edwards wrote: "I cannot but hope that God is about to accomplish glorious things for his church," making him "the more desirous of knowing as fully as may be the present state of religion in the world." Recently

Whitefield had sent him journals detailing his English revivals but he wanted to know more, specifically of "the progress of that affair at Halle in Saxony, begun by the famous Dr. [August Hermann] Francke" and the work of Dutch missionaries in the East Indies, alluding to two regions where large revivals recently had occurred.[20]

Although things went well in England and on the Continent, Northampton continued to be a disappointment. In early October, shortly before Whitefield's arrival, Edwards despondently wrote Eleazer Wheelock, a minister in Lebanon, Connecticut, that it was "a sorrowfully dull and dead time with us." Alluding to the social strife that continued to characterize Northampton, Edwards observed that the town's "temporal affairs" were "most unhappily situated to be a snare to us," and he implored Wheelock, "Earnestly pray for us." And for the benefit of his soul "and the souls of my people," he asked Wheelock's blessing for Whitefield's visit.[21]

NORTHAMPTON REAWAKENED

Edwards's prayers were answered a little over a week later. Whitefield journeyed westward from Boston, through Concord, Worcester, Brookfield, Hadley, and other towns where he preached to appreciative crowds. He finally arrived in Northampton on October 17. He accepted Edwards's invitation to stay with his family and remained for four days before continuing down the Connecticut River valley. In his journal Whitefield recalled Edwards as "a solid, excellent Christian" but very "weak in body." He also was struck by the tenor of his host's family. Sarah Edwards was "adorned with a meek and quiet spirit," he wrote, and "talked solidly of the things of God." Whitefield noted, "A sweeter couple I have not yet seen," a fact that made him renew his prayers for such a helpmeet of his own. He also mentioned the Edwards children, who, with the arrival of Susannah that June, numbered six daughters and one son. The Anglican divine noted approvingly how they "were not dressed in silks and satins, but plain, as become the children of those who, in all things, ought to be examples of Christian simplicity."[22]

Edwards's concern that Whitefield might not be well received could not have been more wide of the mark. He preached publicly four times during his stay and held one private exercise at Edwards's home, and by his and Edwards's reports, these efforts were greatly affecting. During Whitefield's first sermon, when he reminded the townspeople "of their former experiences, and how zealous and lively they were at that time," both they and Edwards wept. Indeed, tears were a staple at Whitefield's services and accompanied each of his appearances in Edwards's pulpit as well as at the private conference with parishioners. During one church meeting, Whitefield recalled, Edwards sobbed the entire time, and his and his parishioners' response to the itinerant's ministrations so impressed Whitefield that he admitted to not having seen "four such gracious meetings together" since his arrival in New England. In his own recollection of the visit, Edwards also recalled the plentiful tears; his congregation had been "extraordinarily melted" by Whitefield's sermons.[23]

And "melted" they were, for Whitefield stirred Northampton (as he had virtually every town in New England where he had preached) to a new and profound engagement with religion. In 1743, in a letter to Thomas Prince, who was gathering accounts of the new awakenings for publication in his monthly religious periodical, *The Christian History*, Edwards sketched the progress of this revival. For one thing, it greatly overshadowed the events six years earlier. Upon Whitefield's departure, interest in religion grew exponentially and spread from "professors" who already had entertained hopes that they were in a state of grace to young people in a "Christless state" and finally to the "very young."[24] In mid-December Edwards happily wrote Whitefield of a Northampton transformed, for religion had "been gradually reviving and prevailing more and more" since his visit. Edwards found it remarkable that after Whitefield's preaching, the Spirit of God had awakened a wholly different portion of the community, young adults who "in that wonderful season nine years ago" had not yet come to "years of discretion." Those who had lived through the previous re-vival without any effect, he reported to Prince, now were "almost wholly passed over and let alone," while the younger generation panted after God, a pattern replicated in many other communities in the course of these revivals.[25]

Edwards's letter to Prince was replete with descriptions of re-markable physical manifestations of the revival. For one thing, con-versions were "frequently wrought more sensibly and visibly." After a sermon in May 1741 two converts were so affected by a sense of God's glory that it manifested itself physically. "The affectation of their minds" overcame their strength, Edwards wrote, and had "a very visible effect on their bodies." Those who saw them soon caught the excitement, so that "the whole room was full of nothing but out-cries, faintings and such like." Others apprised of the events came to see them and were similarly moved, and the meeting went on in this way for several hours. By the middle of the summer such "cryings out" had spread to services in the meetinghouse itself, and many townspeople stayed after services "to confer with those who seemed to be overcome with religious convictions and affections."[26] By late summer such visceral examples of the Spirit's work had spread widely throughout the congregation, and it was "a very frequent thing to see an houseful of outcries, faintings, convulsions and such like, both with distress, and with admiration and joy." Some of these episodes were quite lengthy, and though Edwards went out of his way to as-sure Prince that he had not encouraged all-night meetings (as some revivalists did), parishioners often became so affected by their spiri-tual convictions that they stayed all night at the dwellings where they had gone for religious exercises.

Finally, Edwards remarked on the very public nature of the con-versions. In the earlier awakenings people had wrestled privately with the Spirit; but now "the impressions" were much more "manifest by external effects," with the "progress of the Spirit of God in conviction, from step to step, more apparent." Further, the "transition from one state to another [was] more sensible and plain," so that the progress of someone's conversion "might in many instances, be as it were seen by bystanders." Thus, following Whitefield's visit, conversions occurred more often than not "in the presence of others, at religious meetings, where the appearances of what was wrought on the heart fell under public observation."[27] The converts' public display of their spirituality now contributed to the way in which communities like Northampton and countless others understood their place in God's unfolding plan.

SAMUEL BUELL AND SARAH EDWARDS

Such public demonstration of one's spirituality was novel. But if Edwards did not openly encourage it, neither did he object, for the increase in new church members had rekindled his dream of a regenerated parish and stirred him to reexamine his own spiritual progress. During this period, for example, probably in response to a request from his future son-in-law Aaron Burr, he penned his "Personal Narrative." But matters took a new turn early in 1742 with the arrival in Northampton of Samuel Buell, a young Yale graduate whom the New Haven Association recently had ordained.[28] Among New England clergy, Buell had rapidly gained a name as one of the most stirring itinerants, and when Edwards heard of his impending visit to the area, he invited him to minister in his stead while he was away for a fortnight in Worcester County, Massachusetts, on his own preaching tour.

To say that Buell was effective is an understatement. Relying on the itinerants' now standard modus operandi of preaching nearly every day and spending time in private, protracted meetings, Buell soon wound the Northampton congregation to a high pitch. When Edwards returned, he found the community in "extraordinary circumstances," he wrote Prince, "such in some respects as I never saw it in before." The whole town seemed "in a great and continual commotion." Ominously, there was also some decidedly unusual behavior. Some people, for example, lay "in a sort of trance, remaining for perhaps a whole twenty-four hours motionless, and with their senses locked up." Further, while they were so affected, they often remained as well under "strong imaginations, as though they went to heaven, and had there a vision of glorious and delightful objects."[29] Edwards was hard pressed to square such things with what he hitherto had learned of the way God worked on sinners.

Complicating matters, Buell had greatly influenced Sarah Edwards, who experienced her conversion under his ministry. Her awakening had begun early in 1742, with uneasiness after having disappointed her husband with regard to "some point of prudence, in some conversation" with Uncle Williams of Hatfield. Edwards's admonition evidently initiated evangelical humiliation, and for several days she pondered her worthlessness as a sinner. In this state Sarah looked forward to Buell's arrival, for from what she had heard of him, she hoped that he might do some good in Northampton and perhaps for her too. She was not disappointed. He proved both a powerful, captivating preacher and a compelling spiritual adviser. Indeed, it is not too much to suggest that Sarah became infatuated with this young man and admitted she had "greater success attending his preaching, than had followed the preaching of Mr. Edwards immediately before he went to Leicester." Struggling over whether it was right to rejoice more in Buell's labors than in her husband's, Sarah finally accepted that God might employ "some other instrument than Mr. Edwards, in advancing the work of grace in Northampton."[30]

While not attended with the extravagance of other conversions that Buell's visit initiated, Sarah's clearly displayed the marks of his counsel. The depth of her religious feelings, for example, often sapped her bodily strength, and she spoke of "strong emotions" that accompanied her "intense, and lively, and refreshing sense of divine things." Moreover, even though she clearly had absorbed some of her husband's vocabulary to describe the delights of conversion, she often spoke of her spiritual experience in graphic, almost tangible terms. "I appeared to myself to float or swim," she said of her deepest experience, "in these bright, sweet beams of the love of Christ, like the motes swimming in the beams of the sun, or the streams of light which come in at the window." She added: "My soul remained in a kind of heavenly elysium."[31]

Upon his return, Edwards urged Sarah to record her experiences, and he later used them in his account of the varieties of religious experience that he had witnessed during the revivals. But by his implicit approval of the manner of her and his parishioners' spiritual growth, he condoned behavior that eventually brought him (and the revival movement as a whole) much difficulty. Even in the revival's first year he recognized that faced with such extravagant behavior, he was on new ground. To his friend Moses Lyman, for example, he described "the great stir that is in the land, and those extraordinary circumstances and events that it is attended with." He knew, he continued, that word had gotten out of "persons crying out, and being set into great agonies, with a sense of sin and wrath, and having their strength taken away, and their minds extraordinarily transported with light, love and comfort." Yes, he had seen such things among his own parishioners, he admitted, but he assured Lyman that most of what he observed had had "the clear and incontestable evidences of a true divine work." He then proclaimed: "If this ben't the work of God, I have all my religion to learn over again, and know not what use to make of the Bible."[32] Unfortunately, in time Edwards would indeed have to reexamine some of the premises on which he based his approval of such emotionality.

After Buell's visit Edwards was troubled by his increasing inability to control such behavior. "When people were raised to this height, Satan took the advantage," he explained, and he therefore had to take "a great deal of caution and pains" to keep them "from running wild."[33] To capitalize on the ongoing revival even as he sought to control its excesses, Edwards in early March led his congregation in a covenant renewal ceremony. Another attempt to rein in the backbiting and worldliness that had marked the town until the recent "wonderful outpouring" of God's Spirit, the renewal, in which the entire community publicly reaffirmed its Christian duties, closed with an injunction to police itself with regard to the promises that it had just made, especially before participating in the sacrament of the Lord's Supper.[34] Attempting to put back in the bottle the genie of self-agency that the revivals had unleashed, Edwards signaled by his invocation of the Supper his continuing worry that his ongoing difficulties in Northampton were linked to the lax requirements for communion that his grandfather Stoddard had championed.

Edwards genuinely believed that the recent revivals had been "pure," even more so than in "the former outpouring of the Spirit in 1735 and 1736." But beginning about 1742, it began to appear otherwise, particularly after his people became more "dazzled with the high profession and great show [of religion] that some made who came hither from other places."[35] With the covenant renewal he tried to bind his people anew while they still were under the influence of the Spirit, to maintain the revival's momentum even as he sought to control untoward behavior.

EDWARDS AND THE AWAKENINGS

Northampton's experience in the wake of Whitefield's arrival was replicated in hundreds of communities, from New Hampshire to Georgia. And as reports of revivals in Scotland were added to word of those in England and on the Continent, many colonists began to believe that they were indeed participating in truly extraordinary events. The American revivals, later glorified with the name the Great Awakening, marked a signal period when individuals, communities, and entire colonies were united in bonds of common purpose as never before.[36]

Unlike five years earlier, when Edwards had been at the center of the Hampshire awakenings, he doubted his effectiveness in these recent events. In the late spring of 1741 he wrote to Wheelock to ask him and Benjamin Pomeroy, both of whom had become prominent itinerants, to come to Northampton to help him stir up his flock. "There has been a reviving of religion among us of late," Edwards told the two, and "your labors have been much more remarkably blessed than mine."[37] They obliged; and through the first years of the Awakening, he frequently tendered other such invitations to itinerant ministers who he thought could effectively fan the spiritual embers in his church.

But although at first Edwards was not fully aware of it, from an early stage of the new revivals he in fact was becoming central to the work through the extensive circulation of his *Faithful Narrative* and his subsequent publications about the events. Account after account of the revivals from the late 1730s and 1740s testified to the Hampshire narrative's pervasive influence, both in inspiring others to pray for comparable blessings and in providing a pattern of what Christians might expect if God answered their prayers.

As early as 1737, in his Connecticut election sermon Israel Loring had in mind Hampshire County when he asked people to pray for another event like that which "God ha[d] wrought in some Parts of this Land," when the people had had "a marvelous Visit from the Lord of Hosts."[38] As excitement for the revivals built in the early 1740s, more and more clergy invoked Edwards's account to stimulate their own evangelical efforts. In Durham, New Hampshire, the Reverend Nicholas Gilman read and remarked on parts of *Faithful Narrative* to his people and later did the same with sermons from Edwards's *Discourses on Various Important Subjects*.[39] Similarly, following prayers at a private meeting at the home of the Reverend John Cotton in Halifax, Massachusetts, this minister read from Edwards's *Narrative*.[40] In Wrentham, Massachusetts, Henry Messinger observed that "the News of *many Conversions* in *Northampton* and *other Towns* in *that Part of the Country some Years before*" were the "Means of stirring up Thoughtfulness in many."[41] In Gloucester, Massachusetts, after John White heard of "God's marvelous Works of Grace at Northampton, and especially upon reading the surprising and affecting Account thereof, drawn up by their Reverend pastor," he prayed that "the God of all Grace" would visit his community too.[42] News from the middle colonies was similar. In New Jersey William Tennent's interest in Edwards's work was shared by fellow evangelist John Cross, who legitimated an account of a work of the Spirit in his community by explaining that it "directly answered the account given by Mr. Edwards of the work in Northampton." So normative had Edwards's description of the earlier awakenings become that by 1743, when Thomas Prince issued a circular letter to clergy throughout New England to solicit their revival accounts, his directions patently derived from Edwards's book.[43]

Undeniably, emulation played a large role in the spread of the revivals, a fact captured pithily by one of Timothy Cutler's informants who had traveled to the Connecticut River valley during the first awakenings. When a resident was asked *"whether He thought the thing was not catching,"* the informant recorded the answer simply as, "He did." Cutler recognized how a desire to experience what others already had—in a sense to imitate their experiences—shaped people's response to the events. He thus believed that while many were genuinely converted in these revivals, many others were merely "led by Example." There was such great pressure on people to conform their experiences to those of others and to attest to their divine origin that some people were shy to give "their Sence [*sic*] of the facts" from fear of "prejudicing" themselves "by their Contradicting what is there counted very sacred."[44]

Once there was outright opposition to (as opposed to mere skepticism about) the revivals, Edwards's role began to change. Criticism now began to intensify among those who viewed the converts' excessive emotionality as a liability, mere "enthusiasm" worked up by Satan. At this point Edwards emerged as one of the revivals' chief apologists, in large measure because he published important new works that treated various aspects of the contemporary revivals. Concerned above all with the irregularities among converts in Northampton, Edwards explored in sermon and discourse the pressing topic of how, in times of heightened emotion, one distinguished between true and false religion. As in 1736, his answers to questions that had arisen from his own circumstances soon brought him a much larger audience.

OLD LIGHT OPPOSITION

Opponents of the awakenings, often called Old Lights, found much to object to in the conduct of New Light supporters, but they were most incensed by actions that disrupted established church order. In particular, attack after Old Light attack focused on three issues: the problem of itinerant ministers and so-called lay exhorters, the tendency of the awakened to display antinomian behavior (particularly in their eagerness to judge whether others were converted), and the converts' excessive emotionalism. In each case, examples of what they objected to had occurred on Edwards's watch in Northampton, and these issues were uppermost in his mind as he refined his understanding of the revivals.

Whitefield, Buell, and Wheelock, among others, epitomized the phenomenon of itinerancy. At its least harmful it meant that rather than minister solely to a parish to which one was formally connected, a minister traveled, sometimes at the invitation of another clergyman or, more problematically, of some group of townspeople, to spread the Word of God. If by a colleague's invitation, the itinerant might preach in a meetinghouse, as Buell did in Edwards's absence; if by the laity, he might speak in someone's home, in another public building, or even, as with Whitefield's great lectures, in the open air. Any appropriate venue served the itinerants' purposes.[45] On one of his peregrinations from Durham, New Hampshire, Nicholas Gilman preached to "some Hundreds of People" in Lieutenant John Emery's "Cornhouse an[d] Malt House."[46]

The behavior of those drawn to the revivals warranted more concerns. One critic described the peripatetic Gilbert Tennent as "a monster" who somehow "charmed" his audience. "In the most dreadful winter that I ever saw," the writer said, people "wallowed in the snow night and day for the benefit of his beastly brayings."[47] Most threatening to the established order was an itinerant's splitting communities into contending parties, rending an already weakened ecclesiastical fabric. At its most harmful, itinerancy had the potential to divide communities through "separation" of the true church from its worldly counterfeit.

This was even likelier when the itinerant was not an ordained clergyman, a more frequent occurrence as the revivals spread and the converted grew impatient with some ministers' unwillingness to entertain revivalists. A direct threat to the control clergymen exercised through ministerial associations, lay exhorting—preaching by those not formally educated for or ordained in the ministry—was one of the Awakening's most divisive issues and particularly so after Gilbert Tennent published his inflammatory sermon *The Danger of an Unconverted Ministry* (1740), wherein he urged Christians to do nothing less than cast from the churches clergy who themselves had not experienced the work of conversion.[48]

Nathan Bowen of Marblehead, Massachusetts, indicated where such arguments might lead. It was now reputable, he wrote, "for Common fellows to preach[,] pray & Exhort in Public, without any other Consideration, than the Gratifying his own Vain pride of hart." Who would pay clergy for preaching, he asked, "when a Lay Brother or Sister, can by ye Immediate Impulse of ye Sperit Teach to better purpose, for nothing?" Given the proliferation of uneducated exhorters, New England was far from having "a Famine of ye Word," he added, for "Carters[,] Coblers & ye many Labourers leave their Honest Imployments & Turn Teachers." Worse still, "women & even common Negroes take upon them to [exhort] their Betters even in the pulpit, before large Assemblys." Bowen hardly exaggerated such exhorters' messages.[49] In the summer of 1742 the *Boston Evening-Post* noted that "one Samuel Green, an itinerant," had been charged with making blasphemous speeches, for he claimed that "he was an emblem and Type of the Son of God" and with his breath "could blow away false Prophets as easily as the Holy Spirit."[50]

Green's behavior bled into another of the most frequent complaints about the revivalists: that they encouraged antinomian behavior—that is, a belief that Christ actually lived in and guided the saint. Critics often linked this charge to the equally antisocial notion (again typified by Green) that saints could unerringly judge the spiritual conditions of others. Such "rash judging" achieved its most notorious example in the itinerant minister James Davenport, who in 1743 led followers to the docks at New Haven and incited them to burn the books of such "unconverted" Puritan divines as Stoddard and the Mathers.[51] Many Old Lights connected such behavior to events a hundred years earlier, when Anne Hutchinson and her followers, eventually charged, tried, and convicted for holding purportedly antinomian views, had rocked the Massachusetts Bay Colony.[52] Given the behavior that some New Lights encouraged and approved, Old Lights reasoned that, without a renewed emphasis on one's social obligations, communities would disintegrate into anarchy.

Many antirevivalists also linked Whitefield's insistence on the necessity of a "New Birth" to this antinomian bogey. Thus, after the itinerant's arrival in Charleston, South Carolina, Alexander Garden, the bishop of London's commissary in that city, told his flock to "take good heed and guard against the first Beginnings of this *fatal* Malady." For once "Men's *Heads* are set a Wandering" and the "Wheels of their heated Imaginations agoing," he warned, "who shall prescribe the bounds?" He went on: "No *Reveries* so monstrous or absurd which shall not be deemed Divine Impulses or Inspirations!" No practices "so wicked or immoral" that could not be justified as "the *Impulse of the Spirit*, the command of God."[53] Reaching a fever pitch two years later in the Boston clergyman Charles Chauncy's *Seasonable Thoughts on the State of Religion in New England* (1743), with its lengthy preface comparing events with those in Hutchinson's day, the charges that converts were reviving "the Antinomian Principle" haunted New Light advocates. "*Few,*" Chauncy wrote, "*will venture to disown* a Likeness *between the Disturbances* then and now: *They are indeed surprisingly similar.*"[54]

In the seventeenth century the "rash judgment" that frequently accompanied antinomian beliefs had surfaced in Hutchinson's condemnation of most of the colony's clergy because they lacked "the seal of the spirit." Predictably, as the eighteenth-century revivals progressed and more communities splintered over the question of whether to welcome them, radical New Lights, following Gilbert Tennent, similarly condemned their enemies as unconverted and, so, benighted. While they most commonly directed such criticism at unsympathetic clergy, occasionally entire congregations were subject to the censure of newly minted converts. Nowhere was this more shocking than in an Anglican parish that the Reverend Samuel Johnson opened in Ripton, Connecticut, in the fall of 1743. There, the local "dissenting teacher," Jedediah Mills, "reviled and disclaimed against" Johnson's inaugural sermon, which in part, appropriately, treated the reverence due the Lord's House. Mills insisted that "there is no more holiness in a Church than under an oak tree," Johnson wrote, and soon thereafter some of Mills's followers acted on his sentiment by, as was delicately reported, "defiling the Church with ordure in several places."[55]

For many Old Lights the root of such behavior lay in the revivalists' untoward encouragement of emotionalism and their concomitant insistence that without it conversion was not genuine. Even in the revivals of 1734 and 1735, heightened emotions had played a large role, and six years later in Northampton, as everywhere else in the colonies, participation in the "work" seemed to demand an emotional response to doctrine. This experience was typical in Edwards's own parish during the earlier revivals. Timothy Cutler reported:

> A Certain Person in Northampton wanted [to] supply his Pile of Firewood which was low, and bad[e] his son go into the Woods and [g]et some Firewood, who said *He could not.* Whereupon his Father argued with Him and bad[e] Him observe the need they were under; but he continued saying *[H]e could not go.* At length his Father told Him that unless He was ill, He would [p]ut forth his Authority, and make Him go. And then his Son took up his Ax and went into the Barn, where He made an hideous Mourning and Noise, that [a]larm'd the Neighbours and they went to Him, and then calld his Father. At [l]ength it was moved to send for Mr Edwards their minister before whom He conti[n]ued in this manner, who thereupon advised the Father to forbear urging his [S]on, telling Him that He was under some extraordinary Influence of the [S]pirit, and was *getting through*: a Phrase much apply'd to such cases.[56]

What under different circumstances would have been dealt with as mere insubordination was here excused—nay, encouraged—because the young man was in the throes of spiritual rebirth.

Early in 1742 another Anglican, Charles Brockwell, reported similar things to his superior. "It is impossible to relate the convulsions into which the whole Country is thrown by a set of Enthusiasts that steal about harangueing the admiring Vulgar in *extempore* nonsense," he wrote. Their uncommon behavior of "groans, cries, screams & agonies must affect the Spectators were they never so obdurate & draw tears even from the most resolute, whilst the ridiculous & frantic gestures of others cannot but excite laughter & contempt, some leaping, some laughing, some singing, some clapping one another upon the back etc." This tragic scene, he observed, "is performed by such as are entering into the pangs of the New Birth; the comic[,] by those who are got thro' and those are so truly enthusiastic, that they tell you they saw the Joys of Heaven, can describe its situation, inhabitants, employments & have seen their names entered into the Book of Life."[57]

No mere critic's fabrication, this neatly corresponded to Gilman's description of his management of his flock during the excitement. When he dismissed the church one evening, he was moved to tell his people that he could "See them flocking to Heaven as they were from Meeting." When they turned around to listen to him, he called them back into the meetinghouse. "We held on thro the Night," he concluded, "Blessing and Praising[,] admiring and adoring God— Sometimes praying, then Singing, Exhorting[,] advising and directing, and Rejoycing together in the Lord." He added: "It seemed the Shortest and I think was the Sweetest Night that I have ever seen." He subsequently reported some of the visions that his parishioners, obviously brought to a high pitch, had related to him. On another occasion he wrote that he had found himself "lively in Sermon" and so continued to preach for "at least eight hours." Toward sunset he invited in another preacher, but the people "Screamed" so much that he returned and continued his discourse.[58]

Critics were particularly upset when such erratic New Lights encouraged comparable behavior in children, who comprised an important part of those "getting through." In his letter to London, for example, Brockwell observed that during the revivals "the sleep of children deprived of rest" was called "a trance" and their "uncouth dreams" (occasioned, he explained, from the confusion all around them, with people "praying, exhorting, swooning, etc.") deemed "no less than heavenly discoveries." Brockwell blamed the adults for misleading the youth, who were greatly affected by their parents' "uneasiness" and talked no less than their elders of "renovation, regeneration, conviction and conversion, tho' neither Children nor Parents understood the meaning of the terms they continually cant about." Children from the age of eight through their early teens often assembled, he added, "to vent the imaginary profusions of the Holy Spirit in disorderly praying and preaching." Another observer reported children of about the age of twelve running in the streets shouting that they were "bound to Zion" and inquiring "the way Zion ward."[59]

One could multiply such examples of extravagant behavior, for undeniably some prorevival clergy had let things get out of hand. A writer in the *Boston Weekly Post-Boy* summed up what critics thought of New Lights in his "Recipe" for a "new kind of Convert":

> Take of the green Leaves of Pretension, Hypocrisy and Ambition, of each three Handfuls; Spirits of Pride three drams; the Seeds of Discord and Dissention, one Ounce; the Flowers of Formality, half a pound; Roots of Obstinacy, Ignorance and Controversy, five Pounds . . . ; and then beat them all in the Mortar of Vain Glory with the Pestle of Contradiction: add a few Drops of Crocodile Tears mixt with the Water of Strife, infus'd over the Fire of Blind Zeal; add to the Composition four ounces of the Spirit of Self-Conceit more than lukewarm, and let the presuming Brother take a spoonful of it, Morning and Evening, before his Devotion.[60]

Nathan Bowen of Salem had seen what happened when communities indulged such "converts." Commenting on an itinerant preacher who had come to his town, he hauntingly evaluated a group of old women whom the visitor had "affrighted into Fits of Screeching . . . & the utmost Confusion." He continued: "Many Actions of the persons affected have put some of the more thinking in that town; in mind of ye worm wood & ye Gall of 1692"—that is, of the notorious witchcraft crisis of that year. He had similar thoughts on another occasion, regretting that for the past two years "We Poor Mortals in New England" had endured a "Scene of Folly." Almost every town had "a Part in the Tragedy, or rather Comedy," he wrote, "which will doubtless have A Particular Place in the History of future Times." He concluded: "Alas, thy fatal [16]92 was the days of thy Ignorance[.] But What Shall Excuse thee now?"[61]

THE DISCOURSE OF RELIGIOUS REVIVAL

As critics invoked the specter of earlier New England radicalism, and even of witchcraft, to smear the Awakening, on both sides of the Atlantic the movement's leaders took stock of their efforts to further God's work. Even before Buell's visit to Northampton early in 1742 Edwards had begun to question the behavior of some of his converts and sought to refine his understanding of how to direct their spiritual growth. The previous summer he had preached his powerful sermon *Sinners in the Hands of an Angry God* in Northampton and other locales, most famously at Enfield, Connecticut, where it electrified the auditors and induced just the sort of emotional outbreak he soon enough began to regret.

Prior to Edwards's reprise of his sermon in Enfield he had traveled to nearby Suffield, where other prorevival clergymen, including Benjamin Pomeroy, Joseph Meacham, and Eleazer Wheelock, had recently evangelized to some effect. The town's minister, Ebenezer Devotion, had died the preceding April, and they had asked Edwards to celebrate the Lord's Supper, as he did on July 5 with great success, with ninety-six participants. The following day he preached in a pri-

vate dwelling, a scene that one anonymous observer described in detail.[62] As this individual approached the house, he heard sobs like
those from "bereaved Friends" and then loud cries and groans
"higher" than those of "women in ye Pains of Childbirth," which
grew only louder as he entered the dwelling, filled with about two
hundred people of all ages. Many were fainting, others so enervated
that "you would have thought there [*sic*] bones all broken," and all
this "Extraordinary" to the senses. He remained for three hours as
Edwards, himself so wrought that at one point he nearly fainted,
prayed with the crowd, asking four or five laypeople to continue the
work when he rested. In all, fifteen to twenty people "were brought
to different degrees of Peace & Joy, Some to Rapture, all extolling the
Lord Jesus Xt all begging and beseeching Each One they could speak
to to come to a Redeemer, who had shewed them his mercy."

Meacham and Wheelock had tried to awaken nearby Enfield as
well but had little success until Edwards arrived fresh from his success
in Suffield. On July 8 in Enfield his cousin Stephen Williams also was
present and in his diary recorded the town's response to what ar-
guably has become the most famous sermon in American history.
Williams recorded a scene virtually identical to what had taken place
in the private residence in Suffield. Before Edwards had finished
speaking, he wrote, "there was a great moaning & crying out throughout the whole house." Some cried, "What shall I do to be saved?" and
others screamed, "O, I am going to Hell!" and "What shall I do for
Christ?" Edwards asked for quiet, but the uproar was so great that
he could not complete the sermon. Almost in tears, he went down
among the people and, with the other ministers, counseled those in
spiritual distress.[63]

What had affected the congregation that day was Edwards's insistence on the utter fragility of their lives in the face of God's omnipotence. His text—Deuteronomy 32:35, "Their foot shall slide in due
time"—led him to the inescapable doctrine "There is nothing that
keeps wicked men, at any moment, out of hell, but the mere pleasure
of God." In image after memorable image, he conveyed the inexora-

bility of punishment for the unawakened. "The bow of God's wrath is bent," he said, "and the arrow made ready on the string, and Justice bends the arrow at your heart, and strains the bow, and it is nothing but the mere pleasure of God, and that of an avenging God, without any promise or obligation at all, that keeps the arrow from being drunk with your blood."[64] Without the requisite change of heart wrought by grace, the arrow could not be stayed.

Even more frightening was Edwards's reminder of how insignificant each sinner was to a God who demanded justice for Adam's transgression. "The God that holds you over the pit of hell," he said famously, "much as one holds a spider, or some loathsome insect, over the fire, abhors you, and is dreadfully provoked; his wrath toward you burns like fire; he looks upon you as nothing else, but to be sent into the fire; he is of purer eyes than to have to bear to have you in his sight; you are ten thousand times so abominable in his eyes as the most hateful serpent in ours." Nothing but God's hand kept a person from falling into that fire at any moment, he continued, no other reason "that you did not go to hell the last night" or this morning—indeed, "why you don't this very moment drop down into hell." At this point the shrieking likely began, as Edwards made the audience consider its "fearful danger." It was, he added, "a great furnace of God's wrath, a wide and bottomless pit, full of the fire of wrath" over which he held them. "You hang by a slender thread," he intoned, "with the flames of divine wrath flashing about it, and every moment to singe it, and burn it asunder." And "nothing that you have ever done, nothing that you can do" will induce God "to spare you one moment."[65] This end awaited any congregant with Arminian tendencies, Edwards implied, and on this occasion his auditors heeded his message, so much so that he preached this sermon several more times and even published it, as *Sinner in the Hands of an Angry God*. When he did, he associated it only with his delivery at Enfield, where it had had its greatest effect, the sermon's rhetoric a triumph of his mature preaching style.

In the late summer of 1741 Edwards again stepped into the public arena but, perhaps troubled by the excessive emotionalism of the revivals in which he had participated, struck a different tone. He had gone to New Haven to deliver the address at Yale's commencement and took as his subject *The Distinguishing Marks of a Work of the Spirit of God*, or his first formal evaluation of the recent awakenings. Just before traveling, he had delivered the funeral sermon for his uncle William Williams, after whose passing Edwards became the de facto leader of the prorevival faction in the Hampshire Association. At Yale he took it upon himself to "try the spirits" of the recent awakenings and in so doing refined the discourse of religious revival that he had first scripted five years earlier. With such soon to be influential clergy as Samuel Hopkins and Samuel Buell among its auditors, *The Distinguishing Marks of a Work of the Spirit* became the first major volley in the battle to control the direction and meaning of the Great Awakening.[66]

The immediate occasion for his topic was the increased polarization of pro- and antirevivalists within the Hampshire Association, for by 1741 William Rand of Sunderland (who already had shown his Arminian stripes), Jonathan Ashley of Deerfield, and Benjamin Doolittle of Northfield had emerged as caustic critics of the revivals. Hence Edwards's invocation of the curse of Meroz against those who, while "the Lord is going forth so gloriously against his enemies," sit "silent and inactive." In his laudatory preface to the published version of the address, Boston's William Cooper openly named those who deserved the curse. Fruits of the revival, he noted, "do not grow on Arminian ground."[67]

Cooper was convinced that the revivals were "extraordinary." For one thing, the events were remarkable in their extent, for by then they had spread over "several provinces that measure many hundreds of miles on this continent." They were also unusual with respect to the number awakened and "the various sorts of persons that have been under [their] influence," including all ranks and degrees, but particularly the young. Finally, Cooper pointed to the Awakening's uniformity, for it was "the same work that is carried on in one place and another." He urged those conversant with the revivals to write their own narratives, as Edwards had five years earlier, for the benefit of others. "I can't but think it would be one of the most useful pieces of church history the people of God are blessed with," Cooper added, "the nearest to the Acts of the Apostles of anything extant."[68]

Two years later the first issue of Thomas Prince's monthly *The Christian History* appeared as an earnest of Cooper's wish. In the interim, people could peruse another publication, by the minister who through his *Faithful Narrative* had contributed so greatly to the initial progress of the awakenings. Edwards divided his new work (substantially enlarged for publication) into two parts. In the first, he addressed what were *not* signs by which one could judge whether something was a genuine work of the Spirit. Here he discussed converts' experiences being carried on in very unusual or extraordinary ways; the revival's effects on the participants' bodies, in crying out or groaning; its eliciting in others "a great deal of noise about religion"; and its subjects' having "great impressions of their imaginations."[69] None of these, he insisted, were truly distinguishing marks of a genuine religious experience. They neither confirmed nor denied it.

But Edwards had more to say. Even if those under the work of the Spirit sometimes were "guilty of great imprudences and irregularities," even if they showed too great "a forwardness to censure others as unconverted," even if Satan might have instigated errors in judgment, even if some who were affected fell away "into gross errors and scandalous practices," such things too neither confirmed nor denied that the events were caused by God.[70] Supported with plentiful examples from Scripture, this part of Edwards's address made clear that any who condemned the work on such grounds had to rethink their criteria, for the work comprised much more than such behavior.

What confirmed the Spirit's presence in such matters was the things that Edwards had insisted on for a decade. When conversion raised people's esteem of Jesus, and when it operated against the interests of Satan, or when it brought men to a higher regard of the Holy Scriptures and led them to divine truth, but most important, when "the spirit that [was] at work among a people operate[d] in a spirit of love to God and man," engendering Christian humility and not spiritual arrogance, it was surely a sign of divine presence.[71]

Given this taxonomy, Edwards concluded that God had initiated "the extraordinary influence" on the minds of people then abroad in the land, causing in them an "uncommon concern and engagedness of mind about the things of religion."[72] As Cooper had noted, the revivals occurred throughout the colonies and affected all sorts of people, young and old, high and low. If some had gotten overly excited and others had followed exhorters into extravagance and error, this should not discredit the entire Awakening. Further, having talked with many who had lived through his grandfather's harvests, Edwards concluded that the new events were but a continuation of this earlier revival, although, he admitted, there were "some new circumstances." He stated confidently to his New Haven audience, "We must throw by all talk of conversion and Christian experience; and not only so, but we must throw by our Bibles, and give up revealed religion, if this be not the general work of God."[73]

Edwards begged critics to proceed prudently, to wait to see the fruits of the Awakening in people's "lives and conversation." He also urged both "humility and self-diffidence" and, in a slap at lay exhorters, respect for education that aided one properly to "try the spirits," as he had attempted to do. "We have confined ourselves too much to a certain stated method and form in the management of our religious affairs," he explained, and thus religion had degenerated into mere formality. Even though innovation might frighten and alienate well-intentioned Christians—hence Edwards's counsel to avoid "that which is very much beside the common practice, unless it be a thing in its own nature of considerable importance"—Christians had to remain open to drinking such old wine from new bottles.[74]

CHAUNCY V. EDWARDS

Edwards's address at Yale was a plea for moderation and toleration, but these were not the temper of the times, and, rather than promote ecumenicalism, his sermon became a lightning rod for renewed debate. For revivalists, Edwards had provided an invaluable guidebook, widely read in New England and quickly reprinted in London and Edinburgh. In New Hampshire, for example, Gilman made good use of it with his flock, and from New Jersey, Jonathan Dickinson wrote that Edwards's new discourse had "met with deserv'd Acceptance, and been of great Use."[75] But Old Lights, convinced that "getting through" meant nothing more than taking the wide road to hell, found *Distinguishing Marks* muddled nonsense that only encouraged more erroneous and unchristian behavior. One critic called the recent conversions nothing more than "an epidemical distemper."[76]

Edwards's *Distinguishing Marks* received a formal reply from the Old Lights in Charles Chauncy's *The Late Religious Commotions in New-England Considered*. Two years younger than Edwards and a graduate of Harvard College, Chauncy had entered the fray the previous year with his *Enthusiasm Described and Cautioned Against*, coincidentally delivered at virtually the same time (the day after Harvard's commencement) as *Distinguishing Marks*.[77] The most powerful antirevival sermon of that era, it signaled the beginning of an intense pamphlet war among Edwards, Chauncy, and their respective supporters.

In Chauncy the Old Lights had found a champion intellectually up to the challenge of going head to head with Northampton's minister; and from this point on he was the undisputed leader of the Arminian clergy. From his position at Boston's First Church, Chauncy wielded great influence over the publication of antirevivalist literature. Indeed, as he later admitted with pride to Yale president Ezra Stiles, "there was scarce a piece against the times but was sent to me, and I had the labour sometimes of preparing it for the press, and always of correcting the press."[78] Chauncy also was not loath to offer advice to potential allies across the Atlantic. In 1742 part of his attack on the revivals included a condemnation of the New England events published in Edinburgh, where a similar evangelical movement flourished.[79]

But his main battleground was New England. Acting on Cooper's suggestion for broad inquiry into the revivals, Chauncy solicited information for and prepared a book-length response to Edwards's *Some Thoughts Concerning the Present Revival*, a lengthy defense of the awakenings, which appeared early in 1743. In September, Chauncy replied in *Seasonable Thoughts on the State of Religion in New England*, an unrelenting attack on the revivals. These two books, so opposed in their conclusions, constitute the most sustained intellectual debate over the recent events.

Written late in 1742, *Some Thoughts* was Edwards's final attempt to win support for the ongoing awakenings among those still confused by the events' untoward direction.[80] Much longer than *Distinguishing Marks*, *Some Thoughts* found Edwards more apologetic of (though not yet chastened by) the recent behavior of radical New Lights and thus willing to grant that his opponents deserved fuller answers to their objections. Such critics had emerged even in Edwards's own backyard. Late in 1742, as Edwards was completing *Some Thoughts*, Jonathan Ashley, minister to Deerfield and husband of one of William Williams's daughters, used an invitation to preach at Cooper and Colman's Brattle Street Church, a bastion of prorevival sentiment, to vent his spleen against the awakenings. Within the year Benjamin Doolittle of Northfield and William Rand of Sunderland had joined his cause in print, rending any unanimity to which the Hampshire Association pretended.[81]

More than an elaboration of *Distinguishing Marks*, Edwards's new book raised new concerns. In an early section, on taking scripture as the rule by which to judge credible conversion experiences, Edwards decried his opponents' confusion over the role of raised "affections" or emotions in religion. He insisted that they were "the very life and soul of all true religion" and, moreover, were indistinguishable from the will. His opponents, he explained, claimed the affections "as something diverse from the will, and not pertaining to the noblest part of the soul." To the contrary, Edwards insisted, "all acts of the affections" were in some sense acts of the will, and "all acts of the will [were] acts of the affections."[82] He also reconsidered church membership, so long his concern, observing that no one had the right to judge absolutely whether another was of the elect. "I have seen that which abundantly convinces me," he stated, "that the business is too high for me." Such discrimination was best left to God, "who is infinitely fit for it."[83]

These could have been Stoddard's sentiments, for he had based his liberalization of church membership requirements on similar premises. As Edwards considered the great complexity of religious experience he had witnessed during the revivals, he could not but agree with his grandfather, who had not presumed to separate the saints and the sinners in any absolute way. "God seems so strictly to have forbidden this practice of our judging our brethren in the visible church," Edwards wrote, for "we were too much of babes, infinitely too weak, fallible and blind, to be well capacitated for it." To attempt to do so would be "setting us vastly too high, and making us too much lords over our fellow creatures."[84] For the moment, however, Edwards left unexamined the still vexing question of who, precisely, should be given sacramental privileges, an oversight that returned to haunt him.

As a practical matter, Edwards *did* judge the behavior he witnessed, and nowhere more movingly than in his inclusion in *Some Thoughts* of a lengthy narrative that he proposed as an example of the height of evangelical piety. It was Sarah Edwards's account of her religious experience, written at his request in the aftermath of Buell's visit and now presented anonymously and without any indication of the convert's sex. Edwards remained fully convinced of Sarah's piety, for "if such things are enthusiasm, and the fruits of a distempered brain," he exclaimed, "let my brain be evermore possessed of that happy distemper!" And "if this be distraction, I pray God that the world of mankind may be all seized with this benign, meek, beneficent, beatifical, glorious distraction!"[85] Despite the problems that Buell had raised for Edwards, in Sarah he saw the genuine fruit of the work of the Spirit.

One other point in *Some Thoughts* bears notice, if only because of the embarrassment it eventually caused Edwards. In his discussion of why people should acknowledge and support the awakenings, he allowed himself a moment of hubris. It was not unlikely, he wrote, "that this work of God's Spirit, that is so extraordinary and wonderful, is the dawning, or at least a prelude, to that glorious work of God, so often foretold in Scripture"—that is, of the millennium—for there were "many things that make it probable that this work will begin in America."[86] Citing a bevy of scriptural passages that argued his case, Edwards here revealed his greatest hope: that the history of the work of redemption might culminate in his own time. Others demurred. In England, Isaac Watts found that Edwards's ideas on this issue "want[ed] force."[87] In Boston, Chauncy ridiculed the notion as "absolutely precarious," citing an informant who purportedly heard Edwards claim that the millennium actually had begun in Northampton in 1734 and 1735.[88]

Through almost four hundred pages Edwards marshaled scriptural and historical arguments to convince doubters to support the awakenings. Through an equal number of pages Chauncy in his book argued exactly the opposite. Substituting the word *passions* for *affections*, Chauncy argued for their rational control by the "understanding" and so incorrectly separated (as Edwards had claimed his enemies did) the affections from the will. "One of the most *essential* Things necessary in the *new-forming* Men," Chauncy claimed, "is the Reduction of their *Passions* to a proper Regimen, i.e. The Government of a *sanctified Understanding*." Thus, "when Men's *Passions* are raised to an *extraordinary* Height," as they obviously were during awakenings, "if they have not, at the same Time, a due Balance of *Light* and *Knowledge* in their Minds," they are "in Circumstances of extreme Hazard." He concluded: "The plain Truth is, an *enlightened Mind*, and not *raised Affections*, ought always to be the Guide of those who call themselves Men."[89]

These two large intellects and their respective parties could not be reconciled, for they did not speak the same language. Through the remainder of 1743, positions hardened and tempers flared. After the annual clerical convention in Boston in May, the antirevivalists caucused and published a sharp denunciation of the recent events, a document that fostered much ill will because though it was presented as the opinion of the convention as a whole, only a small group of the total number of ministers in attendance in fact had signed the document. Following the Harvard commencement, the prorevivalists answered with a pamphlet of their own, with a different, and larger, set of signatories in support of the revivals. Charges of antinomianism and Arminianism were hurled back and forth, and with the behavior of radical New Lights like Davenport and Andrew Croswell (another champion of lay exhorters) each day more vexing, the awakenings fell into more disrepute.[90]

By the spring of 1743 Edwards thought the battle lost because the New Lights had not exercised enough control over its dynamic. He wrote to the Reverend William McCulloch of Glasgow, in the hope that he (and Scots evangelicals generally) would profit from seeing the errors of the New England churches. "We have run from one extreme to another, with respect to talking of experiences," Edwards observed. Before, "there was too great a reservedness in that matter," he wrote, but now "many have gone to an unbounded openness, frequency, and constancy in talking of their experiences, declaring almost everything that passes between God and their souls, everywhere and before everybody." Among some of the converts, in other words, religion had been subsumed in religiosity, mere outward display. Among the ill consequences of this practice, he warned, is that "religion runs all into that channel," with other components of spirituality neglected or denigrated.[91]

"There is a great decay of the work of God amongst us," Edwards wrote to James Robe, another Scot, the same day, "and the prejudices there are [against it], in a great part of the country, are riveted and inveterate." Robe recently had overseen a revival at Kilsyth, which Edwards hoped was "less mixed with error and extravagance" than those in America. He described in detail how, in New England, people now were so divided over the revivals that "there [was] at length raised a wall between them up to heaven," an estrangement he blamed squarely on the "imprudent management in the friends of the work, and a corrupt mixture which Satan has found means to introduce." In particular, many had been ready to think that "all high raptures [were] divine," while in fact clergy should have carefully distinguished "such joys and raised affections" from those that were only part of "a noisy show of humility."[94]

In December Edwards wrote a lengthy epistle to Thomas Prince, in response to his request for an account of the Northampton Awakening, for his monthly periodical *The Christian History* (the first issue of which had appeared the previous March). Edwards obliged with many details and, for the most part, remained positive. But while he pointed to people whose behavior subsequent to their conversions demonstrated a true change of heart, he also admitted that there were some others who, swept by raptures and visions, afterward returned to their selfish ways. Such individuals, he wrote, had "a strange influence on the people, and gave many of them a deep and unhappy tincture, that it was hard and long labor to deliver them from, and which some of them are not fully delivered from to this day."[93]

RELIGIOUS AFFECTIONS

The battle for a general Awakening all but lost, Edwards tried to salvage what he could in his own congregation. Late in 1742 and into the next year, he preached a series of sermons on a topic that he had broached in *Some Thoughts* and that eventuated in 1746 in publication of *A Treatise Concerning Religious Affections*, his major evaluation of the effects of conversion. He had come to attribute the revivals' demise primarily to a misunderstanding among both antirevivalists and more radical New Lights over the role of the affections in a work of the Spirit. All the other problems—the censuring, the cries and swoons, the visions, the ranting of lay exhorters, the schisms—derived from not being able to discern truly gracious affections. For almost a decade Edwards had gathered his thoughts on the subject. By 1743, when he completed his sermons, he had preached on the nature of the affections and their importance in religion, once again dissected what were not certain signs that affections were gracious, and, finally, opined on the "distinguishing signs of truly gracious and holy affections." The treatise was his most important work to date, unassailable proof that "True religion, in great part, consists in holy affections."[94]

Herein Edwards aimed "to show the nature and signs of the gracious operations of God's Spirit, by which men are the subjects of, which are not of a saving nature." The key lay in proper regard for the religious affections, which he defined as nothing else but "the more vigorous and sensible exercises of the inclination and will of the soul," not the mere emotions or passions, not outward manifestations of excitement, but something at the very core of our motivation and thus of our being.[95]

Edwards defined his terms precisely. In a discussion of the affections, he noted, language often was "somewhat imperfect, and the meaning of words in a considerable measure loose and unfixed, and not precisely limited by custom." Thus, he took great pains to distinguish between the mere *understanding*, that by which one was capable of perception and speculation, and the *will*. The latter was the faculty, he explained, by which the soul did not merely perceive and view things but was in some way "inclined with respect to the things it views or considers; either is inclined to 'em, or is disinclined, and averse from 'em." The will was the faculty, in other words, by which the soul did not merely behold things "as an indifferent unaffected spectator, but either as liking or disliking, pleased or displeased, approving or rejecting." Some people termed this faculty the *inclination*, he noted, "and the *mind*, with regard to the exercises of this faculty, [was] often called the *heart*."[96] He reemphasized that the will and the affections were not two distinct faculties but one and the same.

True religion, then, was but the "vigorous and lively actings of the inclination and will of the soul, or the fervent exercises of the heart." God had made the affections the "spring of men's actions," he observed. Critics of the revivals, however, tragically confused the affections with mere passions and then discounted all emotional behavior as "enthusiasm," whether or not it stemmed from God's Spirit. Edwards also observed that just as now too many disregarded any behavior that stemmed from the affections as erroneous, so three or four years earlier he and his cohort had erred in being too willing to go to the opposite extreme. "As on the one hand," he counseled, "there must be light in the understanding, as well as an affected fervent heart, where there is heat without light, there can be nothing divine or heavenly in that heart." But so too, "where there is a kind of light without heat, a head stored with notions and speculations, with a cold and unaffected heart, there can be nothing divine in that light, that knowledge is no true spiritual knowledge of divine things." He concluded: "If the great things of religion are rightly understood, they will affect the heart."[97]

Edwards then turned to some familiar intellectual ground. Just because affections were raised high, he noted, or altered the body, or made people constantly talk of religion, or brought scriptural texts to mind, this did not mean that they were truly gracious. Nor were affections necessarily genuine if the comforts and joys that followed them occurred in a certain predictable sequence or made people zealously engage in the external duties of religion. Such actions could all be counterfeited.

Further, it was not necessarily a sign that affections were truly religious if they made one "exceeding confident that what they experience is divine, and that they are in a good estate," for this too easily led to "evangelical" hypocrisy and the sins of censure and rash judgment. Having in mind New Lights who presumptuously claimed knowledge of their salvation, Edwards explained that "it is with professors of religion, especially such as become so in a time of outpouring of the Spirit of God, as it is with the blossoms in the spring." There are vast numbers of them, he continued, "which all look fair and promising; but yet very many of them never come to anything." Many of those soon enough will wither, drop off, and rot, "for a while look as beautiful and gay as the others" and smell as sweet, "so that we can't, by any of our senses, certainly distinguish those blossoms which have in them that secret virtue, which will afterwards appear in the fruit." But it is the "mature fruit which comes afterwards, and not the beautiful colors and smell of the blossoms," by which we must judge them, he continued. So new converts might talk of things of religion, and "appear fair, and be very savory," yet "all may come to nothing."[98]

What were the distinguishing signs of truly gracious and holy affections? Edwards enumerated twelve. In treating some, he elaborated on topics that he already had explained from the pulpit or in print; in others, he announced new criteria drawn from his ongoing dissection of spiritual experience. Thus in his first sign he returned to what he had treated so memorably in *A Divine and Supernatural Light*. Affections that were truly gracious arose from "those influences and operations on the heart, which [were] *spiritual*, *supernatural* and *divine*." Here Edwards recurred to the language of Lockean empiricism in which he had described his own conversion a few years earlier. In the minds of saints, he explained, was "a new inward perception or sensation of their minds, entirely different in its nature and kind, from anything that ever their minds were the subjects of before they were sanctified." This perception is of an entirely new sort and could not be produced by any "exalting, varying or compounding" of the kinds of perceptions that people had before, for it was quite simply "what some metaphysicians [that is, John Locke and his party] call[ed] a new simple idea." It followed, then, that if grace was, in this sense, "an entirely new principle," the exercises of it were "entirely new kinds of exercises."[99]

But even more important, this new spiritual sense was not a "new faculty or understanding" but rather a new *principle* in the saint, a natural habit or foundation for action "so that to exert the faculties in that kind of exercises, may be said to be his nature," an inextricable part of him, who he was, ever after. It was thus "a new foundation laid in the nature of the soul, for a new kind of exercises of the same faculty or understanding." This was another way to say that the change was perfectly natural—that is, explicable through the discourse of contemporary natural science.[100] A "natural" man simply lacked this principle and so was not inclined to God in the same way as one who had it. For those who did have it, all behavior changed, for this new principle transformed the very sense of heart, one's basic character, as the sinner became a saint.

Much followed from the saint's apprehension of this new, simple idea. For one thing, he saw the "transcendentally excellent and amiable nature of divine things as they are in themselves," not through any relation such things had to mere self-interest. He saw the moral excellence of divine things and came to understand with conviction their justness and beauty. Further, truly gracious affections were attended with evangelical humiliation and "the lamblike, dovelike spirit and temper of Jesus Christ." Such affections also had a "beautiful symmetry and proportion," as when the saint displayed love toward others and in which he manifested his piety in varied ways toward all creation.[101]

Also, the higher gracious affections were raised, the more one's spiritual appetite increased. The true saint thus never rested but always yearned for more ways to live the Christian life. Complacency was the sure sign that one was not of the elect, for a saint tended to goodness, he observed, "as bodies [that] are attracted to the globe of the earth, tend to it more strongly, the nearer they come to the attracting body, and are not at rest out of the center." He connected this metaphor from physics to his twelfth and final sign, for gracious and holy affections also had "their exercise and fruit in Christian practice," the very "business" of the saint's life. This Christian practice, Edwards maintained, was "the chief of all the evidences of a saving sincerity in religion," for by their fruits one could know them.[102]

A Treatise Concerning Religious Affections provided a remarkable synthesis of Edwards's thoughts on the revivals. Here he defined spirituality as internal and private, a matter of one's feeling and disposition. Buttressed by both scripture and a wide range of Protestant authors (most notably, his grandfather Stoddard and, among the New England divines, Thomas Shepard), *Religious Affections* is testament to its author's understanding of how the divine impinges on the human. Unlike Edwards's *Faithful Narrative* or *Distinguishing Marks*, however, *Religious Affections* did not make an immediate mark, nor did it do so in his lifetime. By 1746 the awakenings were a receding memory, and his book spoke to controversies that many sought to put behind them. And although eventually republished in England and Scotland, it had less immediate effect there than some of his earlier works, perhaps because it was linked so profoundly to the dysfunction and disintegration of the American revivals.

In *Religious Affections*, however, Edwards had enshrined a unique way to understand the religious life, one that emphasized spiritual experience as a transformation of the inner self that later eventuated in good works. Coupled with his *Account of the Life of David Brainerd* (1749), a biography of a young missionary who exemplified the work of piety, *Religious Affections* provided a new understanding of how one experienced and demonstrated one's religion.

SIX

Northampton in Turmoil

(1744–1750)

PARISH TENSIONS

Between 1739 and 1743 Edwards was busy on many stages. Locally he continued to promulgate revival through his weekly sermons and frequent meetings with his parishioners as they sought greater understanding of their spiritual experiences. But he also was active regionally, for because of his reputation as a revivalist, he was often invited to preach in other communities in Massachusetts and Connecticut. Thus his famous visit to Enfield, Connecticut, in the summer of 1741, when he delivered a reprise of *Sinners in the Hands of an Angry God*, and his trip to Leicester and other parts of Worcester County, Massachusetts, early in 1742, when the itinerant Samuel Buell stepped into his Northampton pulpit. Moreover, after William Williams's death in the summer of 1741, Edwards assumed a larger role in the Hampshire Association and, through it, in the affairs of the province's churches, as other clergy also struggled with the effects and implications of the awakenings. Finally, through his published works as well as a growing private correspondence, Edwards participated in the transatlantic discussion of the revivals, particularly with clergy in the Boston area and in Scotland.[1] By any standard, he was busy.

After 1744, with the end of internecine debate over the revivals,

Edwards's role as an evangelist contracted. His continuing efforts to reinvigorate Northampton's spiritual Awakening yielded little fruit, and he returned to disciplinary matters, trying to hold his community to the standards to which it had committed itself in its recent covenant renewal. But his influence clearly was weakening, for the period between 1744 and 1750 brought escalating tension between him and his church, a painful situation for one who had witnessed the deference this flock had given his grandfather. Indeed, although Edwards remained in Northampton until the end of the decade, his effectiveness as a spiritual leader diminished with each passing year as parochial concerns estranged him from his constituency.

The town's growing disenchantment with its minister was most evident in several years of bickering over his salary, a subject not usually associated with a clergyman who often inveighed against Mammon. But with a large family to support, Edwards depended on his yearly stipend as much as any other head of household. Complicating matters, the 1740s marked a time of inflation and scarce currency in the province, a situation manifest in frequent calls for the creation of a provincial land bank—that is, a fund of money available for loans that was backed by mortgaged lands as collateral.[2] Reluctant to guarantee any salary whose value finally depended on the province's unstable economy, the church resisted Edwards's desire to fix the amount permanently.

Edwards's problem was not with the amount of his salary but rather with the recalcitrance with which the town approved his yearly allotment, a situation exacerbated by what some viewed as the extravagance of their minister's household expenses. In a letter to a precinct committee in 1744, Edwards remarked that the church's addition of fifty pounds to his salary seemed to have "occasioned many jealousies" among his parishioners, as though he and his family were "lavish of what we received and of a craving disposition." The townspeople, he continued, seemed not to like his family's "manner of spending" or the "clothes that we wore and the like," a charge for which there evidently was some basis.[3] To eliminate the need for holding out his hand each year as he justified his requests, Edwards shortly thereafter proposed a set annual salary. In other words, if he and the church could agree on an amount, he never would expect any other increase and promised "never to complain that I have no more." He continued: "The affair of your minister's support, and the consideration of his family's circumstances, won't come over every year, to exercise your minds, and to occasion various opinions and speeches, and to be a constant temptation to persons to look into the way in which the minister spends his money." Indicative of how much suspicion existed between the parties, he also assured the committee that he did not intend to lead them into any "snare." Four years passed, however, before they agreed in principle to his wish and voted him seven hundred pounds a year, the largest clerical salary in the valley, subject to adjustment depending on the market value of certain chief commodities.[4]

THE "BOYS" AND THEIR "BAD BOOKS"

Edwards's estrangement from his parishioners was also painfully evident in his attempt, in the spring of 1744, to discipline several young adults for lewd and insubordinate behavior.[5] Long considered the match that lit Northampton's powder keg, the case was symptomatic of Edwards's frustrating inability to capitalize on the revivals. In the awakenings of both the mid-1730s and the early 1740s, Edwards had found the young people's heightened interest in religion so remarkable that he featured it in his published accounts of the awakenings. More recently, in his community's solemn renewal of its church covenant, the young people had vowed "never to allow ourselves in any youthful diversions and pastimes" that might "sinfully tend to hinder the devoutest, and most engaged spirit in religion."[6] Ironically, at that very time some of the youths began to engage in what Edwards and other adults considered lascivious behavior. That most of the young men involved were church members made the situation all the more embarrassing.

In retrospect, the situation that Edwards faced seems fairly cut-

and-dried. A score of young men had acquired two popular medical books and then used their newfound knowledge of female anatomy to taunt young women, behavior that Edwards thought warranted censure. But when he tried to discipline them, he encountered an emergent challenge to clerical authority that had begun to characterize Northampton's—indeed, all New England's—social structure. Empowered by their centrality to the revivals and now eager to challenge traditional patterns of deference, young parishioners assumed an agency hitherto restricted to those of higher rank. In particular, the young people grew impatient with restrictions imposed on them by those who were not their betters, at least in any spiritual sense.[7] Such difficulties with those whom he numbered among the converted made Edwards aware of what he subsequently codified in the *Religious Affections*. True virtue was manifest most clearly in outward, godly behavior, not in mere profession of experience. The "bad books" case made this painfully evident.

Edwards's troubles began when he asked the parish to appoint a committee to investigate complaints against a number of young men, most in their early twenties, who had gained access to the anonymous and commonly reprinted *Aristotle's Masterpiece: or, The Secrets of Nature Displayed in All the Parts Thereof* and Thomas Dawkes's *The Midwife Rightly Instructed* (1736) and used them both for their own titillation and to harass some of the young women in town.[8] Focusing on reproduction and pregnancy, these texts included verbal descriptions (and, in the case of the former work, graphic illustrations) of the female reproductive organs. These were not the sorts of things young men were supposed to read, a fact they were well aware of. In her deposition in the case, for example, Elizabeth Pomeroy reported that she found one of the books hidden "in their house up the chimney, on the backside of the chimney on the press," where her brother Ebenezer Pomeroy, one of the accused, had hidden it. Another of the group, Noah Baker, had secreted his book in the lining of his coat.[9]

The controversy started predictably enough when the young men, all converts in Edwards's recent awakenings, began to lend the pro-scribed texts to one another for private reading and then to meet in small groups to make "sport of what they read in the book."[10] Ebenezer Bartlett admitted that he sat up until midnight reading one of the texts when it came to him, and added, "Don't you think I would sit up again if I had the opportunity?" Several different female deponents testified that they had come upon the young men in just such behavior, engrossed in a book "that they were provoked about" and telling them "what nasty creatures they was." One "Bathsheba Negro" reported that one of the offenders, Timothy Root, was particularly irreverent, mockingly calling the book the "young folks' bible."[11]

The young men used their newly acquired knowledge to harass young women, "run[ning] upon the girls" and "boasting how much they knew about them." They further humiliated them by claiming that they could tell whether they were pregnant and if they were menstruating. Oliver Warner asked, "When does the moon change girls?" He continued: "Come, I'll look at your [face] and see whether there is a blue circle 'round your eyes." Some of the men got more physical. The same Bathsheba who testified that Root had laughingly read from the book to her and Naomi Warner, reported that after he finished, he was ready "to kiss them" and "catch hold of the girls and shook 'em."[12]

Shocked at such "unclean and lascivious expressions," Edwards moved to discipline the young men. He appointed a committee to investigate the evidence and kept his own notes on the testimony as the inquiry unfolded. In late March, for example, he solicited information from "Eleazar Hannam's Wife" on whether when she was at a friend's house, two of the accused, Oliver Warner and Medad Lyman, were "reading in a book about womenkind" and "[made] sport" of it before other women.[13] The evidence that Edwards gathered was unequivocal: The young men did not deny that they had done exactly what others said they had.

The incident should thereupon have ended with the chastisement of the accused, but it did not. Most revealing was how the young men comported themselves when confronted with the charges. Timothy and Simeon Root were particularly obstreperous during the proceedings. When the committee first met to examine them, the Roots, with "an air of contempt," asked, "What do we do here?" and added, "We won't stay here all day long." Indeed, before the examination started, they actually left for the nearby tavern, where they "called for a mug of flip [an alcoholic beverage] and drank it," and at another point during the proceedings they engaged in a game of leapfrog. Most shocking, however, was their open disdain of the examiners themselves, particularly evident in Timothy Root's utter disregard of the deference expected of the accused to their social betters. "I won't worship a wig," he haughtily exclaimed when first brought before the church committee, and added that his examiners were "nothing but men molded up [of] a little dirt." He continued: "I don't care a turd, or I don't care a fart, for any of them." He had wasted enough time in this matter, he thought, and if they had any business with him, he wasn't "obliged to wait any longer on their arses."[14]

Edwards's handling of the case—cut-and-dried as it seemed—exacerbated divisions in a town already chafing at his demands for a permanent salary. Edwards's first biographer, Samuel Hopkins, claimed that Edwards put the town "all in a blaze" because he read aloud a list of names without discriminating the accused from those who were only witnesses; Hopkins also suggested that some "considerable families" were particularly incensed at his heavy-handedness in the matter.[15] Despite the heightened emotions the case raised, a situation that one historian suggests was related to the increased stratification of gender roles characteristic of the period, Edwards was mortified at the behavior of those whom he once had proudly considered his converts.[16]

Three of the young men were eventually disciplined: The Roots were convicted of contemptuous behavior toward the church, and Oliver Warner was found guilty of public lewdness.[17] But a lack of unanimity in the public's response to the minister's zeal only made more difficult his oversight of a community whose social divisions were typified by the Roots' quasi-democratic insults. Moreover, to

Edwards the "bad books" case proved that Northampton's family government was in shambles. So too its church government, for under current ecclesiastical policy most of those implicated could continue as church members and receive communion. If Edwards attempted to tighten membership qualifications and thus keep such morally offensive individuals from participating, would the town support him, given that such an action would challenge what its revered Stoddard had instituted? Before long he had an answer.

ECUMENICAL PRAYER

In 1745 George Whitefield returned to New England, reopening divisions among Old and New Light factions. He spent a week visiting the Edwardses in the valley before moving on, seeking to replicate his earlier evangelical success. Fortuitously, the itinerant's arrival coincided with the recent success of a British expedition to capture the strategic French fort at Louisburg on Cape Breton Island, a campaign with twoscore Northampton men among its number. The fort's collapse on June 17, 1745, and the subsequent failure of the "Young Pretender," a Catholic Stuart, to consolidate power in Scotland and England left Edwards and other Protestants excited at the possibility that God was again smiling on their cause (and specifically on New England) as he prepared the way for the overthrow of the Catholic Antichrist.

The British government thereupon laid plans for the conquest of Canada, and Northampton became an important garrison. For the next two years the town lived in constant fear of attack by the French and Indians, with depredations occurring as near as Saratoga in New York, Fort Massachusetts in the western part of the province, and even neighboring Southampton, where settlers from Northampton recently had formed a new church. Hostilities in this phase of the ongoing wars ended on October 18, 1748, with the signing of the peace at Aix-la-Chapelle.[18]

Prior to that date, Edwards had contributed to the war by his support of another evangelical effort, an international concert of prayer to unite New England's Protestants with like-minded brethren in Scotland and elsewhere who each quarter joined in either private or communal prayer.[19] The idea for such concerts had originated among Scots clergy who had recently experienced their own great revivals, but the notion of such communal prayer was not new to Edwards. In *Some Thoughts Concerning the Present Revival*, for example, he had written that he had often thought it very desirable and likely to be followed with a great blessing "if there could be some contrivance that there should be an agreement of all God's people in America, that are well affected to this work, to keep a day of fasting and prayer."[20] By 1743 he had acted on this idea locally, establishing "many societies for prayer and social religion [that] were all along kept up."[21] But with the collapse of the New England phase of the awakenings, as well as his disappointment at the deteriorating situation in his own church, Edwards advocated the extension throughout the colonies of such prayer, particularly after he heard of his Scots correspondent John McLaurin's great success in reuniting his people through just such special events. By 1745, Edwards reported to one of McLaurin's compatriots, he had "taken great pains to promote a falling in with this [the Scots'] Concert in New England."[22]

By 1747 Edwards had formalized his plea for Christian union in *An Humble Attempt to Promote Explicit Agreement and Visible Union of God's People in Extraordinary Prayer*, a tract that mixed exhortations toward that end with millennial speculation on the need for Christian cooperation.[23] He admitted that his encouragement of the concerts stemmed in part from disappointment at the condition of the churches in the aftermath of the revivals. "How many errors and extremes are we liable to," he exclaimed, and "How quickly overtoppled, blinded, misled, and confounded!" But those same revivals, as well as the recent victories on the battlefields, also were signs that God might be about to do something more glorious "and would, before he finishes, bring things to greater ripeness." Such commotions as recently had shaken the churches were but "forerunners of something exceeding glorious approaching."[24]

Rev. JONATHAN EDWARDS,
President of Nassau-Hall College.
NEW JERSEY.

Drawn and Engraved by Abner Reed, from an original Portrait, in the possession of J.W. Edwards, Esq. Hartf.

Engraving of Jonathan Edwards by Abner Reed, from an original painting. (Collection of the author)

"I walked abroad alone, in a solitary place, for contemplation."
Page 5.

Edwards in solitary meditation during the time of his conversion. (*Conversion of President Edwards* [American Tract Society, c. 1820s])

Engraving of Benjamin Colman (1673–1747), minister at the Brattle Street Church who helped Edwards publish his *Faithful Narrative of the Surprising Conversions* (1737). He was a strong supporter of the eighteenth-century revivals. (Ebenezer Turell, *The Life and Character of the Reverend Benjamin Colman, D.D.* [1749; reprint Delmar, N.Y.: 1972])

Engraved on Steel by Bradshaw

The Rev.d George Whitefield. A.M.

Engraving of George Whitefield (1714–1770), an English evangelist whose visits to the colonies spurred widespread revivals. (Collection of the author)

Engraving of Gilbert Tennent (1703–1764), a prorevival minister from New Jersey who read his flock excerpts from Edwards's *Faithful Narrative* to stir their revival hopes. (Joseph Tracy, *The Great Awakening* [Boston: 1842])

Whitefield preaching to a large gathering outdoors. Whitefield was one of the first itinerant preachers and pioneered the idea of holding services outside meetinghouses if the crowds so demanded. (Samuel G. Goodrich, *Pictorial History of America* [Hartford: 1846])

Engraving of Samuel Buell (1716–1798), an itinerant evangelist who early in 1742 stayed at Edwards's home and greatly influenced the conversion of Sarah Edwards. He later was associated with more radical elements of the revivals. (Collection of the author)

A crowd of people during the Great Awakening singing on their way to a meetinghouse, presumably to hear a revival sermon. (Samuel G. Goodrich, *Pictorial History of America* [Hartford: 1846])

Engraving of Eleazar Wheelock (1711–1779), friend of Edwards's and a popular itinerant minister during the 1740s. He later founded what became Dartmouth College. At one point Edwards invited him to Northampton to try to revive interest in religion among his flock. (David M'Clure and Elijah Parish, *Memoir of Rev. Eleazar Wheelock, D.D.* [Newburyport: 1811]

Meetings, often in a clergyman's home, provided opportunities for clergy and laity to speak to issues raised during revivals. Edwards frequently hosted such gatherings. (Samuel G. Goodrich, *Pictorial History of America* [Hartford: 1846])

David Brainerd (1718–1747), missionary to the Native Americans. Edwards edited his diary and wrote his biography. (Samuel G. Goodrich, *Pictorial History of America* [Hartford: 1846])

Thomas Prince (1687–1758), the Boston minister who edited the monthly *Christian History*, a periodical devoted to news of the revivals.
(Joseph Tracy, *The Great Awakening* [Boston: 1842])

Engraving of John Sergeant (1710–1749), a missionary to the Housatonic Indians at Stockbridge. Edwards assumed Sergeant's duties in 1750, moving to Stockbridge after his ouster from Northampton. (Sarah Cabot Sedgwick, *Stockbridge, 1739–1939* [Great Barrington, Mass.: 1939])

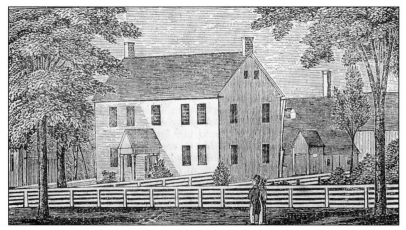

The house built by John Sergeant in Stockbridge and later occupied by Jonathan Edwards. This is where Edwards wrote his great treatises on original sin and the freedom of the will. (John Warner Barber, *Massachusetts Historical Collections* [Worcester, Mass.: 1839])

How could one forward the Gospel plan? "Union," Edwards explained, "is one of the most amiable things, that pertains to human society." All around he saw schism and hard feelings, the antithesis of that "which indeed makes earth most like heaven." The churches were increasingly fragmented into factions, including Separates, New Lights, and Old Lights. Worse still, even in his own community and among those who had been judged saints, selfishness again had the upper hand, a fact strikingly evident in the disruptive behavior of the Roots. It is "the glory of the church of Christ, that she, in all her members, however dispersed, is thus *one*, one holy society, one city, one family, one body," he wrote. So it was very desirable that such union should be manifested in such rituals as days of fasting and prayer. In short, Edwards counseled ecumenical love, for "union in religious duties, especially in the duty of prayer, in praying one with and for another, and jointly for their common welfare, above almost all other things, tends to promote mutual affection and endearment."[25] Clinching the argument, such union also forwarded God's kingdom, so long prophesied in Scripture.

After the book's publication Edwards continued to solicit interest for its central idea, reporting to William McCulloch as late as 1749 that when he sent news of revivals to different parts of the colonies and Europe, he always ended with encouragement "to promote extraordinary, united prayer in the method proposed in the Memorial from Scotland."[26] But *An Humble Attempt* brought Edwards nowhere near the attention that had followed his treatises on the revivals, nor did his and other American clergymen's efforts ever make the concert of prayer as successful a ritual as it had become in Scotland. In 1749 his friend and colaborer Joseph Bellamy admitted as much, writing that "to this day I believe not half the Country have ever So much as heard of Mr. Edwards peice [*sic*] upon the *Scotland Concert*."[27] The implication of his observation was nowhere more clear than in Northampton, where Edwards saw progressive diminution of Christian love and union.

An Humble Attempt is an important signpost in Edwards's career. Written toward the end of a decade when he struggled to salvage what he could of the awakenings, the book displays his unshakable belief in the advancement of religion through an even greater outpouring of the Spirit of God than the world had yet seen. In the privacy of his study, Edwards spent countless hours deciphering the prophecies that had led him to that conclusion, and thus he exhorted parishioners to yearn for something other than mere self-interest. But by the 1740s, in large part because of the freedom offered through spiritual awakening, the degree of one's individual agency and self-worth had become part of what many thought made a life significant. Asking his people to act for Christian union, to make community the highest goal, Edwards challenged them to exercise that agency (as they presumably had during the revivals) to promote the Gospel plan. It was a noble appeal, but neither the colonies nor Northampton were yet willing to embrace it.

DAVID BRAINERD

Concerts for prayer focused Edwards's attention on the international dimensions of Christian union, but closer to home he found an example of the truly gracious piety so much on his mind. In the fall of 1747 David Brainerd, for several years a New Light missionary to Native Americans along the Susquehanna and Delaware rivers, visited Northampton, but in such ill health from tuberculosis that, after a monthlong visit to Boston, he returned to Edwards's home to die.[28] Nursed by Edwards's family, particularly by his second oldest daughter, Jerusha, who had accompanied Brainerd on the Boston trip and, tragically, having contracted his disease, died a few months later, Brainerd indelibly marked the Northampton minister, so much so that after the young evangelist's death he decided to edit his diaries and to assess Brainerd's "very lively instance of the nature of true religion."[29] Published in 1749 with a subscription list of almost two thousand names, *An Account of the Life of David Brainerd* became one of Edwards's most reprinted works.[30]

A Connecticut native, Brainerd was born in 1718 and, destined for the ministry, entered Yale College in 1739, just as Whitefield ignited New England with his powerful preaching. Already melancholy and marked by symptoms of tuberculosis, Brainerd gravitated to students whom the recent religious excitement had touched. With Samuel Buell and David Youngs, he visited other classmates and encouraged them in fervent prayer. By 1741 Brainerd was a leader among New Light students, his commitment deepening when he heard James Davenport denounce New Haven's Old Light minister James Noyes and urge his flock to reject him because of his spiritual deadness. Outraged by this insult to the community's spiritual leader (Noyes was also a Yale trustee), Rector Thomas Clap threatened expulsion of any students who endorsed such criticism.

With his sermon on *The Distinguishing Marks of a Work of the Spirit of God* at the next commencement, Edwards stepped into Brainerd's world and unwittingly redirected the course of the young man's career. Encouraged in his newfound faith, Brainerd unfortunately was overheard privately criticizing tutor Chauncey Whittelsey's leadership of college prayer. Whittelsey, Brainerd had opined to a friend, "has no more grace than a chair."[31] After this dismissive comment reached Rector Clap and Brainerd refused to confess to it in front of the whole student body, he suffered the full penalty of the new college regulations and was promptly expelled. Deeply hurt by this indignity (he never was reinstated), Brainerd sought guidance from other such New Lights as Jedediah Mills of nearby Ripton and Joseph Bellamy, another Yale graduate and disciple of Edwards's, who encouraged the young man to consider a career as an itinerant preacher.

Prohibited from ordination in Connecticut because he lacked a college degree, Brainerd found his calling late in 1742 after a visit to Montauk on Long Island, where he observed the missionary work of Azariah Horton among the Indians.[32] Gravitating to New Jersey and the influential New Light Jonathan Dickinson, Brainerd eventually was ordained by the presbytery. As a missionary he rode hundreds of miles to Indian villages throughout that colony and Pennsylvania.

Although not highly successful as an evangelist, Brainerd remained at this taxing work even as his health failed and he unwittingly infected many of his charges with the tuberculosis that ravaged him. After four exhausting years he decided to revisit New England and, from the home of his friend the Reverend Stephen Williams of Long-meadow, Massachusetts, pay his respects to Edwards. No doubt privy to the details surrounding Brainerd's expulsion from Yale, Edwards had known of his missionary work at least since May 1746, when he had seen one of Brainerd's journals recording his work in Pennsylvania (published earlier that year as *Mirabilia Dei inter Indicos*).[33] On his death, Brainerd left Edwards all of his diaries detailing his missionary work as well as his painstaking examinations of his own spiritual state. These formed the basis for Edwards's elaborate memorial.

As Edwards's canon took shape in the early nineteenth century, his *Life of Brainerd* became immensely popular, rivaled in influence as a personal narrative only by Benjamin Franklin's *Autobiography*. What did Edwards find so distinctive and important about Brainerd? After all, he had not known the young man very well, and it remains a mystery why the missionary appeared in Northampton precisely when he did (legend has it that he and Jerusha Edwards were in love). But Brainerd's biography fitted very well with Edwards's ongoing theorization of the Christian life. *The Life of Brainerd* was much more than an account of the tribulations of a dedicated and selfless missionary.

Compiled during the years when Edwards struggled to remind his community of the lessons they should draw from the recent revivals, his *Life of Brainerd* offered yet another—indeed, the final—installment in a series of works through which Edwards explicated how grace changes one's life. Preceded by other of Edwards's exempla (his accounts, for example, of Abigail Hutchinson and Phebe Bartlett and of his own wife, Sarah), his reprise of Brainerd's life was nothing less than the *Religious Affections* put into objective, tangible form. As Edwards put it to Eleazer Wheelock, he could not help thinking that an account of Brainerd's life taken from his private writings would have a great tendency to promote the interest of true religion and, "more than anything that has ever yet been published, to open the eyes of common people" to the difference between genuine and false piety.[34]

Further, Brainerd's life also fitted with Edwards's larger concerns as he struggled with his congregation's backsliding. Most upsetting to Edwards was the fact that many of his flock embraced the notion that they had it within their own power to effect their spiritual transformation; in other words, they too were becoming Arminian. Early in 1747 Edwards had been increasingly engaged in reading about Arminianism and even had "writ considerably upon it" in his private papers. But he was "diverted from the design . . . by something else that Divine Providence unexpectedly laid in my way, and seemed to render unavoidable, viz., publishing Mr. Brainerd's Life."[35]

Thus, Arminianism was much on Edwards's mind as he prepared his memorial to Brainerd. In his lengthy "Appendix," he pointed out that as much as the young clergyman had struggled with "enthusiasm" in the early phases of his conversion—Brainerd had heard Davenport approvingly and trafficked among other radical New Lights such as Jedediah Mills—Brainerd also "was full of the same cavils against the doctrines of God's sovereign grace which are made by the Arminians."[36] But like Edwards, Brainerd finally embraced the doctrine of divine sovereignty as central to salvation. His religion, Edwards wrote, "was wholly correspondent to what is called the Calvinistical scheme, and was the effect of those doctrines applied to his heart." Where, asked Edwards rhetorically, was there found "an Arminian conversion or repentance consisting in so great and admirable a change" as had occurred in Brainerd? Arminians placed religion in morality, he explained, but they could not muster one example of a life like the one Brainerd had lived after his acceptance of the "Calvinistical scheme." Could the Arminians, he asked, "produce an instance, within this age, and so, plainly, within our reach and view, of such a reformation, such a transformation of a man to scriptural devotion, heavenly-mindedness, and true Christian morality?"[37]

Brainerd had internalized Edwards's understanding of the "New

Birth," proof of how deeply, by the early 1740s, his ideas permeated evangelical culture. But like Sarah Edwards's account of her conversion, Brainerd's needed some tailoring before it fitted Edwards's intentions.[38] Thus, rather than stress Brainerd's ecstatic experiences, Edwards emphasized how the missionary had experienced "a new inward apprehension or view" of God as he had never had before, "nor anything which had the least resemblance of it." His soul had been "so captivated and delighted," he wrote, "with the excellency, loveliness, greatness, and other perfections of God" that he "was even swallowed up in him." Even though Brainerd recorded subsequent doubts about his spiritual state, "the sweet relish" of what he had felt in those moments transformed his life, so much so that Edwards accounted him "a remarkable instance of true and eminent Christian piety in heart and practice."[39]

Edwards did not shy away from Brainerd's faults. He struggled to understand the young man's melancholia, a sensitive topic because by Edwards's admission, his own family was prone to the condition.[40] But just as Brainerd's embrace of "enthusiastical" principles swung him from the depths of his melancholy, so too his utter devotion to practical labor offered another way to exorcise this demon. Thus Edwards stressed the quotidian effects of the Spirit on the young Yale graduate. Even though Brainerd had joined "for a season with enthusiasts," much more important was how grace had given his life a continuing existential thrust. "His work was not finished," Edwards commented, "nor his race ended, till life was ended." He added: "He continued pressing forward in a constant manner, forgetting the things that were behind and reaching forwards towards the things that were before."[41]

Brainerd had experienced nothing less than "a change of nature, a change of the abiding habit and temper of his mind," from "the habits and ways of sin unto universal holiness of heart and practice; from the power and service of Satan unto God." Through the power of divine and supernatural light, in other words, the missionary had moved from self to other, for "his joy was joy in God, and not in himself."

The "new relish and appetite" he received at his conversion made holiness and conformity to God his chief object, and this disposition
manifested itself most commonly in his heroic labors. "His religion,"
Edwards explained, "did not consist only in experience." Rather, "all
his inward illuminations, affections, and comforts, seemed to have a
direct tendency to practice" and were always "of an increasing nature."[42] Such constant growth in grace, always drawing nearer to God
yet never in this life attaining final union, made Brainerd an exemplar
of truly gracious affections. It also marked the spiritual distance, of
which *The Life of Brainerd* served as a permanent reminder, between
the man who had died in Edwards's home and the parishioners outside his doors who defined themselves by mere self-interest.

MEMBERSHIP REQUIREMENTS:
STODDARD REDIVIVUS

In the period between the "bad books" case and Brainerd's arrival,
Edwards had other worries, for the spiritual lethargy and in some
cases outright hypocrisy of his congregation made him rethink the
qualifications for admission to church membership. Through the period of the awakenings Edwards had accepted as sufficient for membership (and, by implication, for sacramental privileges) simple assent
to the cardinal points of Christian doctrine. But his recent experiences
painfully suggested that many on the membership rolls in fact evidenced little outward godliness, their recent reaffirmation of the
church covenant notwithstanding. Moreover, while in the excitement
of the revivals Edwards had eagerly welcomed new members to the
church's rolls, he now realized that in all probability he had admitted
some whose experiences had been mere "enthusiasm." The kernel of
godliness, the evidence of sainthood in Christian practice that he described in *Religious Affections*, too often seemed lacking. Edwards
now wanted stronger evidence before approving church members.

For almost twenty years he had lived with Stoddard's reasoning on the matter. Sometime around 1744, however, prompted by his recent experience with the church over his salary and his prosecution of the "bad books" case, Edwards began to consider requiring for membership not mere assent to sound doctrine but a personal profession that included a description of an experience of saving grace, a test that Stoddard had rejected as unscriptural. Edwards did not consider such a change lightly, and before he made his decision he "search[ed] the Scriptures, and read and examine[d] such books" that pertained to the subject. For two years he kept his opinion to himself. Then, around 1746, he crossed the Rubicon, sharing his opinion with several church members, as well as briefly mentioning the matter in his *Religious Affections*. He also knew that when he acted on his principles, it "would occasion a more general noise and tumult," and thus, before he broached the matter openly, he considered talking it over with Colonel John Stoddard, Stoddard's son and Edwards's longtime supporter. We do not know if he ever did so. Church affairs were at such a low point that no new applicants for membership presented themselves until the early winter of 1748, after John Stoddard's death.[43]

When a candidate finally came forward, Edwards conveyed his new expectations, only to be rebuffed because the man claimed that by the long-established rules of the Northampton church no such individual relation was required. When word of this exchange circulated, there was "great uneasiness" in the town. At this point Edwards finally presented his new opinion about membership to a church committee and asked for the courtesy of explaining his reasoning from the pulpit. His request met with a firestorm of criticism. Worse, Edwards now had to face his opponents without Colonel Stoddard's protection. A church committee refused to allow him to preach on the topic, so Edwards, committed to action, turned to his pen to explain his position. While he was writing, a candidate who was willing to abide by the new procedure presented herself but she later demurred, "afraid, by what she had heard, that there would be a tumult if she came into the church that way."[44] There could be no resolution to the impasse until Edwards's position was fully known and explained, as it finally was in August 1749 with the publication of *An Humble Inquiry into the Rules of the Word of God Concerning the Qualifications Requisite to a Complete Standing and Full Communion in the Visible Christian Church*.

In changing the rules for membership, Edwards directly challenged Stoddard's legacy, which Edwards's opponents claimed (erroneously) had become "the established opinion all over New England."[45] But his real problem lay not so much in his challenge to Stoddard per se as with a laity that daily seemed more intent on flouting clerical authority. In his debates with Increase Mather, Stoddard himself had rebuffed similar attempts at usurpation of ministerial privilege by those—laity as well as clergy—who wrapped themselves in the mantle of tradition to forward their own personal agendas. In 1718, in *An Examination of the Power of the Fraternity*, he had sharply attacked the powers hoarded and abused by the laity through their stubborn adherence to the principles of the Cambridge Platform. Stoddard's arguments therein figured prominently in his grandson's defense of his own course of action.

The occasion for this venting of Stoddard's spleen was a controversy in the Enfield, Connecticut, church where for four years the congregation had quarreled with its minister, Nathaniel Collins, and finally had tried to prevent his administration of the Lord's Supper. Twice the Hampshire Association, created to arbitrate just such cases, urged an amicable settlement to the difficulties, but the congregation persisted in its animosity toward Collins. In 1724 the association concurred in his dismissal, but before that happened, Stoddard weighed in and lambasted the Enfield congregation for forming "an inordinate Veneration" of the principles of its ancestors without having taken the trouble to "make an impartial Examination of them, as if it were a transgression to call them into question, and bordered upon Irreligion to be wavering about them."[46]

Throughout his brief essay Stoddard argued vigorously that the brethren themselves, not the clergy, were the main stumbling block to the progress of Christ's legions. Jealously guarding their congregational prerogative, church members sought to arrogate to themselves yet more power. But "the Community," Stoddard intoned, "are not men of Understanding," and "a crafty man may lead a Score of them by the Nose." Defending the clergy's authority and learning, he noted that if the government of the church were put into the townspeople's hands, things would be carried "headlong by a tumultuous cry." He also stiffly reminded his hearers that it did not become them "to reflect upon the Wisdom of God, as if they had understanding to mend His Institutions."[47] The guidance of the churches should remain in the hands of those with enough wisdom to discern what Scripture counseled.

Given Stoddard's disdain for a laity that used tradition to cover its self-serving ends, he would have had to respect Edwards's principled decision to reverse his own views, even if he had disagreed with the changes themselves. But Edwards knew that for many church members Stoddard's opinions were a lightning rod and in his preface to the *Humble Inquiry* said as much. "Especially may I justly expect," he requested, "that it will not be charged on me as a crime, that I don't think in everything just as he did, since none more than he himself asserted the scriptural and Protestant maxim, that we ought to call no man on earth master." Referring often to Stoddard's *An Appeal to the Learned*, he reminded readers that in it his grandfather had insisted "that it argues no want of a due respect in us to our forefathers, for us to examine their opinions." Indeed, Stoddard would want his successor to question his judgment because he never considered himself an oracle. It was perfectly possible, Edwards explained, to alter some of his grandfather's practices "without despising him, without priding myself in my wisdom, without apostasy," and without "making disturbance in the church of God."[48]

"I have formerly been of his [Stoddard's] opinion," Edwards admitted in his preface, "which I imbibed from his books, even from my childhood, and have in my proceedings conformed to his practice." Moreover, he continued, deference to the authority of someone so venerable, "the seeming strength of some of his arguments," his success in his ministry, and his great reputation and influence "prevailed for a long time to bear down" Edwards's scruples. But now Stoddard's "loose, large principles" hindered the progress of the Gospel, and Edwards was compelled to challenge them, even if it was with "the greatest reluctance, that ever I undertook any public service in my life." Hinting at the conflagration that his opinions had ignited, he also made it known that he had published his thoughts on the controversy only after the church proved unwilling to hear his arguments.[49]

The substance of Edwards's *Humble Inquiry* is easily redacted. He addressed the question "whether, according to the rules of Christ, any ought to be admitted to the communion and privileges of members of the visible church of Christ in complete standing, but such as are in profession, and in the eye of the church's Christian judgment, godly or gracious persons." Edwards argued the negative and, in using the phrase *godly or gracious*, made it clear that he did not claim that anyone could tell *absolutely* whether another was of the elect but only that a candidate for membership should display a "credible *profession* and *visibility* of these things." He explained, "'Tis visibility to the eye of a Christian judgment that is the rule of the church's proceeding" in matters of membership and its privileges.[50] Mere profession, an assent to language (as presently was the case in Northampton), was insufficient and had been so as well for Stoddard, who always had reserved the right to discipline people for unchristian behavior. The difference lay in Stoddard's initial charity of judgment. Because he believed in the efficacy of the sacraments in the process of conversion, he sought to provide each Christian with as many opportunities as possible to grow in grace, but through experience his grandson had learned the cost of such generosity.

Edwards wanted to admit to membership only those who had made "a profession of real piety." But he also struck new emphases, to accord with what he had learned of conversion in the recent awakenings. To own the covenant, he explained, is "to profess the consent of our hearts to it." Or, to put it another way, "'Tis not only a professing of the assent of our understandings, that we understand there is such a covenant, or that we understand we are obliged to comply with it;

but 'tis to profess the consent of our wills, it is to manifest *that we do comply with it*." Here he recurred to what he had observed in the twelfth and final sign of truly religious affections: that godliness should be evident in one's daily Christian practice. Lurking behind his arguments in *An Humble Inquiry*, in other words, was his realization that too many admitted to membership in the heat of the revivals no longer lived through such piety. They had made their profession to serve a turn, to gain sacramental privileges for themselves and their children, and now resisted any restriction of membership because they regarded it and its attendant benefits as a right. Edwards had had enough of such self-serving duplicity. "He that keeps back his heart, does in effect keep back all," he argued, for the heart is the seat of one's disposition, of one's very will.[51]

Against the objection that his new scheme might keep from the church some true saints who doubted that they could meet this standard, Edwards countered that it was better to insist on "some visibility to reason, of true saintship, in admitting members" than to "open the door to as many as please, of those who have no visibility of real saintship, and make no profession of it, nor pretense to it." As he had learned in the "bad books" case and in his difficulties over salary, ungodly men could be "morally sober, serious and conscientious" for a while, when they first came into the church. But if their hearts had not been changed, all was for naught. The results of leniency in membership requirements now were only too apparent: The churches were filled with people like the Roots, "openly vicious in manners, or else scandalously erroneous in opinions."[52]

All this should not have been a surprise, for in his *Religious Affections* Edwards had similarly argued that to accept a profession of Christianity as genuine, there had to be reason to think that the candidate did not make such a profession by merely complying with a prescribed form. Rather, he had to signify honestly what he was conscious of in his own heart. In other words, he had to speak to the transformation of his will that eventuated in godly actions. Edwards did not want to hear just about a person's spiritual experience; he wanted proof of it in the Christian's daily walk. If a saint truly saw the world differently, his behavior would accord with this vision. That is what Edwards sought for admission to his church.

He also attended to one other concern, for his reassessment of the qualifications for membership had implications about not only who came to the communion table but who brought children to baptism. One of the most closely guarded rights of membership, baptism had been the key issue in the framing of the original Half-Way Covenant in the 1660s. But Edwards was convinced that parents often made a mere show of religion to secure the baptism of their offspring and thus sought to reverse the recommendations of the Synod of 1662. "Owning the covenant," he explained, was something people too often neglected until they were married, and then they did it "for their own credit's sake, and that their children may be baptized." It was very much owing to such parents that there were so many young people who, when they matured, made no profession of godliness. Edwards suspected that baptizing the children of those who had never made "any proper profession of godliness" was merely expedient, a way "to give ease to ancestors with respect to their posterity, in times of general declension and decay."[53] So much for the Half-Way Covenant and for Stoddard's more radical innovations.

In a letter to the Boston minister Thomas Foxcroft, Edwards observed that in time his people might be brought around to his views on the qualifications for the Lord's Supper. But with respect to the other sacrament, he wrote, "there is scarce any hope of it." In an eerily prescient moment, Edwards seemed already to read the handwriting on the wall, for he added, "This will be very likely to overthrow me, not only with regard to my usefulness in the work of the ministry here, but everywhere."[54]

But the condition of the churches demanded such a risk. In changing the qualifications for church membership, he did not so much reject Stoddard's ecclesiology as refine it so that ministers might regain the kind of power over their flocks that Stoddard never relinquished over his. His grandfather always had reserved the right to prevent someone from coming to the sacraments if he lacked godliness. In the wake of the revivals of the 1740s, however, such generosity as Stoddard's only contributed to more rending of the community's religious fabric. Edwards was not chary of taking stitches to make the necessary repair.

"A SORROWFUL, STRANGE, SURPRISING AFFAIR"

Edwards's decision enflamed passions, and even though he took the trouble to prepare an elaborate defense of his propositions, the town's course of action seemed set. Its unwillingness even to allow him to address the subject of membership from the pulpit told him what he needed to know. A majority of Northampton's church members would defend to the end the privileges that his grandfather Stoddard had given them, even if it meant rejecting the minister who had made their town famous on both sides of the Atlantic.

About the middle of August 1749, copies of *An Humble Inquiry* finally reached Northampton. To Edwards's recollection, about twenty were distributed, but given the recalcitrance of a majority of the church even to consider his views, few people read the book, he observed, or were likely to, "at least for a very long time." For a while there was "less noise in town," but by October matters had continued to deteriorate. Several people who sought membership had come to Edwards and made credible professions of godliness, but a church committee prevented them from making them public, presumably because by church rule, such action was not required.[55] By mid-month all the talk was of calling a council from neighboring churches to consider Edwards's actions and, if necessary, to speak to the issue of a separation between him and the community.

By late November Northampton's direction had become starkly clear, for a committee had delivered to Edwards a copy of a resolution it intended to bring to the church. Because Edwards had departed from the principles that "the great Stoddard" had practiced regarding the admission of church members, principles that Edwards himself had long followed, and because his rules seemed inconsistent with those of true religion and had destroyed the peace of the church and the town, the committee wished to call a council to help both parties decide if separation was necessary if Edwards did not admit the error of his ways.[56] In a letter late that month to Foxcroft, Edwards wrote what a decade earlier would have seemed unimaginable: He had "not the least expectation of continuing" as Northampton's minister.[57]

The next round of bickering centered on the constitution of any council called to adjudicate the controversy. Edwards requested that some of the clergy come from outside the Hampshire Association because its members were all, save one, on the church's side. By late December, as Edwards wrote to his close friend Joseph Bellamy, the "tumult [was] vastly greater" than when Bellamy had last visited and was "rising higher and higher continually." Edwards vividly described meetings that consumed all his time: "society meetings, and church meetings, and meetings of committees; of committees of the parish and committees of the church; conferences, debates, reports, and proposals drawn up, and replies and remonstrances." He concluded: "The people have a resolution to get me out of town speedily, that disdains all control or check." Particularly worrisome to Edwards, his opponents now openly accused him of duplicity and self-interest. "The state of things," he told Bellamy, "is come to that, that they seem to think it greatly concerns 'em to blacken me, and represent me in odious colors to the world, to justify their own conduct."[58]

At mid-month, after much give-and-take, a preliminary council of five churches from the Hampshire Association met to hear the background to the dispute and to decide if a more formal council should be called. Ironically, behind this jockeying lay Edwards's action in the Robert Breck controversy fourteen years earlier, when he had insisted that the council called to deliberate that matter be composed only of members from the Hampshire Association. Now his church used that example against him, knowing as it did that within the association it had the votes to oust him.

This preliminary council, however, was loath to take action and suggested a cooling-off period, for the controversy already had produced "a great degree of alienation" and "a want of meekness and charity" on both sides. The delegates also recommended that any townspeople who sought admission to the church wait until the controversy between the pastor and his people was settled. This council reconvened in February, again to consider Edwards's request to include churches from outside the association.[59] During this period too Edwards finally got to explain his position from the pulpit, but to little effect. Most townspeople had already made up their minds, and primarily those from outside Northampton attended the lectures. The full advisory council finally recommended that the case be mediated by a more formal body, consisting of representatives from ten churches, with Edwards allowed to choose two of the five allotted to him from outside Hampshire County.

This long-awaited meeting convened on June 19, 1750. In the previous months Edwards had expended an astonishing amount of intellectual and psychological energy on what had begun as a matter of principle but had become deeply personal. He admitted as much after the affair, telling his Scots correspondent John Erskine that during the difficulties he had had "a multitude of distracting troubles and hurries."[60] This situation was all the more troubling because Edwards sincerely believed that he had uppermost in mind the good of his congregation. As he put it to Foxcroft, "I think my people in awful circumstances, and in the highway to ruin, for the present and future generations; and I durst not leave them without first using all proper endeavors that they may be saved from ruin."[61] But they would not listen.

At its core, the church members' dispute with Edwards hinged on whether they could continue to exercise church privileges that by then they presumed as rights. Hence Edwards's defense against the charge that he had arrogated powers that Stoddard never claimed. At his settlement, Edwards wrote, the people in Northampton had given him "the same power in church government which they yielded to

Mr. Stoddard." The church had allowed Stoddard a veto on church members, he declared, "and never, so far as I have heard of it, disputed it, at least never in the present generation."[62] Now, however, the congregants faulted Edwards for wishing to exercise the same privilege. What had changed was their sense of empowerment in the wake of the revivals, an entitlement to rank and standing in a society no longer defined by a member's spiritual capital but rather by his success in a rapidly maturing economy. Edwards was correct. He asked only for what had been granted Stoddard. It also was likely, however, that if Stoddard had lived to preach to these congregants, he too would have run up against their newfound sense of personal agency and been forced to adjust his procedures to the lessons of experience.

Things did not go well for Edwards in the council, particularly because one of the churches that he had chosen refused to send a representative, though its minister attended as a gesture of support for Edwards. That one missing delegate proved crucial, for on June 22, 1750, by a vote of 10–9, the council recommended Edwards's separation from the Northampton church. It also exonerated Edwards of any insincerity or personal animus in the matter. Edwards's friend Samuel Hopkins traced this extraordinary turn of events to the "bad books" case, suggesting that Edwards's loss of influence among the young people had ended his "usefulness" in Northampton.[63] But the issue was larger. After the excitement of the awakenings early in the decade, Edwards had expected that the same experiential transformation that had defined his own Awakening would inform the spirituality of new church members. When their subsequent behavior proved otherwise, he refused to accommodate their hypocrisy and resisted any diminution of his prerogative to make such judgments. As a result, he was ousted from the church that he had made an evangelical beacon, an event so newsworthy that the council reports in toto appeared in July in two consecutive issues of the *Boston Gazette*. Edwards's first biographer aptly described the events as "a sorrowful, strange, surprising affair."[64]

"THROWN UPON THE WIDE OCEAN
OF THE WORLD"

The council's advice did not end the matter. From an early point in the controversy, Edwards's opponents sought to have some able polemicist answer his *Humble Inquiry*. Their first choice was Edwards's own cousin Elisha Williams, the former rector of Yale and a formidable scholar. In late May 1749, Edwards asked Thomas Foxcroft to do what he could to dissuade Williams from the rebuttal. Not that he was afraid of "the strength of any fair arguing against the doctrine," he said, but because of his "peculiarly disadvantageous circumstances." Williams had it in his power to do Edwards "a great deal of hurt, let his arguments be never so weak," probably a veiled reference to how difficult it would be for Edwards to find another pulpit if so influential a figure opposed his ideas. Edwards suggested that Foxcroft "artfully" lead Williams to believe that "his opposing me in this matter would be offensive to learned men" in England and Scotland who saw things Edwards's way and thus that such a work "would not be for his honor."[65]

The town had also asked Peter Clark, Salem Village's minister, to consider the task, but after communicating with Edwards about his ideas, Clark demurred. Williams, now in Wethersfield, Connecticut, then accepted the assignment but, before he could complete it, left for a several years' stay in London. He referred the task (and what he had already written) to his brother Solomon, minister to Lebanon, Connecticut, and another staunch supporter of Stoddard's doctrines.[66] In 1751 Solomon Williams published his answer to Edwards as *The True State of the Question: Truth Vindicated*. The next year, faced with what he feared could be "a long and perhaps almost endless labor of replying," Edwards countered with *Misrepresentations Corrected Concerning the Qualifications Necessary to Lawful Communion in the Christian Sacraments*, in which stifling any personal animus he had toward Williams for his attack on his beliefs, he cogently argued that the Lebanon minister had greatly misrepresented Stoddard's views on membership.[67] These pamphlets only prolonged the sour taste in Edwards's mouth as he sought to address more practical matters.

Most significant, there was his employment, for Edwards knew that the bitterness of the proceeding in Northampton would make many congregations loath to hire him, and more so because many of his opponents were influential people who had gone out of their way to defame him. At this juncture Edwards's self-confidence was at a low point. Almost a year before his dismissal he had lamented his future prospects should a separation be warranted. "I have many enemies abroad in the country," he wrote Foxcroft, "who hate me for my stingy principles, enthusiasm, rigid proceedings, and that now are expecting full triumph over me." He continued: "If I should be wholly cast out of the ministry, I should be in many respects a poor case," unable to serve the current generation but unlikely "to get a subsistence in a business of a different nature."[68] It boggles the mind to think of Edwards as anything other than minister and theologian, yet he obviously had contemplated that possibility, even as he acknowledged that he was "by nature unfit for secular business." Complicating matters, other churches would consider him expensive property, for his salary was as good as that of any minister around Boston.

After the dismissal Edwards viewed his situation as dire. "I am now as it were thrown upon the wide ocean of the world, and know not what will become of me and my numerous and chargeable family," he wrote John Erskine. He had "no particular door in view" that he could open for his "future serviceableness," and he reiterated how unsuitable he was for other employment.[69] Edwards had properly taken his own measure, for it was almost a year before he found a new position. Adding to his uneasiness and embarrassment, Northampton retained him for much of that time, hiring him by the week to preach to a congregation that itself was having difficulty in hiring a new minister, in no small part because of the town's reputation for contentiousness.

Some of Edwards's supporters even considered separating from the Northampton church and offered to install him in their rump

congregation, but by that time he had begun to hear of other opportunities, in churches in Canaan, Connecticut, and Lunenberg, Virginia, for example, and even of the possibility of an appointment in
Scotland, where he had many supporters. He finally accepted the offer of the Commissioners for Indian Affairs in Boston to become missionary to the Housatonic Indians in the frontier settlement of
Stockbridge, Massachusetts, fifty miles west of Northampton in the
Berkshire Mountains. He assumed the position in the summer of
1751, after two more of his daughters had been married and he had
managed to sell some of his Northampton property.

FAREWELL SERMON

Even though Edwards remained in Northampton until the summer
of 1751, on July 1, 1750, he severed his formal connection with the
congregation he had nurtured for more than twenty years. On that
day he stood before it for the last time as its pastor and offered his final words and wishes in an emotional sermon whose doctrine was
"Ministers and the people that have been under their care, must meet
one another, before Christ's tribunal, at the day of judgment."[70] He
drilled home the point that on Judgment Day God's withering eye
would see through the hypocrisy and deception with which people
acted on earth. As powerful a rhetorical effort as any of his better-
known revival sermons, this one must have been almost unbearable to
those in the audience who had had a hand in his dismissal.

He began calmly enough, observing that "we live in a world of
change, where nothing is certain or stable" and where "a little time, a
few revolutions of the sun, brings to pass strange things, surprising
alterations, in particular persons, in families, in towns and churches,
in countries and nations." One such change, he went on, occurred
when ministers and their people, "between whom there has been the
greatest mutual regard and strictest union," dissolved their solemn relationship. But no matter how far from each other the two parties

might remove, they would meet again, on "the last great day of accounts." Then, when Christ came to judgment, "every error and false
opinion shall be detected; all deceit and delusion shall vanish away before the light of that day," and "all shall know the truth with the greatest certainty, and there shall be no mistakes to rectify." No doubt
lamenting the time stolen from other tasks as he had prepared his
Humble Inquiry and then answered Williams's reply to it, Edwards
also observed that on that final day all disputations would end. Then
there would no longer be "any debate, or difference of opinions; the
evidence of the truth shall appear beyond all dispute, and all controversies shall be finally and forever decided."[71]

If these opening words had Edwards's opponents wriggling in their
seats, what followed was even more unsettling. He reminded them of
his many years of labor, how often he had helped them search their
own hearts and how frequently they had rejected his advice. He observed that nothing was more common than for those who are "most
abominable to God, and the children of wrath, [to] think highly of
themselves," as though they were God's precious children. But those
who viewed themselves as the most eminent saints in the congregation were "in a peculiar manner a smoke in God's nose." At Judgment
Day, God would put an eternal end to the self-conceit and vain hopes
of such deluded hypocrites. "And then shall all know the state of one
another's souls," he reminded them, and "the people shall know
whether their minister has been sincere and faithful, and the minister
shall know the state of everyone of their people." On that day "the infallible judge, the true fountain of light, truth and justice," would
judge between the contending parties and declare the truth, who was
in the right, and what was agreeable to his mind and will.[72]

It is hard to avoid the conclusion that Edwards relished the
prospect of that day, even though he spoke only in generalities about
the difficulties through which he had just passed. On Judgment Day,
he told his audience, he would be required to give an account of his
stewardship. Likewise, his people would give an account of their conduct toward him and of the improvement that they had made of his

twenty-three-year ministry. There will be nothing "covered," he warned, and "All errors, falsehood, unrighteousness and injury shall be laid open, stripped of every disguise; every specious pretense, every cavil, and all false reasoning shall vanish in a moment." Then it would appear "what the ends are we have aimed at, what have been the governing principles we have acted from, and what have been the dispositions, we have exercised in our ecclesiastical disputes and contests."[73]

This sermon was an unsparing indictment of those who, for almost a decade, had chafed under his words. Edwards ended with a promise to his flock that he would never forget them and always pray for their prosperity. He also hoped that they soon would find a pastor to guide them (the search for his replacement in fact took more than two years). But in his very last line he again revealed the depth of his emotions. "And let us all remember," he intoned, "and never forget our future solemn meeting, on that great day of the Lord; the day of infallible decision, and of the everlasting and unalterable sentence."[74]

Still faced with the indignity of preaching to the church on a supply basis, Edwards lingered in Northampton for another year. Not until the following summer did he leave, to commence a radically different pastoral assignment. By no wish of his own, Edwards had concluded his pastoral labors in the community he had centered on the map of evangelical Christianity.

SEVEN

Stockbridge and the Housatonics

(1750-1757)

WHY STOCKBRIDGE?

The next seven years of Edwards's life seem incongruous, a combination of the utterly local and petty with the strikingly cosmopolitan. As he began his missionary work to a small band of Housatonic Indians in the wilderness of Stockbridge, he also returned to intellectual labors that put him in conversation with Europe's most advanced philosophers and theologians. Why did he so readily accept the Stockbridge position and embrace it with such enthusiasm? He was not without options. One of his Scots correspondents noted that, in the wake of Edwards's dismissal, two "large churches of New England people much pleasanter as to worldly accommodations" than Stockbridge entertained his ministry, but either nothing came of the offers or he was disposed against them. The summer that he accepted the post in Stockbridge, a church in Virginia called him "with much earnestness and importunity," but before its final offer he had been installed in the Berkshire hills.[1] What was Edwards thinking when he moved from one of the most important churches in Massachusetts to a tiny settlement on the edge of the provincial frontier, to preach to a few white families and a few score Mahicans who could barely understand English?

For one thing, Edwards's decision was practical. He had a large family at home and needed an income, and the move to Stockbridge, sixty miles west, would not be as arduous and deracinating as one to Virginia, or, for that matter, to Scotland, where others of his supporters lobbied for him.[2] In addition, Edwards's acceptance of the post in Stockbridge was linked to his immediate reputation, to his ambition, and thus to the larger contours of his career. As well known as he was for his role in the recent awakenings, outside of a small circle of younger men he had tutored and supported, most New Englanders would not have found him an appealing choice for a vacant pulpit, particularly in the eastern part of the province, where clergy of a distinctly Arminian tinge proliferated. To be sure, Joseph Bellamy, Samuel Hopkins, and others of Edwards's theological circle who had resisted the appeal of the more radical Separates and some townspeople in the valley who had voted against Edwards's dismissal remained utterly loyal. But their numbers were not enough to offset the influence of, say, Charles Chauncy in Boston, or of Edwards's cousins Elisha and Solomon Williams and the River Gods (as the powerful merchants and magistrates were known) in the valley itself. There was no party or school of which Edwards was the center, and the stories that his opponents had circulated of his "stiffness" and "arrogance" had proved effective. His inglorious exit from Northampton marked him as damaged goods, and he was grateful for an opportunity to start anew.

In going to Stockbridge, Edwards did not think that he had been reduced to utter desperation, for with David Brainerd's heroic evangelical labors still fresh in mind, he entered his new role with undeniable enthusiasm and commitment. Although he had not shown any predilection for missionary work, he regarded it as vitally important to both the English Protestant cause and the general progress of Christianity, for he viewed the entire northeastern part of America as a vast theater where the British defended a significant front in the war against the French and their popery. Protestants believed that their triumph in this war, when coupled with their conversion of the native tribes to true—that is, Protestant—Christianity, was essential to the fulfillment of scriptural prophecy. As a missionary Edwards would not only save individual souls but also align himself in yet another way with the work of redemption. Going to Stockbridge was part of the work to which he had dedicated himself since his teenage years. The scene may have changed, but Edwards believed that he still had a role to play in the cosmic drama that so engaged his mind.[3]

THE STOCKBRIDGE MISSION

In the summer of 1751 Stockbridge was a tiny settlement sixty miles west of Northampton, situated in a fertile bottomland of the Housatonic River in the extreme southwestern part of the province. Fifteen years earlier colonists had founded the town as a mission to a small band of Mahican Indians known as Housatonics. Squeezed for land by the Dutch along the Hudson River and threatened by both the French and fierce Mohawk tribes to the north, the Housatonics through the early eighteenth century struggled to maintain their traditional way of life until, ravaged by disease and alcohol, they voted early in 1743 to accept the Province of Massachusetts Bay's offer of a Christian mission. Spearheaded by the Reverends Samuel Hopkins of West Springfield and Stephen Williams of Longmeadow and supported by the London-based Company for the Propagation of the Gospel in New England and Parts Adjacent in America (known as the New England Company), the mission, situated on the Housatonics' land near the settlement of Great Barrington, was to employ both an ordained minister and a schoolteacher to bring the Indians into the Protestant fold.[4]

The Massachusetts government eagerly supported this initiative. For one thing, the new settlement provided a bulwark against further incursions by the French and Indians, who for decades had threatened the province's western and northern frontiers. The British hoped too that the Housatonics' acceptance of the mission might influence other Native Americans, including the more numerous (and belligerent) Mohawks, to side with them in any future hostilities. Such a missionary outpost also made other English settlements in this rich, forested land more secure. Finally, the province's clerical leaders embraced the opportunity to forward what they saw as part of their chartered purpose in the New World: to win benighted souls to Christ. Since the days of the Reverend John Eliot, the "Apostle to the Indians," the formation of "praying towns" for the conversion of the tribes had been a constituent part of the colonists' millennial vision.

Once the tribe consented to the mission, its prime movers cast about for a suitable minister, eventually settling on twenty-four-year-old John Sergeant, a recent Yale graduate and tutor.[5] Converted in the recent revivals and eager to forward such missionary work among the heathen, Sergeant rode to Stockbridge in October 1735 to test the effectiveness of his preaching. A Native American translated his simple sermons, and the Yale tutor was gratified to find that his auditors evinced some interest in his message. Over the next two months he won the tribe's confidence, so much so that when he returned to Yale briefly in November, they allowed him to take two of the tribe's children with him, presumably to tutor him in the Mahican language.

The area clergy selected twenty-five-year-old Timothy Woodbridge of West Springfield to teach the Indian children at the mission school. Woodbridge returned with Sergeant, who eagerly resumed his work and by December 1735 had baptized about forty Indians. "Their whole hearts seem'd to be engaged in the matter," Sergeant wrote, "and I have reason to think that the imperfection of their knowledge is made up by their zeal and integrity."[6]

By 1736 things were going well enough for the Massachusetts government to establish a six-square-mile township that included the site of the mission and to grant plots of land to both Sergeant and Woodbridge as well as to four other white families the government would select to live there. By 1737 Woodbridge and Sergeant had completed houses for themselves and constructed both a meetinghouse and a school. Other English families arrived the same year. One was headed by forty-seven-year-old Ephraim Williams of Newton, Massachusetts, who was a cousin of Israel Williams of Hadley and whose daughter Abigail married Sergeant in 1739. On June 22, 1739, the town was formally incorporated as Stockbridge. The Housatonics now formally lived under the control of the Province of Massachusetts Bay, with Williams, justice of the peace for Hampshire County, their chief magistrate. By 1740 the mission was flourishing, boasting 120 Indians within its borders. Three years later young David Brainerd began his ministry with the Mahicans at the Kaunaumeek village, about twenty miles away.

Throughout this period, however, the area lived in the dark shadow of the French and Indian Wars. Fortunately, Stockbridge was spared any major depredation, although Fort Massachusetts, forty miles northeast, was captured and burned. Their loyalties tugged in every direction by entanglement in the Englishmen's battles, the Housatonics mourned the loss of some of their fighting men and were as glad as their British allies to see hostilities end in the summer of 1744. A year later, however, the tribe suffered an even greater loss, for in July their beloved thirty-nine-year-old Sergeant, who had fallen ill with a fever two months earlier, died.

This loss came as the Indians were bringing a number of complaints against some of the area's white residents before the Massachusetts General Court. Upset by English land claims and by the settlement of more white families than originally had been specified in the town's charter, the Housatonics wanted greater control over the dispensation of their acreage. But with unassigned land in the eastern part of the province increasingly scarce, the Berkshire forests had become important real estate. Situated on prime riverfront, Stockbridge drew the attention of land-hungry colonists who recognized its potential. At the center of this land grab was none other than Ephraim Williams, intent on amassing a family fortune in lumber. To make matters worse, under pressure from merchants, the county court granted a license for the sale of alcohol in the community, a sad corruption of what earlier had been a more idealistic, if not fully altruistic, enterprise.

EDWARDS AND THE WILLIAMSES

For two years after Sergeant's death Stockbridge languished without a minister, its spiritual needs met only sporadically by Moravian mis-

sionaries from nearby New York. As early as November 1749 Edwards had known of the town's difficulties, for he wrote Thomas Foxcroft of his hope that "[c]ommissioners would now take care that
there may be a man sent them [the Stockbridge Indians] of sound
principles, and pious character." Alluding to Woodbridge's and the
late Sergeant's plan to start an Indian boarding school aimed at drawing Mohawks from outside the immediate area as well as the more local Mahicans, Edwards observed that if the project were put "under
the care of a missionary of good character," it would provide "the best
door for gradually propagating the gospel among the Indians that is
opened at present."[7] His difficulties in Northampton increasing daily,
he may well have been thinking of himself for the position.

Stockbridge's inhabitants were divided on Sergeant's replacement.
One faction, led by Woodbridge, threw its influence behind young
Samuel Hopkins (nephew of the West Springfield clergyman instrumental in starting the mission), now settled in nearby Great Barrington. Another group, headed by Williams, championed Ezra Stiles,
another young Yale graduate, as unsympathetic to the cause of the
New Lights as Hopkins was its defender.[8] When Hopkins demurred,
he suggested his friend and mentor Edwards (though whether at Edwards's own suggestion is unknown). Interested, Edwards traveled to
Stockbridge to preach in early October 1750. At the request of both
the commissioners in Boston and the local inhabitants, he returned the
following January to assess his prospects. For his part, Woodbridge
adamantly opposed Stiles's candidacy, both on religious grounds and
because he shrewdly guessed that the young man was in Ephraim
Williams's pocket, and when Stiles's interest cooled, Edwards alone remained in the pool. In February the Housatonics, in good measure
swayed by Woodbridge, issued Edwards a call. He accepted and
moved to a settlement whose population numbered about 150 Native
Americans, joined by thirteen white families.[9]

The move to Stockbridge went well, even though Edwards still
had to liquidate his Northampton property. His duties were demanding. On the Sabbath he preached separately to the English and Native

American members of his congregation, with one of the latter then translating his words into Mahican. Gideon Hawley noted that in speaking to the Native Americans, Edwards was "a plain and practical preacher" who refrained from invoking too much "metaphysical knowledge" in his sermons. His delivery was "grave and natural," and his lessons were "concise and full of meaning."[10] To this audience he stressed the same Calvinist doctrine that he presented to the English families but, as one scholar has noted, struck different emphases. In particular, in his sermons to the Native Americans, meant to encourage those who had not been Christian to come to the faith, Edwards often stressed God's willingness to save sinners, rather than his indifference to those who, already brought to the light of Christianity, persisted in backsliding. He had some success in these labors, for six professions of faith of Native Americans are among his papers.[11]

Early in 1752 he wrote his father from his new home to say, "Here, at present, we live in peace; which has of long time been an unusual thing with us."[12] But the calm did not last. Edwards had walked into another explosive situation, for Williams, the community's largest landowner and an influential politician, had bitterly opposed his appointment and did all that he could to undermine it. When Edwards's name was first raised, Williams had voiced his objections to nearby Deerfield's Jonathan Ashley, one of the valley's crypto-Arminians and a vocal opponent of the awakenings. For one thing, Williams claimed, Edwards was not "sociable" and thus not apt to be a good teacher. Further, he was "an old man" who would have difficulty in learning the Indian language.[13] Presumably, Williams had in mind someone like Stiles, who, though he did not know the Mahican language either, would be more pliant to Williams's wishes.

When the Commissioners for Indian Affairs in Boston approved Edwards, Williams tried to look on the brighter side. At least the Northampton minister's presence in Stockbridge might make that tiny town more alluring to investors. "I would not have him fail of going [to Stockbridge] for [a salary of] £500," Williams wrote Ashley, "since they are so set for him, not that I think he will ever do so much more good than another, but on account of raising the price of my land." But Williams despaired of ever winning Edwards to his side, as he might have Stiles. The Northampton controversy fresh in mind, Williams pronounced Edwards "a very great bigot," not willing to admit any person into heaven "but those that agreed fully to his sentiments."[14]

There was more to Williams's opposition to Edwards than his letter allowed, for not just Ephraim Williams but the extended Williams clan fueled resistance to his appointment. Moreover, behind the scenes they had also undermined his previous ministry in Northampton. During the communion controversy Edwards discreetly had held his tongue and not directly implicated them, though he long had known that they had engineered his ouster. When he resettled in Stockbridge and ran head-on into opposition to his ministry fomented by yet another Williams, he decided to tell his story more openly.

He first broached the matter in a letter to Thomas Hubbard, speaker of the House of Representatives, in the early spring of 1752, when he defended himself against Ephraim Williams's attempts to undercut his effectiveness at the mission. Commenting on the difference between Williams's version of recent events in Stockbridge and his own, Edwards explained that there were "many in New England of a certain family" who were "extremely uneasy" at his being here. He fully expected members of this family to represent him "as very unfit" for the position because he was "a mischief maker, etc, and should not wonder if they strive to remove me."[15]

That July, in a lengthy letter to Isaac Hollis of London, chief patron of the Indian school, Edwards openly named his opponents, providing as well a detailed genealogy of the key players and a chronology of recent events to explain his current plight. "The family of note" that he had mentioned in an earlier letter, he explained, the one "deeply engaged in the controversy on the side of my opposers," was none other than the Williamses. His problems with them, he told Hollis, had begun long before; Elisha Williams, he went on to note, had been "much resorted to for advice" by Edwards's opponents during the Northampton controversy and had acted as their chief adviser until he left for England to pursue his political ambitions. At that point Elisha had left his brother Solomon the task of refuting Edwards on the communion controversy, an effort, Edwards explained, "written with no small degree of bitterness and contempt."[16]

Another brother, Colonel Israel Williams of Hatfield, also had "exerted himself very much with zeal" against Edwards, as had other members of his extended circle of influence, including Jonathan Ashley, and Colonel Oliver Partridge and the Reverend Chester Williams of Hadley, the latter two being "very busy and active in that affair." Finally, in the cabal Edwards included Jonathan Hubbard, minister to Lower Sheffield and moderator of the recent council at Northampton, who had also "shown himself very opposite" to Edwards's coming to Stockbridge.[17]

In short, a group of prominent individuals who, having hounded him from Northampton, now sought to eliminate Edwards's influence over the Housatonic Indians and their supporters lest he block their plans for political and economic supremacy in the region. During Edwards's candidacy for the Stockbridge post, he explained to Hollis, when the Williamses saw that "the stream was too strong for them," they at first "appeared as if they were friendly" even though their hearts were "very opposite."[18] But once they knew that Edwards was going to attempt to maintain control of the missionary enterprise by cultivating his own important contacts in Boston and England, the Williams faction showed its true colors. And believing Edwards to be "empty of politics," the Williamses misjudged.[19] Politics could not have saved Edwards's position in Northampton, when the controversy centered primarily on ecclesiastical concerns. But, considering the importance of the Native Americans to British security in New England, Edwards quickly found friends among those who, alerted to the Williamses' chicanery, were more than willing to entertain his side of the story and eventually to support him.

STOCKBRIDGE INTRIGUE

Edwards's difficulties began with the oversight of Sergeant and Woodbridge's boarding school, which once had numbered fifty-five students but languished as warfare against the French and Indians turned the town into a garrison. By the early 1750s, with attacks temporarily halted, Ephraim Williams, with the support of officials on both sides of the Atlantic who recognized the benefits Britain accrued if the Native Americans thought themselves well treated, promoted the original educational plan, generously endowed by Londoner Isaac Hollis. Never one to miss a chance to extend his influence, Williams proposed a girls' branch of the school, to be taught by his daughter (and Sergeant's widow), Abigail. Working hand in glove with Williams, the Brookfield, Massachusetts, merchant Joseph Dwight forwarded himself as overseer of both schools, his son to direct the boys' branch.

Complicating matters, the New England Company in the late winter of 1752 named Gideon Hawley the official instructor for the boys' branch, haphazardly administered since 1748 by sixty-two-year-old Martin Kellogg, one of Williams's sycophants and against whom the Indian boarders had lodged many complaints. When Hawley arrived, he sought to convince the Indian children to move from Kellogg's tutorial to his own, and his success in this line infuriated Williams and his clique, who continued to back Kellogg. As the confrontation escalated, the Williams family stepped up its efforts to discredit Edwards, Woodbridge (now the town's representative to the General Court), and the young Hawley. But their actions further alienated Native Americans already suspicious of the family's efforts to monopolize the school and resentful of their acquisition of more of the Indians' lands.

As a result, many of the Indians, including some curious Mohawks who had ventured to the village to consider what opportunities the English settlers offered, began to leave the community, an exodus that gained momentum after a suspicious fire early in 1753

had burned a new school building to the ground. With the local
Housatonics disgusted by this turn of events, Woodbridge brought
the cause of the Indian mission before the legislature, a move that further infuriated the Williams clan, which redoubled its efforts to rid itself of those who did not support its vision for the town. Having lost
his Northampton position to the machinations of this family, Edwards did not relish the thought of losing another. Because of what
Woodbridge and Hawley already had done for the Native American
children, he threw his energy and reputation behind them. The re-
sulting political brawl stretched from Stockbridge to Boston and
eventually across the Atlantic.[20]

If a few years earlier Edwards had been reluctant to personalize his
difficulties, now he brought matters into the open at the highest levels. In the late winter of 1752 he wrote Andrew Oliver, secretary of
the commissioners, about the suitability of Joseph Dwight and
Sergeant's widow for the positions that the elder Williams had earmarked for them. In particular, he pointed out how Mrs. Sergeant's
disposal of Hollis's bequest for the school had eventuated in severe financial improprieties. The greater his insight into the "management
of these affairs," Edwards told Oliver, the more he was "filled with astonishment." At the root of all these troubles, he added, were simply
"[s]elfish designs and intrigues for private interest," which would be,
he concluded, "the ruin of our affairs."[21]

In March, with Elisha Williams in London lobbying the New England Company for the appointment of Sergeant's wife, Edwards offered Jasper Maudit, treasurer of the company, his views of her
candidacy and of the Williams axis in general. After praising Hawley's
success as an educator, Edwards raised the issue of the Williamses' opposition to his own labors and pointed out that the attendant
brouhaha had now "been made very public all over New England."
Needless to say, this was not the kind of publicity the missionary enterprise needed. A few days later Edwards continued his campaign,
this time with Speaker of the Massachusetts House Hubbard, to
whom he reported the natives' "rooted, universal prejudice" against

Williams because of his persistent attempts to gain their lands. Reiterating the charges of malfeasance with regard to the Hollis funds, Edwards noted that Kellogg's business, "if it can be called a business, is not that for which Mr. Hollis has hired him."[22]

Such reports infuriated Williams and his cohort, which stepped up their efforts to drive Hawley from his position and to discredit Edwards's depictions. Not intimidated, Edwards continued to alert the officials charged with oversight of the Stockbridge mission to the difficulties that he and Hawley faced. In July, for example, he himself described the whole imbroglio to Hollis in an attempt to persuade his patron to support those who had the Indians' best interests at heart. In particular, Edwards urged him to rebuff Elisha Williams's attempts to install Dwight and his daughter as bona fide trustees of the mission. In a letter written the same day to Josiah Willard, secretary of the province, Edwards complained more forthrightly than ever of Dwight's attempts (sanctioned by Williams) to control the school for his own selfish ends. Edwards doubted that there ever could be any reconciliation of the difficulties because Dwight was "naturally a person of too sovereign and arbitrary a disposition, naturally exceedingly inclined to engross all power and manage all things by himself."[23]

Such missives continued through the summer, and in the early fall they culminated in Edwards's report to Oliver that Ephraim Williams's activities were now beyond the pale. Among other things, he was trying to pack the community with his own supporters, offering to buy "out at once the old inhabitants" so that he could sell their land to people who shared his own economic plans for the area. Shortly thereafter Williams's ill health resulted in his departure from the area, but his son Ephraim Jr. continued to oppose Edwards. Indeed, the younger Williams was so adamant about Edwards's removal that he "declared he would gladly spend £500 of his money to accomplish it," and he displayed a similar animus against Hawley.[24]

Such threats were not idle. In February 1753, when the boarding school for Mohawk children burned to the ground (and with it Hawley's living quarters and possessions), many thought it arson perpetrated by Hawley's opponents. The situation in Stockbridge was becoming so intolerable that Edwards thought it "high time the Honorable Commissioners had full information of the state of things" and asked Oliver to expedite their involvement before all efforts to run the mission foundered. Even more upsetting because Edwards was addressing the highest level of colonial government, Joseph Dwight attempted to persuade his old commander in chief, Sir William Pepperell, to write to London opposing Edwards. In turn, Edwards also wrote to this distinguished official, imploring that he listen to his side of the story before taking any action.[25]

In late November 1752 Dwight presented the Massachusetts House with a lengthy report in which he attacked Edwards's stewardship. Edwards rebutted in a letter sent directly to Speaker Hubbard. He minced no words, asking Hubbard to consider the difficulty under which he labored to defend himself. "You doubtless, Sir," he began, "are sensible what vast disadvantage a person lies under when one has a personal quarrel with him" and is not allowed to be present when such charges are made, "being all the while 150 miles off" in the wilds of the Berkshires. "How easy it must be," he continued, "for a gentleman of Col. Dwight's abilities, when animated with that high degree of resentment he has long expressed towards me, and the great resolution if possible to procure my removal from Stockbridge—I say, how easy must it be for such a gentleman, under these circumstances, to make another appear very odious."[26] Dwight's report, in other words, was so personal and partisan that Hubbard owed it to Edwards to hear his side of the story.

Charges and countercharges at the highest levels of the provincial government and in London continued for more than another year. Affairs in Stockbridge degenerated so much that the Williams/ Dwight faction stopped attending first the administration of communion and then church services. That most of the church sided with Edwards in the lengthy and rancorous dispute no doubt contributed to why he was unable to convince the Williamses to air their grievances before the whole congregation. With the family now increasingly marginalized, the commissioners and the provincial officials accepted Edwards's version of events. Unfortunately, their support came too late to prevent many of the Mohawks, once willing to believe in the worth of an English education, from abandoning that prospect and quitting the area in disgust.

The tide turned decisively in Edwards's favor late in 1753, when Hollis, finally convinced of the Williamses' malfeasance, appointed Edwards the chief superintendent of the mission school, a decision that so angered Joseph Dwight that he wrote Governor William Shirley an outright lie, blaming the Mohawks' departure from the mission on their dislike of Edwards. When this charge became public, Edwards endured another barrage of criticism, even from his good friend Thomas Prince. Confident that with Hollis's endorsement he now could administer the mission and school on truly Christian principles, Edwards ably defended his own activities to Prince and others, spelling out the true reasons for the Mohawks' disenchantment. It was finally the Williamses' self-serving attempts to monopolize the area's land and trade and their attendant lack of interest in the native tribes that had driven the Mohawks away.[27] From that point, under Edwards's sure hand, the Indian mission and school attained some degree of stability, even if it never gained the prominence that Hollis and others had envisioned.

HAWLEY'S REPENTANCE

Not all went poorly during Edwards's Stockbridge years. In the midst of his battle with the Williamses, he was surprised by an unexpected confession from Major Joseph Hawley, instrumental in hounding him from his Northampton pulpit a few years earlier. Hawley was no mean person, for he was Solomon Stoddard's grandson and, when he led the charge against Edwards, had been a Northampton attorney and justice of the peace. He was also the son of the Joseph Hawley who in the midst of Edwards's first Northampton Awakening had cut his throat and so dampened the revival's flames. The younger Hawley had been at Yale during the second wave of awakenings in the early 1740s but soon thereafter had become "very open and bold" in his support of Arminian ideas.[28] In 1749 he had become the chief mouthpiece of Edwards's Northampton detractors and lobbied vigorously for an immediate separation between pastor and church.

We do not know whether the despair and suicide of Joseph Hawley's parent had spawned or contributed to the son's original animus, but by the late summer of 1754 he had had a change of heart. He sent Edwards a letter in which he wrote of his own role in the dismissal proceedings and asked Edwards's forgiveness. Edwards received the letter in the midst of one of his debilitating illnesses and did not answer for three months. As Hawley had requested, he did so "with true candor and Christian charity."

Edwards admitted that Hawley's request was intrinsically distasteful to him, obliging him to revisit "that most disagreeable and dreadful scene." He also said that he believed himself greatly injured by the townspeople who had sought his dismissal because despite his insistence that he had acted in good faith, they continued to impugn him with selfish motives. Even when he addressed his detractors "in the language of moderation and entreaty," he went on, they had interpreted it as "a design to flatter the people, especially the most ignorant, so to work upon their affections, and so to gain a party." Any good Christian, he wrote, should have wanted to moderate the passions raised. Instead Hawley had blown on the fire, an action "the less becoming" given how young he then was.[29] Moreover, Edwards added, in Hawley's remonstrance to the council called to adjudicate the Northampton difficulties he had said things that were "uncharitable and censorious" and "full of direct, bold slanders, asserted in strong terms, and delivered in severe, opprobrious language." Edwards then repeated the admonition of his *Farewell Sermon*: that the entire church was guilty in the sight of God and in need of humble repentance. "I must leave you to judge for yourself, concerning what I say," he concluded, insisting that he had no interest in carrying on "any paper or letter controversy with you on the subject." He trusted that Hawley would respect his account of the events and asked that God might enable him to "view things truly, and as he views them."[30]

Soon thereafter the two resumed a cordial relationship, linked as they were by the memory of the elder Hawley's death. But despite Edwards's goodwill, the younger Hawley's guilt tortured him for the remainder of his life. As late as 1760, two years after Edwards's death, he wrote the Reverend David Hall of Sutton, Massachusetts, a member of both Northampton councils called to look into Edwards's relation to the church, to admit his errors. He had long taken it as his duty, he wrote, "not only to humble myself before God for what was unchristian and sinful" but openly to confess his faults to members of both councils and so to "take shame" for his role in the Northampton proceedings. In a confession freighted with the same kind of drama as Judge Samuel Sewall's sixty years earlier, admitting before his church his errors in condemning to death the Salem witches, Hawley confessed to sinning "exceedingly in consenting and laboring that there should be so early a dismission of Mr. Edwards," particularly through his "groundless and slanderous imputations" against him. Feeling the pangs of conscience and perhaps the fraying band of his mortality, Hawley asked the clergyman to make his repentance known as widely as possible, and Hall obliged by printing the missive in its entirety in the *Boston Evening-Post* on May 19, 1760.[31]

IN THE STOCKBRIDGE STUDY

Even as Joseph Hawley's 1757 letter reminded Edwards of the similarity of his present difficulties to what he had earlier endured for several years in Northampton, it reinforced his belief that whatever resistance he incurred, he had to continue to defend the Calvinistic scheme. But his situation was hardly conducive to a return to the study. Stockbridge itself, for example, remained in turmoil because of threats of Indian warfare, so much so that the province fortified the town, filling it with soldiers (some of whom were domiciled in Edwards's own home) who formed a front line against incursions from the north. The pressures he was under from this new threat of violence as well as from the opprobrium of the Williams clan took a toll on his health. Beginning in midsummer, Edwards suffered from "a most severe attack of the ague and fever," his constitution "so enfeebled" that he even suspended his correspondence.[32]

Early in 1755, however, Edwards began to recover, even as the region to the immediate north erupted in the next phase of the French and Indian Wars. The missionary enterprise finally in his control and the attention of his virulent enemies diverted at least temporarily by the warfare to the north, Edwards returned to projects long contemplated but delayed by personal exigencies. Foremost among these tasks was his public refutation of the Arminianism that had continued to take root in the colonies.

Since the earliest days of his ministry Edwards had in mind such an attack on Arminianism, and his preaching on the topic had been crucial to the emergent culture of revival in the Connecticut Valley in the 1730s. The subject continued to engage him through the 1740s, particularly as he recognized its poison in the arrogance and selfishness of many of his wealthier Northampton parishioners. As early as the summer of 1748, when Edwards was firmly in place in Northampton, he alluded, in a letter to John Erskine, to his wish to write on the topic. He also mentioned that living "in this remote part of the world," he needed to be told "what books there are that are published on the other side of the Atlantic" that might help him consider the topic. By the following summer Erskine had obliged and provided new reading material germane to the controversy.[33]

But the time for this undertaking still had not been propitious, in light of what Edwards faced in Northampton. As he put it to Thomas Gillespie, around 1750 he "had begun to write something against the Arminians" but soon was embroiled with the difficulties over the qualifications for communion. Not until his settlement in Stockbridge did he again consider the prospect of completing a book on the subject. Adept at multitasking, even as he struggled to put the mission and its school on firmer footing and sent to press *Misrepresentations Corrected*, his final word on the Northampton difficulties, he returned to his plan to battle Arminianism as it was embodied in a cadre of English apologists whose works Erskine had sent him.

He thanked Erskine in particular for an account of the writings of the English divine John Taylor. Erskine probably had described Taylor's decidedly liberal and increasingly popular notions of the doctrine of original sin. Edwards knew what had to be done to turn this tide. He first wanted to treat the issues of free will and moral agency, "endeavoring, with as much exactness as I am able, to consider the nature of that freedom of moral agents, which makes them the proper subjects of moral government, moral precepts, counsels, calls, motives, persuasions, promises and threatenings, praise and blame, rewards and punishments." To accomplish this, he would strictly examine "the modern notions of those things" and demonstrate their "palpable inconsistency and absurdity." For the moment, he would leave aside Taylor's writings on sin and focus instead on the writings of Daniel Whitby and Thomas Chubb, as well as of a few others whose notions of free will, though not properly Arminian, still fed the invidious scheme.[34] By late November he reported to Erskine that he had begun "to write a little on the Arminian controversy" but because of the imbroglio with the Williams family "had not had time to set pen to paper since."[35]

Despite the ongoing difficulties at the mission (this was about the time he wrote to Pepperell and William Hogg, the Scots merchant and his patron, at such length), Edwards again commenced work on the project, and within six months he was far enough along to ask Thomas Foxcroft to assist him in gathering subscriptions for his book. Although in mid-October Edwards complained to Thomas Gillespie that he was still meeting with trouble in Stockbridge, later that fall he had completed his *Careful and Strict Enquiry into the Modern Prevailing Notions of That Freedom of the Will, Which Is Supposed to Be Essential to Moral Agency, Vertue and Vice, Reward and Punishment, Praise and Blame*, his most lengthy work to date.[36]

He was anxious for its appearance. "I long since sent away my book against the Arminians," he wrote the Boston minister Foxcroft, his de facto Boston publishing agent, on February 5, 1754, "and want to know very much what is become of it." A month later, around the time that Hollis put him in charge of the Indian school, the book was still in the press, and Edwards sent Foxcroft what appears to have been a second round of additional materials and asked whether it might not be best "to put the papers containing my additions . . . into the ms. at the places where they are to be inserted, to prevent their being overlooked or forgotten." He added his wish that the printing of his book "might be hastened."[37] The volume finally appeared later that spring.

Edwards hardly paused to enjoy its reception, however, for as his manuscripts show, he viewed all his work from this period as of a piece. His treatise on the will was only an opening volley. He immediately turned to other, related theological and ethical questions. In his section on "Original Sin" in his "Book of Controversies," Edwards had noted the following: "Perhaps in more volumes than one a treatise the first part concerning the nature of true virtue, and in this treat of God's end in creating the world, and in the next part concerning original sin . . . , and then concerning infused habits and concerning grace's differing from common grace in nature and kind." The manuscripts further reveal that by 1753 and 1754, he had virtually drafted the first two of these, which he came to view as integral parts of a separate volume that eventually comprised the posthumously published *Two Dissertations, I. Concerning the End for Which God Created the World. II. The Nature of True Virtue*.[38] When Samuel Hopkins and Joseph Bellamy visited their mentor early in February 1755 and heard him read from "The Last End of God in the Creation of the World," Edwards had shared a work that would not be published until 1765.[39]

He reported the completion of these works to Foxcroft on February 11, 1757, and noted their importance to his attempts to place Christianity on a rational basis. As things now appeared, he wrote his colleague, "the modern opinions which prevail concerning these two things"—that is, God's end in creation and the nature of true virtue—stood "very much as the foundation of that fashionable scheme of divinity [Arminianism], which seems to have become almost universal." He had in mind particularly the notions of Lord Shaftesbury (Anthony A. Cooper) and George Turnbull, "calculated to show that all mankind are neutrally disposed to virtue, and are without any depravity." He also found such ideas epitomized in the recent publications of Jonathan Mayhew, who was a rising star among liberal clergy in Boston and one of the topics of his missive to his Boston correspondent.[40]

What of the other proposed treatises? Although Edwards may have wanted to codify once and for all what he had come to know of the operations of grace, he had written already on this topic, in bits and pieces, sermons and volumes, from the 1730s on, as he had considered the effects of the awakenings. Instead he turned to the question of original sin and particularly to Taylor's increasingly popular views, with which by now he was totally familiar. As early as the summer of 1748 Erskine had sent him Taylor's *The Scripture-Doctrine of Original Sin*, the work that more than any other set the terms of contemporary debate on this topic.[41] Over the next few years, as he watched Taylor's opinions pass as common currency in America as well as in England, Edwards knew that he would have to address his arguments. In his perusal of Solomon Williams's response to his own *Humble Inquiry*, for example, Edwards had detected Taylor's unmistakable influence, and in the letter to his church appended to his *Misrepresentations Corrected* he reminded his people of the congruence of some of Williams's views in his rebuttal to those of the English author "who lately has been so famous for his corrupt doctrine."[42]

Edwards began his new treatise in the summer of 1756 and the next February told Foxcroft that the book was "almost prepared" for the press. Why he chose to publish it before the already completed *Two Dissertations* is not clear, but it may have had something to do with a recent flurry of pamphlets pro and contra Taylor's Arminian notions that were issuing from New England presses (one of them, a contribution from Edwards's own disciple Joseph Bellamy). In any event, Edwards described his new work to Foxcroft as a refutation of Taylor's ideas, with the book about as "large" as his effort on free will.[43] Edwards completed his work on original sin on May 26 and then spent a few months drumming up subscriptions for it, writing to Bellamy to circulate handwritten circulating "proposals" to enlist more subscribers, now that they had run out of the printed forms.[44] The book appeared early in 1758.

Thus in a few short years in the mid-1750s Edwards completed four lengthy theological treatises on topics of transatlantic interest and concern. That he accomplished this in the virtual wilderness of Stockbridge, his attention (and health) drained not only by preaching to and administering a school for Native Americans but also by the need to defend himself against the incessant intrigues of those who sought his removal from the area, is remarkable. Buying or borrowing books on his infrequent trips to New Haven or Boston, or requesting them of his various correspondents on both sides of the Atlantic, Edwards struggled to keep abreast of the most advanced religious, philosophical, and scientific discourse. Through his own writing, he redirected the course of such thought.

EIGHT

Transatlantic Debate

(1754-1758)

THE PROBLEM OF MORAL AGENCY

Sereno Edwards Dwight, one of Edwards's earliest biographers with access to much family material, reckoned that his subject, remarkably, spent only about four and a half months writing *Freedom of the Will*, the cornerstone of his response to the Arminian controversy.[1] He had contemplated writing such a response at least since the summer of 1747, or shortly after he had published his *Religious Affections*. But he had mulled over the topic much longer, since his days at Yale. The question of whether man was capable of choosing between good and evil, and thus was responsible to the moral law, seemed to him the central stumbling block to the further progress of religion. After all, Edwards's sermons on man's utter dependence on God and on justification by faith alone had done so much to initiate Northampton's first awakenings in 1734 and 1735. Now, as he saw members of the current generation stray from those points of doctrine because of their inflated sense of personal agency, he wished to revisit the subject and settle it for all time.

As early as the fall of 1723, in one of his "Miscellanies," he had proposed what he spent a lifetime pondering: that freedom of the will and divine omnipotence were congruent, not mutually contradictory.

As he put it, "'Tis very true, that God requires nothing of us as [a] condition of eternal life but what is in our own power; and yet 'tis very true at the same time, that 'tis an utter impossibility that ever man should do what is necessary in order to salvation, nor do the least towards it, without the almighty operation of the Holy Spirit of God."[2] All is from God and of God, and unless man believed this, he misunderstood his obligation to the Supreme Being.

But precisely how did one reconcile freedom of the will with belief in an almighty God? Or concomitantly, in a predetermined universe, what precisely do terms like *liberty* and *agency* mean? This was to form the nub of Edwards's *Freedom of the Will*, yet in this "Miscellany" Edwards demonstrated that at the age of twenty he was already close to cracking the code to this mystery. There were many things entirely within our power, he explained. Undeniably, man can do what he pleases, for that is the way people usually understand their freedom. Edwards here insisted on linguistic precision. When someone says that a man cannot "will" such a thing, people take it to mean that this person might truly wish to do something but is unable to do it. But this was verbal chicanery, the wrong way to think about freedom of the will. For while something—some circumstances or ideas, for example—might cause someone to *want* to do something, through no act of his own power does a person actually "will" it, in the common understanding of the term. Rather, to do something or not depends solely on one's "disposition." A little later, in another entry, he explained this through analogy. Jesus, Edwards wrote, had as much liberty as any man to do what he wanted, yet it was "absolutely impossible" that he should sin because he was not disposed to it. It was not in his constitution.[3]

As the young Edwards commenced his ministry with Stoddard, he revisited the issue, observing in his notebooks that many found it against their natural notions of justice to believe that they should be punished for actions that they had to do against their wills. But here too the difficulty stemmed from a confusion of language. Because people did not use such words as *necessary* and *impossible* with precision, Edwards explained, it was natural for them to wonder how they could be punished for what they could not avoid doing. But they missed the real question: Should men be punished for voluntary actions that in fact God had determined ahead of time? Edwards's answer was yes. To address the question properly, one had to consider a person's disposition, that which "determined the will to determine itself this way," to understand why an individual willfully performed any action.[4] In his great *Freedom of the Will* Edwards expanded what he had postulated in his "Miscellany."

When he took up his pen to address the matter more formally, Edwards had behind him decades of experience with the disastrous effects of men's believing in their own agency and thus aggrandizing themselves at the expense of others. The now-repentant Joseph Hawley, leader of the group that had sought to oust Edwards from his pulpit, proved a memorable example of one who had progressed from "lax principles in religion" to "falling in in some essentials things with Arminians," and the behavior of the Williams clique in Stockbridge brought home only more vividly the dangers inherent in believing that people might act as independent agents.[5] In both cases what these individuals thought was right derived from their corrupt wills, an inability to see that their actions were selfish and thus ungodly. Thus, despite the trying physical and psychological environment in which Edwards labored in Stockbridge, by 1753 he had tried to synthesize once and for all a proper understanding of the relation of liberty to necessity.

The main foils in his treatise were three English writers who recently had addressed the freedom of the will from very different positions. The first was the proto-Unitarian Thomas Chubb, a Benjamin Franklin–like character who had begun life as a self-educated artisan and through his anti-Trinitarian writings brought himself to the attention (and for a while even the patronage) of prominent cosmopolitan dissenters.[6] Inspired particularly by the writings of Arminian churchmen such as Samuel Clarke and William Whiston, Chubb's first work, *The Supremacy of the Father Asserted* (1714), had been a defense of Arianism—that is, a belief that Christ was not the same substance as God the Father but, rather, had been created as his human agent. He soon progressed to other topics, coming precariously close to advocating deism. Chubb was particularly troubled by the Calvinist view of man as inherently evil, for he believed that the hopelessness this doctrine engendered led man to atheism. Consequently, he emphasized man's inherent nobility. In particular, Chubb denied that God in any way was responsible for moral evil; man, through his own free will, created it. Also drawing Edwards's ire was Chubb's understanding of the relation of man's actions to his motives and particularly man's presumed ability to set them aside if he so wished.

Daniel Whitby, a Church of England clergyman who had made a name combating the recidivist Calvinism of his fellow Anglican divine John Edwards, also was in Edwards's sights.[7] Whitby was distressed by the noxious doctrine of innate depravity, for to believe that God had made the entire human race corrupt by nature did not seem congruent with the supreme goodness that God embodied. Rather than regard man as utterly depraved, Whitby postulated him to be in a state of trial or probation during which he was free to exercise his will for his good and thus align himself with the history of redemption. A well-regarded churchman, Whitby provided Edwards with an important example of how insidiously Arminianism could contribute to the debasement of God's grandeur even as with flimsy arguments it provided a scaffold on which man purportedly could climb to heaven.

Edwards's final target was the dissenting Calvinist divine Isaac Watts, instrumental in the publication of Edwards's *Faithful Narrative* in the mid-1730s.[8] Earlier in the century Watts had not been afraid to combat the emergence of the English deists, but his ecumenicalism had made him soften his understanding of Calvinist doctrine, particularly regarding the extent of human reprobation. He was important to Edwards as an enemy (perhaps even an unwitting one) from within the ranks of revivalists, his willingness to accommodate the rationalist spirit of the age particularly destructive to the faith once delivered to the saints. What drew Edwards's attention was Watts's

Essay on the Freedom of the Will in God and in Creatures (1732), particularly Watts's notion that because the mind was "active," to some degree it was self-determining. The will, Watts argued, could make the understanding do what it knew was wrong. Equally problematic was Watts's conception of a God who demanded our praise because of what he did in the world rather than from our comprehension of what he in essence *is*, the fount of creation. Although Edwards treated Watts with the respect due someone who was, on many other points, on his side, he obviously was disturbed that the Arminian poison had tainted so eminent a dissenter.

From his letters to John Erskine and others, it is evident that Edwards wished to be kept apprised of any transatlantic publications germane to his interests, and in the course of *Freedom of the Will* he addressed as well the ideas of such Church of England divines as Samuel Clarke and John Taylor and the Scots moralist George Turnbull.[9] But Chubb, Whitby, and Watts represented three "voluntaristic libertarians" who differed primarily in degree and thus presented a spectrum of how one could think about man's self-determination. They thus afforded Edwards representative targets as he attempted to strike a decapitating blow against Arminianism.[10]

The results were intellectually staggering. Since its publication *Freedom of the Will* has been regarded as one of the most convincing arguments for the Calvinist view of the relation between freedom and necessity.[11] Most important, Edwards's success derives from the remarkable congruence of his theological speculation with his practical experience as an evangelist. If to some the book's conclusions seemed totally out of step with what they took as the bedrock of human nature, the sheer power of Edwards's intellectual formulation, based as it was in psychology rather than in Scripture or theology, demanded their attention.

Although *Freedom of the Will* is lengthy, its key premises are few and elegant. The will, Edwards explained in his first section, simply is "that by which the mind chooses anything." More precisely, the will is "that faculty or power or principle of mind by which it is capable of choosing." An act of the will, then, is itself "the same as an act of choosing or choice." In other words, "In every volition, there is a preference, or a prevailing inclination of the soul," and with every action thus "some preponderation of the mind, an inclination, one way taken rather than another." To Edwards this seemed an unexceptional, commonsense understanding.[12]

When he proceeded to discuss what an act of will is, he concluded that "what determines the will" is the motive that, "as it stands in the view of the mind, is the strongest." Drawing on John Locke's writings, Edwards explained that in this sense "motive" is what the understanding apprehends. We act, then, as we apprehend something and in accordance with the agreeableness of that stimulus. A voluntary and rational agent chooses that which appears to him "good," that which pleases him or is for his benefit. There is "scarcely a plainer and more universal dictate of the sense and experience of mankind," he wrote, than "that, when men act voluntarily, and do what they please, then they do what suits them best, or what is most agreeable to them." Therefore, Edwards concluded famously, "The will always is as the greatest apparent good is." We do what our understanding tells us is best to do, if we mean by *understanding* how we perceive and apprehend, apart from what merely is called reason or judgment.[13]

This distinction is crucial, for Edwards's understanding of how a man wills was based in the notion that with regard to an act of the will, there is no deliberation, no rumination over whether something is good or bad. Rather, the will is determined instantaneously; once an external stimulus is apprehended as agreeable, motive, will, and act instantly follow. To accept this is to go far toward accepting Edwards's whole theology, for his notion of the will related directly to his understanding of the religious affections and of the concept of grace itself. The natural man who has not been renovated by God's grace cannot help acting sinfully, for all his actions stem from the way things affect him. As a fallen creature he perceives selfishly. Even though he attempts to act "good," his final motivation, his "sense of heart," is that of a natural, fallen man. Concomitantly, what God bestows through free grace is a new spiritual sense that thenceforth makes one's actions flow from a fount of goodness. The saint is the person for whom the glory of God and not self-interest always determines the greatest good.

Edwards explained this fully in his section on "Natural and Moral Necessity." For him, moral necessity is that "which arises from such *moral causes*, as the strength of inclination, or motives, and the connection which there is in many cases between these, and such certain volitions and actions." On the other hand, natural necessity pertains to what one must do because of natural causes, what pain forces him to do when his body is hurt, or what he must conclude because he knows that two and two make four or that black is not white. Moral necessity is of a wholly different order; it governs our relation to God. Thus we have a moral obligation to love God more than anything else, but the fallen man, given his corrupt sense of heart, his selfishness, cannot do so. One may try to love God because of some natural necessity—because one is ill and afraid of death, for example—but no matter how deep that love, it carries no weight. Moral inability thus consists of a "want of inclination" or the offsetting "strength of a contrary inclination."[14] Moral inability prevents a sinner from doing what is just in God's eyes. Only grace can do that. And in the revivals, Edwards believed, he had seen time and time again the change of heart that made people see (and thus act) differently, their greatest good now defined by godliness.

The Arminians' proposition that under such moral inability people were not "free" did not trouble Edwards. "Liberty," he told his readers, is simply "that power and opportunity for one to do and conduct as he will, or according to his choice," without taking into account "anything of the cause and original of that choice; or at all considering how the person came to have such a volition." Let a person, he explained, come by his volition or choice by whatever means; "if he is able, and there is nothing else in the way to hinder his pursuing and executing his will, the man is fully and perfectly free." On these terms, saints and sinners are free, at liberty to act from their inclinations. What they cannot control, and what does not enter the equation of their freedom, is *how* their inclination got to be the way it is and *why* they apprehend as they do. This was set at creation.

Edwards covered all this essential ground in the first of his book's four parts and spent the remainder demolishing the arguments and potential objections of Chubb, Whitby, Watts, and others. As important as this material was to the contemporaneous debate over the relation of liberty to necessity, Edwards's more lasting contribution was his seemingly unassailable defense, on Enlightenment principles, of the Calvinist notion that God demands obedience to the moral law and condemns to everlasting punishment those who disobey it. In his other sections, he parried arguments about God as the author of sin, squared his understanding of man's "liberty" with the omnipotence of divine will, and defended Calvinism against charges that it ends in a materialism, a "necessity" as dispiriting as that which Thomas Hobbes theorized.

Edwards's *Freedom of the Will* was a tour de force that immediately redefined the international debate over its subject and did so for the next century.[15] Response to the work was quick. In late July 1757, at John Erskine's request, Edwards responded to supporters of Lord Kames, who Erskine thought had twisted the meaning of Edwards's arguments for their own purposes. Edwards's lengthy response was considered important enough to be issued as a separate pamphlet in 1758 and then appended to the third and subsequent editions of *Freedom of the Will*, published in 1768. Edwards simply dismissed Kames out of hand. "It must be evident to everyone," Edwards wrote, who "has read both his *Essays* [*on the Principles of Morality and Natural Religion*] and my *Freedom of the Will*, that our schemes are exceeding reverse of each other."[16] In a second letter to Erskine sent the very next week, Edwards similarly demolished Kames's response to his critics in England and Scotland.

Edwards's book clearly was making waves and marked his reentry to a stage on which he had last played with his writings on the revivals. To him, of course, *Freedom of the Will* was of a piece with his earlier work. Once again he had shown God glorified in man's dependence on him, the necessity of justification by faith alone, and the transforming power of a divine and supernatural light. But for his polemic to be persuasive, he had to name the enemies of the work of redemption and display in the most uncompromising ways their errors and their tendencies. The result was exhilarating and whetted his desire to complete other parts of his defense of Christianity.

GOD'S END IN CREATION

His *Freedom of the Will* at the printer, Edwards turned his attention to two other dissertations that he viewed as related and integral to his theological edifice. He had hinted at the subject of one of them in the fourth part of his book when in a discussion of moral necessity and moral responsibility, he observed that God himself is in "the highest possible respect an agent, and active in the exercise of his infinite holiness." God's actions, Edwards added, thus "are in the highest, most absolutely perfect manner virtuous and praiseworthy; and are so, for that very reason, because they are most perfectly necessary." But to what end were God's "perfect" actions? Why did he dispose things as he did?[17]

Edwards first noted the unexceptional: All comes from God, and all is of God. Humanity thus is part and parcel of God's creation and thus also of God. Edwards linked this to his belief that nothing a human does contributes to God's splendor, for "if the creature receives its all from God entirely and perfectly, how is it possible that it should have anything to add to God, to make him in any respect more than he was before, and so the Creator become dependent on the creature?" Thus the whole universe, "including all creatures animate and inanimate, in all its actings, proceedings, revolutions, and entire series of events," proceeds "from a regard and with a view to *God*, as the supreme and last end of all."[18] But what, then, was the purpose of the universe?

To Edwards the answer was obvious, if also utterly mystical in its beauty and grandeur. God's end in creation simply was "to communicate of his own infinite fullness of good," or, to put it another way, to "diffuse his own fullness." God had made the world, Edwards explained, so that "there might be glorious and abundant emanation of his infinite fullness of good *ad extra*." Being so good, so beautiful, so true, God in essence spilled over into more of the same, and this effulgence was creation. As Edwards put it, "*A disposition in God, as an original property of his nature, to an emanation of his infinite fullness, was what excited him to create the world; and so that the emanation itself was aimed at by him as a last end of the creation.*" In its lowest as in its highest forms, the universe thus eternally testifies to God's primary purpose, to display his glory.[19]

Edwards saved for this work's companion treatise an answer to what such an understanding of God's creation demands of his creatures. In the remainder of this work he elaborated on the "fullness" that was pushed into creation by God's will. One result of this action was "the communication of virtue and holiness to the creature." Virtue and holiness are the very substance of God, and so what is distributed through the universe, including to human creation, by God's will is more of the same. At the same time, when humans act in agreement with this holiness, they fulfill their highest purpose, reflecting such virtue. But in so doing, Edwards reiterated, they do not add to God's luster but exemplify it. "His rejoicing therein is a rejoicing in his own acts," Edwards reiterated, not a joy derived from the creature's actions per se.[20]

When the saint evidences such refulgence, in other words, it simply is what God intended by the original emanation of his goodness. It isn't that God discovers beings originally "out of" himself and embraces them from his goodness but, rather, that he "enlarges himself in a more excellent and divine manner." How? By communicating himself "and so[,] instead of finding, making objects of his benevolence." God does not take into himself what he finds distinct from himself, Edwards explained. Rather, "by flowing forth, and expressing himself" in his creatures "and making them partake of him, and rejoicing in himself expressed in them, and communicated to them," he displays his utter primacy.[21]

Although in this treatise Edwards was not sparring with specific opponents as he had done in his *Freedom of the Will*, this work dovetailed with his arguments concerning the will. He also knew that herein his thoughts might seem particularly abstruse, but this necessarily arose, he said, from the subject's "infinite sublimity" and "the incomprehensibleness of those things that are divine." This straining of language until it was almost at its breaking point, so much meaning did it have to bear, only increased as Edwards elaborated his central premises and reached a crescendo in his struggle to explain "the glory of God," the "emanation and true external expression of God's internal glory and fullness." Obscurity here was unavoidable, he explained, "through the imperfection of language, and words being less fitted to express things of so sublime a nature."[22]

This immeasurable distance between language and meaning did not stop Edwards from trying to describe how it is that God's creation reflects his glory. Thus "not only the creature's seeing and knowing God's excellence" but also his "supremely esteeming and loving him" was part of the communication of God's fullness. In the highest sense, worship is part of the glory of God. In the creature's "knowing, esteeming, loving, rejoicing in, and praising God," Edwards stated, the glory of God is exhibited as well as acknowledged. God's fullness is received and returned in what "is both an emanation and a remanation," for his "refulgence shines upon and into the creature, and is reflected back to the luminary." Giving ourselves to God in this way through selfless worship is integral to his intention in creating the world. When we yearn to be with God, we acknowledge not only our but God's highest intention. Not to yearn to be part of this "remanation" indicates a disposition, a sense of heart, at cross-purposes with God's intent. "God's respect to the creature's good, and his respect to himself" are not different matters, Edwards explained. Rather, both are "united in one, as the happiness of the creature aimed at is happiness in union with himself."[23]

Edwards left his most profound and challenging insight for the final pages of the treatise. "The more happiness" for man, he wrote, "the greater union" with God. And if such happiness is to continue eternally, this union will become more "strict and perfect," more like that of God and Christ, the Father and Son, only as time goes on. Because God made the universe as he did, all that had gone out from him would return to him. But logically, because creation is eternal, an utterly perfect union presumably can never be attained. Edwards put it memorably:

> Let the most perfect union with God be represented by something at an infinite height above us; and the eternally increasing union of the saints with God, by something that is ascending constantly towards that infinite height, moving upwards with a given velocity; and that is to continue thus to move to all eternity. God who views the whole of this eternally increasing height views it as an infinite height. And if he has respect to it, and makes it his end, as in the whole of it, he has respect to it as an infinite height, though the time will never come when it can be said it has already arrived at this infinite height.

For creation to be as grand as it is, in other words, the time will never come when one can say that his union with God is consummated.[24]

The saint finds further proof of God's infinite power and wisdom in so disposing of his creation, even if it means that he will never "know" God as perfectly as he wishes. For just as God aims at satisfying justice in the eternal damnation of sinners, punished as they are for sinning against an infinite God, so he glorifies his saints in heaven with "eternal felicity," allowing them, as saints, "the bestowment of a good infinitely valuable." Yet "there never will come the moment, when it can be said, that now this infinitely valuable good has been actually bestowed."[25] Eternity is just *that*, utterly central to the end for which God had created the world, and the Christian life thus is one of constant movement toward a center the saint can never reach.

THE NATURE OF TRUE VIRTUE

If creation is emanation and "remanation," how is one to behave in the world to accomplish this "reflection" of God's will? What constitutes true goodness? For Edwards, this question was linked closely to his discussion in the *Freedom of the Will* of one's *disposition*—that is, of whether one sees the world as a saint, and so is inclined to gracious actions, or as a sinner, motivated only by self-interest. Edwards addressed the implications of this in *The Nature of True Virtue*, the companion piece to *The End for Which God Created the World*.

In this work Edwards had in mind specific philosophers, notably Francis Hutcheson (and, to a lesser extent, William Wollaston), who recently had gained ascendancy for their own views on the subject.[26] In particular, Edwards felt the need to address Hutcheson's *Inquiry into the Original of Our Ideas of Beauty and Virtue* (1725), in which he posited in humankind a universal "moral sense" that was equal and operating in a way comparable to the other senses and that allowed an individual to judge virtue and vice. Hutcheson thus invested "conscience," which Edwards viewed as only a version of self-interest, with a power that led further into the Arminian tangle. If the universe is but an exfoliation of divinity and our divinely ordained role is inexorably to move back toward its mystical center, the judgment of any merely human "sense" cannot adequately end in true virtue.

How, then, did Edwards define true virtue? For him it connoted beauty or "excellency." Another way to ask this question is, what was it that "renders any habit, disposition, or exercise of the heart truly beautiful"? Distinguishing between "particular" beauty—that is, beauty limited to some particular things within an essentially private sphere—and "general" beauty—that is, when something is viewed "most perfectly, comprehensively and universally, with regard to all its tendencies"—Edwards proposed that "True virtue essentially consists in benevolence to Being in general." More accurately, it involves action, "that consent, propensity and union of heart to Being in general, that is immediately exercised in a general good will."[27]

True virtue never consists solely in our love of particular beings, no matter how profound our sympathy for them, but rather in our love of being, "simply considered." Love of particular beings can arise from such a disposition but finally is too limited to be true virtue, for no affection can be such unless it stems from consent to "the universal system of existence," to creation. This is, after all, the reason man has been created, for, as Edwards argued in *The End for Which God Created the World*, our highest calling is to reflect the very glory that constitutes God's presence in our everyday lives. The best evidence of such a love, Edwards declared, thus arises from "the temper of mind wherein consists a supreme propensity of heart to God." Such virtue is "the agreeableness of the kind and degree of our love to *God's end* in our creation and in the creation of all things, and the coincidence of the exercises of our love, in their manner, order, and measure, with the *manner* in which *God* himself exercises love to the creature in the creation and government of the world."[28] This is what Edwards meant, in his previous dissertation, when he said that God had created the world so that humankind could reflect his glory.

Edwards spent the bulk of this treatise discussing such propositions in practical terms and how they related to what others—most notably Hutcheson and Wollaston in his *Religion of Nature Delineated* (1726)—had propounded in their schemes of virtue. Edwards took great pains to distinguish a disposition to true virtue (another way of describing how a saint "sees" the world) from the "secondary" beauty that Hutcheson had mistakenly invested with moral value. Further, it was only this secondary beauty, according to Edwards, that Wollaston had in mind when he resolved all virtue into "an agreement of inclinations, volitions, and actions, with *truth*."[29] Beauty that is defined only as the harmony or fitness or suitability of one thing or one being to another—something that pleases man by a congruity he recognizes—never constitutes true virtue.

The main problem with secondary beauty, Edwards argued, lay in its origin in and relation to self-love, the opposite of love to Being in general. As early as the 1730s Edwards had addressed this topic in one of his "Miscellanies," but now it was of greater concern because some contemporary philosophers argued that self-love was the very foundation of the moral sense.[30] Edwards rejected this proposition outright. Self-love, he said, is nothing but "a man's love of his own happiness."[31] In this regard, love for another is but a love that in some way pleases us. Men love those who are like them, who hold the same views, who are attractive to them, who give them a good feeling if they aid them. In all these cases no larger principle is at work than self-interest. Even though such notions are congruent with an understanding of a God who loves harmony, they represent only what Edwards termed secondary beauty. Consistency and harmony are great laws of nature, but they have nothing to do with true virtue.

Edwards understood that people have no way to conceive of anything that others do or suffer except by "recalling and exciting the ideas" of what they themselves feel and understand; we consider the pain or pleasure of others by putting ourselves in their places. This comparison forms the basis for what Edwards terms natural conscience: either the disposition to approve or disapprove of the moral treatment of someone from how we would view such treatment of ourselves or the "sense of desert" that arises from the "natural agreement, proportion and harmony" between injury and punishment for it, or loving and being loved, or showing kindness and being rewarded.[32]

Anyone who argues that this implies a moral sense "distinct from what arises from self-love" deceives himself. If the approbation of the conscience is the same as the approbation of the heart, Edwards said, conscience would always make one act in direct proportion to that "virtuous temper of the mind." Such is not the case, as man's frequently sinning against his conscience abundantly proves. "The conscience may see the natural agreement between opposing and being opposed, between hating and being hated, without abhorring malevolence from a benevolent temper of mind, or without loving God from a view of the beauty of his holiness."[33] Only those ruled by a supreme taste for virtue, not by a wish to please themselves (however altruistic their pleasure seemed to them), were truly virtuous.

Another category of benevolent action flows through what Edwards termed natural instinct and has to do with the general preservation of the race—the natural affection that evidences itself as love between the sexes, for example. Edwards admitted that here he agreed with Hutcheson and David Hume (in his *A Treatise of Human Nature* [1739]) that "there is a foundation laid in the soul for kind affection between the sexes."[34] But such feelings are patently private and have nothing to do with our union to Being in general. So too that pity is "natural to mankind when they see others in great distress," for as with the pangs of conscience, such reactions arise from uneasiness at the comparison of the other people's plights with our own.[35] Natural pity is very different from true virtue. It benefits the race but does not stem from the benevolence to being that marks truly virtuous actions.

Finally, Edwards observed that men mistake such private affections for true virtue because of the "narrowness of their views." When they extend private affections to a large number of people, they delude themselves into thinking that they are truly benevolent, but they still only consider "a small part of the related system." All that was left, then, was for Edwards to show that the nature of true virtue is "founded in the reason and nature of things." Being affected "with the immediate presence of the beautiful" does not depend on argumentation and rationalization but only on "the frame of our minds whereby they are made so that such an idea, as we have it, is grateful, or appears beautiful." In this sense, a taste for the beautiful is perfectly natural—that is, according to the laws of nature. Our inclination to happiness is the key, happiness defined as the greatest possible good, to God himself. Through our benevolence God seeks nothing less than "to agree with himself, to be united with himself, or to love himself," and so "he gives the same temper to his creatures, this is more agreeable to his necessary nature than the opposite temper."[36] True virtue consists in nothing less than consent to the universe, demonstrated by an unqualified desire to live according to God's laws.

In this dissertation, one of Edwards's most influential, he set the bar for human behavior as high as one possibly could. He argued nothing less than that the quotidian good that men do to and for each other, the "love" that we show our spouses, families, communities, and nations, as well as our pity for tragedies, small and large, exemplify only secondary virtue, *unless* God has transformed our hearts from selfishness to selflessness. To put it another way, unless one "sees" the world as a saint, thus disposing oneself to true virtue, anything that he wills is only from his selfishness, no matter what seeming good comes of it. Thus nothing that man does can mitigate the eternal punishment that God has in store for sinners whose behavior flows from such a source. Harsh as this seems, the fall of man after he transgressed God's law in Eden demands it.

MAN'S SINFUL NATURE

Edwards next turned his attention to the doctrine of original sin, corollary to the nature of true virtue, for it too required defense against the Arminian onslaught. In the summer of 1748 Edwards's Scots correspondent John Erskine sent him John Taylor's works, books of which Edwards knew but did not yet own. These works, he told Erskine, would help him as he answered the Arminians' attacks on Calvinist doctrine.[37] Over the next decade, as Edwards framed his arguments in his various notebooks, he focused particularly on Taylor's *The Scripture-Doctrine of Original Sin, Proposed to Free and Candid Examination* (1740), a book that to many readers (sympathetic or not to its arguments) seemed unassailable and that by the 1750s was exerting a large influence even over New England clergy, particularly in eastern Massachusetts.[38] There liberal ministers like Lemuel Briant and Jonathan Mayhew added Taylor's propositions to those of Samuel Clarke and other English latitudinarian clergy to forge a theology more in line with the enlightened principles the New Englanders espoused.[39] Commenting in 1752 on the spread of such "new divinity," Edwards noted that "these modern, fashionable opinions, however called noble and generous," were commonly attended by not only "a haughty contempt, but an inward, malignant bitterness of heart towards all the zealous professors and fenders of the contrary spirit of principles."[40] This certainly was the case five years later, for with Edwards already at work on his own treatment of the topic of original sin, a nasty and lengthy pamphlet war on the subject erupted among New England clergy. This extended discussion, to which

Edwards's close associate Joseph Bellamy contributed, may well have moved him to delay publication of two already completed manuscripts, as he readied his treatise on sin for the press.[41]

By the time Edwards wrote Thomas Foxcroft in February 1757, he was well along in his *Great Christian Doctrine of Original Sin Defended* and assured his correspondent that he had "particularly considered everything, of any consequence in Dr. Taylor's book." He had studied it so carefully, he explained in his preface, because no other volume had done "so much towards rooting out of these western parts of New England, the principles and scheme of religion maintained by our pious and excellent forefathers."[42] Edwards had worked as well through the books of other latitudinarian thinkers, particularly George Turnbull, whose *Principles of Moral Philosophy* (1740), based as it was in considerations of natural law (and thus of scientific reasoning of the sort in which Edwards was well versed), came under fire in Edwards's lengthy treatise. Other apologists for a more "enlightened" view of man, including Francis Hutcheson, also came into Edwards's focus, but the Scots Presbyterian Taylor and his countryman Turnbull absorbed most of Edwards's blows.[43]

Taylor's book against original sin was the centerpiece of the Arminians' assault on Calvinism because it appealed to those who found the doctrine of an inherent universal evil abhorrent to their notion of man's true worth and dignity. Those who agreed with Taylor viewed man as intelligent and rational, possessing the free will to choose between good and evil. To propose instead that from birth and because of Adam's initial transgression, man is doomed to a life of sin and thus is worthy only of eternal condemnation to hell's torments seemed patently absurd. So too other conclusions that flowed logically from this doctrine: that, in so creating man with a propensity to evil rather than good, God is the veritable author of sin, a notion that did not accord with views of the deity as the source of all benevolence. Edwards had his work cut out for him.

In his recently published *Freedom of the Will*, however, he already had laid some of the groundwork for a rebuttal, but as he always did, he first cleared the air by precise definition of his terms. "By original sin," he wrote, he meant "the *innate sinful depravity of the heart.*" Thus his primary task, given that "all moral qualities, all principles, of virtue or vice, lie in the disposition of the heart," was to discover if the heart of man was naturally "of a corrupt and evil disposition."[44] Edwards's answer was unequivocal. It was indeed corrupt.

As a good scientist might, Edwards argued first from observation and experience. "A steady effect argues a steady cause," he explained. And when he looked about him, everywhere he saw a "prevailing propensity" to sin. Of course, man does much good in the world, but the question is not, how great is man's tendency to sin, but, rather, is his *prevailing* tendency to do good or evil? Here Edwards made a striking analogy. One would not say that the state of a ship about to cross the ocean was "good" if it could not hold together for the whole voyage, for it might sink before it went partway over. Considering its general condition, no matter how far it goes, it is going to sink. So it is with the generality of humankind. It argues nothing for man's essential goodness that now and then, or even more often than not, he performs good deeds if his general disposition is not to true virtue. Man's general tendency toward sinfulness thus demands eternal punishment as a just desert.[45]

Edwards's argument from experience was powerful. "I must leave it to everyone to judge for himself," he wrote, "from his own opportunities of observation and information concerning mankind, how little there is of this disinterested love to God, this pure divine affection, in the world." His tour through ancient and modern history revealed instead affections that "perpetually . . . keep the world, through all nations and ages, in a continual agitation and commotion!" Edwards himself had seen enough of this, on the frontier between the French and British, where these nations sparred for North America. All history brought evidence of man's depravity. What could someone like Taylor possibly be thinking when he proposed that man was as capable of good as of evil and had the power to choose between the two? "There have been so very few in the world," Edwards concluded, "from age to age, ever since the world has stood, that have been of any other character" than those that tended toward the self and thus to sin.[46]

Edwards was satisfied that his arguments from experience offered unanswerable proof of man's innate depravity, but in Part Two he corroborated them by ranging widely through Scripture. The least interesting section to the twenty-first-century reader, it was essential to his project, for he had to demonstrate that Taylor and his cohort's doctrines were not only irrational but also unscriptural. Dividing his argument between relevant passages in both the Old and New Testaments, Edwards made it clear that as with Taylor's failure to prove his notion of sin through an appeal to experience, his attempt similarly to enlist the Bible did not bear exegetical scrutiny.

Thornier was Taylor's proposition that God would not condemn to everlasting hell newborn infants who died without ever committing sin, a topic that Edwards addressed in his third part. In a period of increasing humanitarian sentiment, the thought that an innocent child could go to hell struck many as proof that Calvinism was divorced from any rational notion of justice. But here too Edwards demonstrated Taylor's fatuousness, for Scripture taught that "*all* whom he [Christ] came to redeem, are *sinners*." The mere fact that newborn children are under the curse of death indicates that they too are subject to the same satisfaction of the law as adults. Further, Taylor's argument diminished—indeed, made superfluous—the meaning of Christ's redemption, for, through Taylor's logic, Christ had not died for *all* sinners. Thus, from Taylor's principles flowed the unscriptural notion that there was no need of Christ's redemption, for if God "has made other sufficient provision for that, viz., a sufficient power and ability, in all mankind, to do all their duty, and wholly to avoid sin," as man presumably could if he had free will, the crucifixion was irrelevant.[47]

In Part Four, Edwards answered objections raised against the Calvinist notion of innate depravity and in so doing touched on two issues that further demonstrated the cohesion of his thought. The first had to do with the notion that if sin is understood as intrinsic, as Calvinists implied, and not as the result of man's free will, God is the author of sin, an incongruous proposition if one views the deity as the primary source of benevolence. Edwards replied that his doctrine did not imply (as the Arminians suggested it did) that God infuses a "*taint, tincture*, or *infection*" in every human, for this argued an erroneous understanding of sin. To account for man's sinful nature, Edwards explained, one did not need not to believe that some evil quality is "*infused, implanted*, or *wrought*" into his nature. Rather, evil is privative, "the withholding of a special divine influence to impart and maintain those good principles, leaving the common natural principles of self-love, natural appetite, etc." to themselves without the government of superior principles. The inevitable result was the total corruption of the heart.[48] Innate depravity thus meant spiritual emptiness, a lack of something that only grace could restore as it disposed one to true virtue.

Edwards's elaboration of this concept was striking. When man sins, he said, the superior principles leave his heart, as "light ceases in a room when the candle is withdrawn." He is thus "left in a state of darkness, woeful corruption and ruin," like "a fatal catastrophe, a turning of all things upside down, and the succession of a state of the most odious and dreadful confusion." To compensate for this loss of spiritual compass, man acts predictably, immediately setting himself and his natural inclinations in God's place. The result is tragic, for now "the objects of his private affections and appetites" reign supreme, having taken the place of God. If one understands the corruption of the heart in this way, Edwards continued, God is not the creator of depravity. "Only God's withdrawing, as it was highly necessary and proper that he should, from rebel-man" and man's ensuing reliance on his natural principles for moral guidance are necessary to explain his utter corruption.[49]

And so it was with everyone, from Adam on, a genealogy and argument to which the Arminians raised one final objection. How could God punish *all* men for the sin of Adam? It made no sense, they claimed, that humankind subsequently was responsible for what their first ancestor had done. In what way could Adam and his posterity be looked on as equally complicit and so dealt with accordingly? Here Edwards demonstrated that such objections to the imputation of Adam's sin were simply founded on a wrong notion of "what we call sameness or oneness, among created things." Such "identity or oneness with past experience," he patiently explained, depended only on "the sovereign constitution and law of the Supreme Author and Disposer of the universe."[50]

Some things, Edwards went on, *seem* distinct in time yet are united by the law of the Creator. Think, for example, of "a tree, grown great, and an hundred years old." In one way it is the same plant as "the little sprout, that first came out of the ground, from whence it grew, and has been continued in constant succession." Perhaps not one of its original atoms remains the same, he explained, "yet God, according to an established law of nature, has in constant succession communicated to it the same qualities, and most important properties, as if it were one." So too the body of a forty-year-old man is "one with the infant body . . . from whence it grew," though it has "changed" in a hundred ways. Citing John Locke on how personal identity is defined just by such a personal consciousness maintained over time, Edwards observed that such "communication or continuance of the same consciousness and memory to any subject, through successive parts of duration, depends wholly on a divine establishment." Identity of consciousness thus wholly depends on a law of nature and so, by extension, on the sovereign will and agency of God.[51]

This explains our oneness, our sameness, with Adam, as well as our complicity in his transgression, for which God can exact the punishment of eternal misery. As a corollary, Edwards offered the remarkable proposition that "God not only created all things, and gave them being at first, but continually preserves them, and upholds them in being." The existence of God's creation in any moment and each successive one is "the effect of the *immediate* agency, will and power of God." It followed, Edwards set out for the less philosophically astute among his readers, that "God's upholding created substance, or causing its existence in each successive moment, is altogether equivalent to an immediate production out of nothing, at each moment." There is no identity or oneness in creation, unless God "so unites these new effects, that he treats them as one, but communicating to them like properties, relations, and circumstances." In other words, at any given moment it is as though God again were creating all from nothing. "All is constantly proceeding from God" and so is maintained by him.[52] Arguing for the concept of our oneness in sin with Adam, Edwards drew on his deepest understanding of the utterly arbitrary power of God, on whom all creation depends. Such was the Being whose exfoliation defined the world and its purpose. Also, he reinforced his sense that all humanity's complicity in sin argued an equality that made no one any better than another, man or woman, master or slave, European or Native American.[53]

Completing his treatise on original sin, Edwards put to rest Arminian arguments for the inherent dignity and worth of man. But as he showed people their utter insignificance and worthlessness, he was at odds with the tendency of his age to locate in man all that is noble and good. Edwards believed that the verifiably observable universe coincided with the scriptural account of its origin and purpose and of man's place in it. To him, there was nothing irrational about the end for which God created the world or of man's utter depravity yet eternal obligation to true virtue. Those who thought differently (and they had become legion, even in western Massachusetts) did so because of their limited vision, which was overt proof of their sinfulness.

All that now remained for Edwards to write was the massive history of the work of redemption, showing the congruence of all recorded history with Scripture, a task he had outlined in his sermon series of 1739. After his astonishing productivity at the Stockbridge mission one had every reason to believe that as soon as his three recently completed treaties were published, the world would soon enough have his summa.

NINE

Princeton

(1757–1758)

AARON BURR AND THE COLLEGE OF NEW JERSEY

During Edwards's tenure at Stockbridge, he was also preoccupied with family matters. Not long after the family's arrival in the Berkshires his twenty-year-old daughter, Esther, married the Reverend Aaron Burr, pastor of a Presbyterian church in New Ark, New Jersey, and president of the infant College of New Jersey. Founded by moderate New Light Presbyterians as a seminary at which to train pro-revival clergy, the college always had had Edwards's support, and he welcomed the Reverend Burr, scion of a wealthy Connecticut family, as a new family member.[1]

But the marriage was unusual, for Burr was sixteen years Esther's senior, and their courtship brief. Burr had met her when she was a young teenager and, although he had kept in contact with Edwards, had not seen her for many years. Intent on making her his wife, however, he traveled in the late spring of 1752 to Stockbridge to inform her and the family of his intentions and to ask for her acceptance and their blessing. He was successful, and within two weeks Esther was on her way to New Jersey to be wed; Sarah Edwards was the only family member at the ceremony. Did the isolation of and primitive conditions at the Stockbridge mission contribute to her rapid accept-

ance of Burr's proposal? Even within the family her precipitate decision raised eyebrows. Two years later Esther's younger sister Lucy still
wrote of it, noting that pockets of the family spoke disapprovingly of
Esther's "way of marrying."[2] Outside the family circle, however,
people were delighted with the match. In the fall after the wedding,
Edwards wrote the Scots revivalist William McCulloch that his
daughter's marriage seemed "very much to the satisfaction of ministers and people in those parts, and also our friends in Boston, and
other parts of New England."[3]

Esther's next few years were difficult, for until she found other
young women of comparable sophistication and interests, she was
frequently homesick.[4] Moreover, her health was fragile. In the spring
of 1753 her father sent a long letter of concern and consolation in
which he recommended several herbal and folk remedies (including
the flesh of "rattlesnake," a widespread homeopathic remedy) for her
condition. "And above all the rest," he suggested, "use riding in pleasant weather; and when you can bear it, riding on horseback; but
never so as to fatigue you." He was concerned enough to report Esther's illness to his friend Thomas Foxcroft.[5] The next spring, attended by her mother, Esther was well enough to give birth to the
Burrs' first child, Sally; but her second pregnancy, three years later,
was more difficult, with Aaron Burr, Jr., arriving prematurely. By late
summer, however, Esther, feeling stronger, brought her son to Stockbridge for the blessing of his grandparents.

Through these years Aaron Burr was busy with college affairs. The
school had been chartered in May 1747, and Burr had acceded to its
presidency later that summer, after the death of the fledgling institution's first president, the prominent middle colonies revivalist Jonathan
Dickinson. Until his congregation released him from his pastorate,
however, Burr held both demanding positions. When he finally was
able to devote all his attention to the school, he did it much good.
Over his ten-year tenure he put the college on a solid financial base,
traveling widely to raise funds, and in 1756 he oversaw its move to
Nassau Hall in the town of Princeton. An admirer of Dickinson's

evangelical labors as well as his writings—next to Edwards's, his accounts of the revivals were the most important to issue from the colonies—Edwards heartily supported his son-in-law's efforts. Even before Burr's marriage to Esther, for example, Edwards had welcomed news of Burr's planned fund-raising trip to England and Scotland. By spending a year or so in such a venture, Edwards counseled him, "There doubtless might great advantages be obtained." Given what lay in Edwards's own future, he appended a caution that is haunting. "One thing I will venture to give you my thoughts in," he wrote. Since Burr had not had "the smallpox," he should find himself "a skilled, prudent physician" from whom to receive an inoculation before he traveled.[6]

Burr never made the trip to England, but over the next several years he worked indefatigably for the school's welfare. Edwards contributed his mite as well, so confident in the education the college could provide that in 1753 he sent his fourteen-year-old son, Timothy, there. Around the same time, Edwards hosted a young Scotsman, about to take his Bachelor of Arts degree at the college and of whom Burr thought highly, at the homestead in Stockbridge. Edwards was particularly excited by Burr's account in the late winter of 1757 that a sizable religious awakening had begun in Princeton. The president described "a growing concern about the things of religion among the students for sometime past," with many remarkably reformed. Further, some students had initiated a religious society for prayer that eventually included "above half" of the student body. "I never," Burr added breathlessly in a postscript, "saw anything in the late revival that more evidently discovered the hand of God." Esther concurred. "Certainly a glorious work of God is going on," she wrote her father.[7]

Later in February, Burr was even more effusive in his comparison of the Princeton revival to the earlier awakenings, his missive so like Edwards's own descriptions of the awakenings of the 1730s that one imagines him with *Faithful Narrative* in hand. For a week, he wrote, a religious concern had been universal, "not one student excepted." The minds of students "were taken off from their vanities and vicious courses," and their conversations now were all about religion. "The utmost harmony" prevailed, Burr noted, and most important, the work had been carried on "by the still voice of the spirit," not through any "boisterous methods" or "special pathetic addresses to the passions." Alert to the excesses that had spoiled the fruit of previous revivals, he took pains to lay before his charges what he thought had "obstructed the work before." He was pleased to report that as a result, all the converts' conduct was "very prudent."[8]

This news deeply moved Edwards. But all this excitement, coupled with his incessant fund-raising, took a toll on Burr's health. On September 2, 1757, he left for Elizabethtown to preach the funeral sermon of his friend and the school's patron Jonathan Belcher. Already weakened, Burr contracted malaria and died three weeks later. Esther was left alone with the children, far from the support of her parents, and her letters to them show her struggling to accept the blow fate had dealt her.

EDWARDS AT PRINCETON

In a letter of consolation to Esther, Edwards broached another, unexpected topic. "As to removing to Princeton [as the college now was called]," he wrote, "to take on the office of president, I have agreed with the church here, to refer it to a council of ministers," to determine if it was his "duty" to assume this new position.[9] Two days after the premature death of Edwards's son-in-law, the trustees of the institution had decided that Edwards was his most suitable successor and had issued the invitation. Edwards admitted to being greatly surprised at the offer, but in retrospect, the trustees' choice seems logical, in view of the college's mission to train evangelical clergy and Edwards's record as a revivalist. For Edwards, the job's appeal was self-evident. The position at Princeton afforded him the opportunity to work in a safe and congenial environment as well as the gratification of training a cadre of young men for the Christian ministry.

But he did not easily reach his decision. One sticking point, confided to the grieving Esther, was the family's depressed financial situation. No doubt thinking of the wealth her husband had brought to the position, Edwards admitted: "I know I can't live at Princeton, as a president must, on the salary they offer." He was, however, interested enough to ask his friend William Tennent, well regarded at Princeton, to lobby the trustees on his behalf. Edwards also worried that his supporters in Stockbridge would not want him to leave his work among them, now that he had derailed the Williams clan. He wondered if the townspeople might sway the council of ministers by advising that Edwards's departure would be greatly against Stockbridge's "temporal interest."[10]

Edwards's lengthy reply to the Princeton trustees reveals much of his ambition at this point in his life, immersed as he was in the preparation and publication of his great theological works. He noted, for example, how difficult it would be to pull up stakes and move to distant Princeton, particularly because he and his family had just begun to get their affairs "in a comfortable situation for subsistence in this place." More important considerations, however, were the "defects" that he believed made him unfit for the position.[11]

With a degree of self-analysis he had not undertaken since he had written his "Personal Narrative," Edwards confessed to a constitution "in many respects peculiar unhappy, attended with flaccid solids, vapid, sizy and scarce fluids, and a low tide of spirits." This humoral disposition occasioned "a kind of childish weakness and contemptibleness of speech, presence, and demeanor" and "a disagreeable dullness and stiffness" much unfitting him for conversation, "but more especially for the government of a college." As well as he may have performed in the pulpit, he shrank at the thought of taking on, "in the decline of life, such new and great business, attended with such a multiplicity of cares, and requiring such a degree of activity, alertness and spirit of government."[12]

Edwards raised another matter: He regarded himself more a scholar than a teacher or administrator. Thus his acceptance of the position, he told the trustees, would not well "consist, with those views, and that course of employ in my study, which have long engaged, and swallowed up my mind, and been the chief entertainment" of his life. He admitted to having spent great amounts of time in writing "on innumerable subjects" and thought it particularly important that he continue to address "the prevailing errors of the present day." He also mentioned what the trustees presumably knew: that he had published something "on one of the main points in dispute between the Arminians and Calvinists"—that is, his *Freedom of the Will*—and had it in view "in like manner to consider all the other controverted points, and have done much towards a preparation for it."[13]

He then outlined in great detail his future scholarly projects, among them "a great work" that he titled "A History of the Work of Redemption," "a body of divinity in an entire new method, being thrown into the form of an history, considering the affair of Christian theology, as the whole of it, in each part, stands in reference to the great work of redemption by Jesus Christ." This history, which he had outlined in the series of sermons he gave to his Northampton congregation in 1739, would be "carried on with regard to all three worlds, heaven, earth, and hell" and would consider "the connected, successive events and alterations, in each so far as the Scriptures give any light." The result would allow the reader to see "in the brightest light, in the most striking manner . . . the admirable contexture and harmony of the whole" of God's plan. Nor was this all. He described a second project, "The Harmony of the Old and New Testament," to be written in three parts and intended to "lead the mind to a view of the true spirit, design, life and soul of the Scriptures, as well as to their proper use and improvement."[14]

Edwards also mentioned that he had in hand a few other works—presumably the treatises on sin, the end for which God created the world, and true virtue—on which he had made great progress and that he meant to publish soon. The larger point, he explained, was that so far as he could judge his talents, "I think I can write better than I can speak." From what he knew of the demands of the presidency he worried that if he accepted the position, he would put himself into "an incapacity" to pursue his writing any longer. In addition, if he accepted, he told them, rather than be responsible (as Burr had been) for instruction in all the languages and having the care of one of the classes in all parts of their learning, he wanted instead to devote himself primarily to the senior class.[15]

Edwards admitted that he understood the importance of the position and "the regard due to so worthy and venerable a body, as that of the Trustees of Nassau Hall." He ended by saying that unless the trustees were discouraged by what he had written, he would seek the advice of friends and colleagues, ascertain what the commissioners in Boston thought of the prospect, and then discuss the matter with his church.[16] Obviously, he was intrigued.

As his letter to Esther indicates, within a month things progressed enough for him to call a council of representatives from neighboring churches to consult on the advisability of his removal. Having already obtained permission from the commissioners in London to relinquish his duties at the Indian school, he filled the council's seats with his friends, and on January 4, 1758, they assented to his removal. To the end Edwards remained conflicted. Hearing the council's recommendation, he was so "uncommonly moved and affected with it" that he fell into tears, something, one of his early biographers wrote, "very unusual for him, in the presence of others." But it is unclear whether his were tears of joy or sadness. Evidently Edwards had been surprised that the council so readily dispensed with the arguments he himself had made against his removal.[17]

The candidate's own doubts notwithstanding, the trustees were eager to have Edwards assume the position, and on January 14 he wrote his old coworker Gideon Hawley, now a missionary to Indians in another part of Massachusetts, that he was about to set out on his journey southward. He traveled alone (his family was to join him in the spring, presumably when travel was easier), and he was met in Princeton by his daughters Esther and Lucy, his eldest child, still unmarried. Shortly after his arrival he received the sad news of the death of his father, Timothy, at the age of eighty-nine.[18]

The Princeton trustees quickly installed Edwards as the institution's third president, and he plunged assiduously into his duties, preaching in the college hall each Sabbath and setting questions in divinity for the senior class. He was well received by the students, who spoke of these classes "with the greatest satisfaction and wonder." For his part, Edwards seemed to enjoy himself and told his daughters that although he had been apprehensive of moving to Princeton, "he was called of God to that place and work."[19]

SMALLPOX

When smallpox visited the Princeton area, on the advice of his physician, William Shippen, and with the consent of the Princeton corporation, Edwards willingly submitted to inoculation. On February 13 Shippen administered the vaccine to Edwards, Esther, and her children, and for a few days all went well. But Edwards soon developed a severe fever and a large number of pustules in his throat, which so obstructed it that his physician could not administer medicine to stop the infection. Though Edwards could say very little during his illness, he was lucid to the end. Those gathered around him in his final moments, discouraged by what his loss would mean for both the college and religion in general, were surprised to hear him say, "TRUST IN GOD, AND YE NEED NOT FEAR." These were his last words; he died on March 22.[20]

Shippen immediately wrote to Sarah Edwards to apprise her of her husband's last days and assured her that he had safely inoculated the other members of her family. But he spoke too soon. Esther, who had seemed in fine health, was seized by a "violent disorder" and died sixteen days after her father. The family's tragedy only continued. In September, Sarah left Stockbridge to see Esther's two children, then being cared for in Philadelphia and awaiting her arrival before they all returned to Massachusetts. She traveled through Princeton and arrived in the city on September 21 in good health. However, five days later, severely ill from dysentery, she died. Her remains were brought to Princeton and buried alongside her husband's.

Princeton's ill fortune continued too, for its next president, the well-regarded Virginia Presbyterian Samuel Davies, who had kept Edwards informed of revivals in the Virginia backcountry, died after only two years in office. The next choice, the Reverend Samuel Finley, another middle colonies evangelist, served but five years, and it was only with his successor, the distinguished Scots theologian John Witherspoon, that the trustees stabilized the institution.

Just before he assumed his new position, Edwards had completed *The Great Christian Doctrine of Original Sin Defended* in late May 1757 and sent the manuscript to the printer later that year. At Princeton he proofread some of its pages but did not see it published.[21] The remainder of his great "body of divinity in an entire new method" lay unfinished, its outline and elements sketched in thousands of manuscript pages.

KEEPERS OF THE FLAME: HOPKINS AND BELLAMY

On January 18, 1758, shortly before he left for Princeton, Edwards had traveled to Great Barrington, Massachusetts, and left a great many manuscripts in Samuel Hopkins's safekeeping. He meant to retrieve them in the spring when travel by carriage was easier. On his death, his other manuscripts passed to his wife, who also deposited them with Hopkins and asked him to publish a biography of her husband. She did not live to see more of his works in print, but Hopkins's cache of materials was immense: Edwards's probate inventory listed fifteen folio volumes, and as many in quarto, including almost eleven hundred sermons and the notebook "Miscellanies."[22]

Hopkins had graduated from Yale in 1741. While there he had been swept up in the revivals and given spiritual counsel by none other than David Brainerd. After graduation he had found his way to Northampton to study with Edwards. Arriving unannounced in the early winter of 1741, Hopkins found Edwards away but was welcomed by Sarah. Soon Samuel Buell, who was to have such an important influence on Edwards's congregation and family, joined him. The young man remained with Edwards off and on until the summer of 1743, when he accepted a position in what became Great Barrington, not far from the Stockbridge mission. In 1769, Hopkins removed to the church in Newport, Rhode Island, where he ministered for the remainder of his career, a chief defender of the theological edifice that Edwards had constructed. His *System of Doctrines* (1793), along with Joseph Bellamy's works, is a cornerstone of what, with Edwards's corpus, became known as the New England Theology or the New Divinity.[23]

Hopkins took seriously his custodianship of Edwards's manuscripts, which he controlled until 1767, when (following the provisions of Sarah's will) they passed into the hands of Edwards's son, Jonathan. Later in the century, Edwards, Jr., was responsible for the publication of some of his father's still-unpublished materials. In the decade immediately following Edwards's death, however, Hopkins, with the help of his friend Bellamy, did the most to bring Edwards's writings to a larger public. Bellamy, a graduate of Yale in 1735, had been Edwards's first tutee in Northampton and early on had proved a stalwart in the revivals.[24] In 1750 his teacher had supplied a preface to his important treatise *True Religion Delineated*. Spending his entire career in western Connecticut as pastor to Bethlehem, Bellamy was widely known for taking in students in a "school of the prophets" to prepare them for the ministry. Before his death, in 1790, he trained more than sixty ministers in Edwards's system of divinity.

Hopkins immediately set about preparing the "life" that Sarah Edwards had requested and finished it, according to the dated preface, late in August 1764. When he published *The Life and Character of the Late Reverend Mr. Jonathan Edwards* the next year, he appended eighteen "Sermons on Various Important Subjects." Concomitantly, he and Bellamy divided the work of preparing the manuscripts of the two treatises, on the end for which God created the world and on the nature of true virtue, that Edwards had finished but temporarily put aside. Both men had been in Stockbridge in 1756 to hear Edwards read from the former work, which now fell under Hopkins's purview. Bellamy was responsible for its companion.[25]

Work on these went quickly, and early in 1764 Hopkins wrote Bellamy that he still waited for some word from the Boston printer Kneeland and might have to go to Boston himself "to forward the matter." His preface to the two works, signed simply "The Editor," was dated July 12, 1765. Despite Hopkins's control of the manuscript archive for another decade, no new Edwards materials appeared until later in the century, under Edwards Jr.'s tenure as custodian of his father's unpublished legacy. A letter from Hopkins to Bellamy dated April 4, 1768, sheds some light on why, despite Edwards's considerable reputation, publishers shied away from investing in his works. Hopkins reported that while plans were going ahead for a Scottish reprint of *Freedom of the Will*, there had been little interest in the sheets of *Two Dissertations* and Edwards's *Life* that Kneeland had forwarded across the Atlantic. In the interim, Hopkins explained, William Hogg, the Scot who had requested the sheets, had died. Now, they were being returned as some of the subscribers reneged and the projected cost of the volumes became too dear. Hopkins went on to note that Kneeland's house was full of sheets from the two works, "which must soon be sold for waste paper."[26]

As Hopkins's letter suggests, in view of Edwards's reputation abroad (particularly in England and Scotland), there had been initial interest in the publication of his works. His *Freedom of the Will* and *Original Sin*, treating topics that engaged English philosophers and theologians, were reprinted in London, Edinburgh, Dublin, and elsewhere. Also, as early as June 1759 the Scot John Erskine, Edwards's longtime correspondent, wrote to Bellamy that he thought he could raise subscriptions for two volumes of Edwards's "practical works."[27] Next, an English clergyman expressed interest in issuing first an abridgment of *Religious Affections* and later all of Edwards's printed works.[28] But nothing came of further efforts to issue the hitherto unpublished manuscripts until 1774, when Edwards, Jr., now starting his clerical career, published *A History of the Work of Redemption*, the series of sermons that Edwards had delivered on that topic in 1739 and that he had hoped to expand into a large treatise. The work was first published in Edinburgh, with Erskine's assistance. As Edwards, Jr., explained, the Scot had removed "the difficulty of getting any considerable work [of his father's] printed in this infant country" by locating an Edinburgh bookseller who undertook the publication and thus brought another of Edwards's important (albeit unfinished) manuscripts to general notice.[29]

Six years later Edwards, Jr., convinced a Hartford, Connecticut, printer to issue a volume of his father's hitherto unpublished sermons (*Sermons on the Following Subjects*), but this work still did not open the gates for more manuscripts. As Edwards, Jr., noted, in British North America there evidently was no large market for Edwards's works. And while the colonies were preoccupied with the deteriorating imperial situation, few printers thought it opportune to issue lengthy books by someone who, in the eyes of many, seemed out of step with the times. Thus, when in 1778 Yale president Ezra Stiles observed in his diary that in another generation Edwards's works would "pass into as transient notice perhaps scarce above oblivion," he reflected a common sentiment. In the future, Stiles wrote, the "rare character" who read and found wisdom in Edwards's books would "be looked upon as singular and whimsical." His works would constitute, Stiles opined, "the rubbish of Libraries."[30] Only a coterie of western New England ministers headed by Bellamy and Hopkins, as well as a few from the middle colonies who had welcomed Edwards's leadership of Princeton, kept Edwardsean theology before the public.

THE NINETEENTH-CENTURY INVENTION OF "EDWARDS"

America's greatest evangelical and one of its greatest thinkers seemed doomed to oblivion. But it was not to be so, for beginning in the 1790s, Edwards's reputation was rehabilitated until in the 1840s his was a household name, America's evangelical.[31] Moreover, unlike those dark days when Hopkins had to placate printers who stored reams of unbound pages of Edwards's treatises, his various devotional works now were reprinted scores of times in thousands upon thousands of copies, having become what, in the printing trade, were called steady sellers. In this period Americans discovered the "Edwards" of whom we think when we invoke the Great Awakening. What he had written of the religious life now resonated in new and powerful ways, so much so that for antebellum America it is not amiss to speak of the flowering of a particularly Edwardsean culture.[32]

Bellamy, who had gone to the Connecticut Valley to study with Edwards and had trained scores of young clergymen in Edwards's New Divinity, was the chief figure in this reinvigoration of Edwards's reputation. After the Revolutionary War and in the wake of the disturbances and debates that led to the forging of the Constitution, Bellamy's tutees and others inclined to the New Divinity oversaw a new series of revivals, centered in rural parts of western Massachusetts and Connecticut. These events were the first flowering of what became known as the Second Great Awakening, and the second- and third-generation Edwardseans who directed them looked back to the master's writings to explain their parishioners' religious experiences.[33]

During this period reprints of Edwards's works found a new and receptive American audience. In 1794, Edwards's *An Humble Attempt to Promote Explicit Agreement and Visible Union* was reissued, along with Bellamy's own treatise from 1758, *The Millennium*. So too Edwards Jr.'s edition of his father's *History of the Work of Redemption* was finally reprinted in the United States in 1792. A bellwether of Edwards's future fame and influence was the republication of *The Life of David Brainerd* in 1793, for its presentation of his notion of benevolence soon permeated nineteenth-century evangelical culture. Further, in the pages of the monthly *Connecticut Evangelical Magazine*, begun in 1800 and for more than a decade the chief mouthpiece of those who led the Connecticut revivals, Edwards's example and works were always front and center, particularly as a new cohort of ministers found their own revival experiences cognate to what Edwards had described in Northampton sixty years earlier.[34]

After 1800, as Methodist ministers claimed more and more evangelical success in the western and southern parts of the United States, New England revivalists increased their efforts to wrap themselves in Edwards's mantle, enlisting his carefully wrought criticism of the excesses of the eighteenth-century revivals against what they viewed as the comparable disorder of frontier camp meetings. Now significant numbers of clergy, mainly New Divinity men, self-consciously saw themselves as part of an evangelical tradition that had originated in the mid-eighteenth century with Edwards and the colonial revivals. In 1808 a contributor to the *Connecticut Evangelical Magazine* reviewed Edwards's life and works in a lengthy piece that ran to two issues, and in the same year the renowned printer Isaiah Thomas began to issue the first uniform edition of Edwards's works, in eight volumes, from his Worcester, Massachusetts, press. In 1818 Benjamin Trumbull, writing in his *Complete History of Connecticut, Civil and Ecclesiastical*, spoke of the colonial revivals as central to the history of the whole region and pointed to Edwards as their prime mover.[35]

By 1830 Jonathan Edwards had a new and vital presence in the lives of many New Englanders. As the Second Great Awakening spread, Edwards's reputation grew with it, particularly through the interdenominational republication of his Pietistic works, most famously his *Religious Affections*, which the American Tract Society first reprinted in 1831 in a heavily edited and abridged edition.[36] Masking (or eliminating outright) the more mystical and markedly Calvinistic passages in this work, the Tract Society serviced an interdenominational united front committed to evangelical religion and reform and, as part of its work, reinforced Edwards as the progenitor of the revivals that swept many parts of the nation. The *Religious Affections* and others of Edwards's works that spoke to the emergent interest in the culture of sentiment now became iconic texts to those who promulgated a religion of the heart.[37] Soon thereafter enterprising publishers (as well as various religious tract societies) republished Edwards's *Faithful Narrative* and *Some Thoughts Concerning the Revival*, works that informed people's expectations of a whole new set of revivals, a hundred years after Edwards first had analyzed comparable phenomena. This canonization of Edwards and the events in which he had participated reached its apogee in 1842, on the centenary of the colonial revivals, when Joseph Tracy published his seminal *The Great Awakening,* forever naming what in their own time had been seen as discrete, if related, events.[38]

By 1840 those responsible for the cultural renovation of Edwards were offering the example of his life to a nation tired of (and perhaps disenchanted with) Benjamin Franklin's ubiquitous version of self-fashioning. Thus, in addition to the frequent reprinting of his *Life of David Brainerd*, Edwards's own "Personal Narrative," first packaged in 1827 as *The Conversion of President Edwards*, was frequently reissued, particularly by the American Tract Society, in thousands of inexpensive copies.[39] Edwards's personal piety, as well as his works that spoke to emotional engagement with religious doctrine, had made him central to American evangelical culture (and to American Protestant Christianity generally) in ways that, fifty years earlier, would never have seemed possible.

Ezra Stiles's prediction of Edwards's obsolescence had indeed been premature. But it is *this* Edwards, the rehabilitated, highly edited, and "Romantic" Edwards—not the eighteenth-century theologian who spawned the New Divinity—who came down to us as America's evangelical. Bellamy and Hopkins had done their office honestly and, finally, with remarkable diligence; they kept alive the grandeur of Edwards's theological summa. But it was only because Edwards had written what the nineteenth century could appropriate for its own purposes that his subsequent influence in American culture was so remarkable. In 1776, for all intents and purposes, Edwards had seemed doomed to obscurity. He was subsequently resurrected and put to use in new and important ways by a culture that saw its own aspirations in his language and example. Remarkably, each generation has been able to do likewise, appropriating Edwards for its own needs.

TEN

Coda:
Thinking Through Edwards

CLEARING THE AIR

What did subsequent generations discern and embrace in Edwards, beyond his defense of increasingly unpalatable doctrine like the imputation of Adam's sin to all humanity or a freedom of the will defined so that things beyond human control determined our decisions and behavior? What was his appeal to nineteenth-century Christians of all denominations, so that on the eve of the Civil War he remained the champion not only of Congregational and Presbyterian theologians but also of Methodists like David Sherman, who said: "Take him all in all, he may be reckoned with as the mightiest mind that ever has appeared in the modern world"?[1] What is Edwards's importance to us? What accounts for his continued influence?

In the context of Edwards's abortive career, his work as a minister and theologian seems to have failed outright. By the mid-1740s Edwards had lost control of the religious revivals that he had promulgated and defended. As a result, his own congregation slipped back into its self-righteous ways, and the moderate clergy relinquished control of the energy and direction of the spiritual awakenings. Edwards also had a difficult time in his pastorates in Northampton and Stockbridge, the communities in which he spent the majority of his

years as a minister. In both places, opposition to him became so virulent that in light of his subsequent importance, it seems explicable
only as he understood it, as evidence of man's utter depravity.

After Edwards's death, the American public evidenced little interest in the publication of his voluminous theological manuscripts or
even in the republication of his great treatises, so that before 1800
one was more likely to find his appreciative readers across the Atlantic
rather than in Massachusetts or Connecticut. Even by the late 1740s
his champions had realized that only a small audience was interested
in his writings. In a letter to the Boston clergyman Thomas Foxcroft,
Joseph Bellamy observed that "not half the country" had "even so
much as heard" of Edwards's new work (his *Humble Attempt*) and
noted that to ensure that the press run would be worth the printer's
effort, he had had to find five men who guaranteed to purchase fifty
copies each. More surprising, given how popular the book later became, Bellamy reported that Edwards's other recent work, *A Treatise
Concerning the Religious Affections*, sold poorly.[2]

The problem had to do with what many perceived as Edwards's
abstruseness. In 1752, for example, as Edwards was planning his
great philosophical treatises, Bellamy wrote to Edwards's other chief
acolyte, Samuel Hopkins, with an idea about how to make their tutor's published works more popular. If Hopkins would write a cate-
chetical text to simplify Edwards's ideas, this would render them
more accessible. Such a collection of two or three hundred questions
and their answers would assist younger students in the study of divinity and Edwards's thought, Bellamy explained, for "at present
[even] the learned do not understand him."[3] The plan spoke to the
plain truth that by 1780 few regarded Edwards as America's most influential theologian. Yet within a generation all this changed, his obscurity and unpopularity forgotten as a united evangelical front
trumpeted him as the progenitor of a remarkable American spirituality. It remains to synthesize and summarize what in Edwards's work
(and, to a lesser extent, in the example of his life) remained so durable
and influential.

Except to a small number of cognoscenti in American theology and, later, philosophy who kept his flame alive, the Edwards who became most influential in American culture was not the theologian and metaphysician who published several lengthy and, in small circles, well-received doctrinal treatises. Nor was he the Edwards who in 1741 in Enfield, Connecticut, preached *Sinners in the Hands of an Angry God*, a sermon that few eighteenth-century admirers regarded as exceptional. Samuel Hopkins, Edwards's first biographer, never mentioned it, nor did Sereno Edwards Dwight in the life of Edwards he published in 1829. The clergyman and historian Benjamin Trumbull was the first to bring this piece wide attention, in 1818 in his *Complete History of Connecticut*, a central artifact of the Second Great Awakening.[4] Like a burr that will not be shaken, the notion that somehow this sermon represents the apogee of Edwards's art has persisted, particularly through the efforts of earlier twentieth-century critics, who, bent on disparaging Edwards by associating him with an outmoded Calvinism, valorized it in accounts of Edwards or reprinted it in influential anthologies of early American literature.

The cornerstone of Edwards's legacy and his subsequent import for American culture is his writing about personal religious experience and how it is constituted and evaluated. As one nineteenth-century admirer put it, "Piety was the mainspring of [Edwards's] exertions, the moving force of his existence, the volcanic fire that fuses his theology, and that broke up the primary strata of philosophical truth."[5] This is not to deny the enduring interest of his doctrinal work among philosophers and theologians. But what most powerfully engaged subsequent readers of Edwards's theology was how he understood the spiritual life.

The writings that pertain most directly to this latter subject grew from his own experience, both personal and institutional, in the two awakenings in which he participated. As much as Bellamy, Hopkins, Stephen West, and other second-generation Edwardseans sought to keep his New Divinity before the public, the import of Edwards for the Second Great Awakening and for later generations lay emblematically in those of his works most frequently reprinted in antebellum America. Some of these—his *Life of Brainerd* and *Religious Affections*—were even selected for inclusion in the fifteen-volume American Tract Society's Family Evangelical Library, the only volumes by American authors in the series.[6] Edwards's Pietistic works defined and codified a certain religious sensibility and engendered a novel way of thinking about human worth and self-empowerment. His attempt to close the container labeled "religious experience," undertaken as he watched many misunderstand his counsel and forward their own personal agencies at the expense of God's omnipotence, failed. For the past two and a half centuries people have gone to Edwards to understand what it means to embody spirituality and make it evident in their daily lives. He did nothing less than script how modern American evangelicals understand these concepts. In so doing, he also liberated other ideas, unaffiliated with any explicitly religious tradition, that allow his readers to reconceive the tenor of the spiritual life.

EDWARDS AND PERSONAL AGENCY

Ironically, Edwards himself had qualms about his guidance of the great spiritual awakenings that preoccupied him through the mid-1740s. In a letter to the Reverend Thomas Gillespie written in 1752, Edwards admitted that in the revivals of 1734 and 1735 he had sailed in treacherous waters without a good compass. Contributing to the Northampton debacle of 1750, he explained, were his youth and "want of more judgment and experience." "In some respects," he explained, "my confidence in myself was a great wrong to me," just as had been his "diffidence" in not acting earlier against "received notions and established customs" (presumably those of his grandfather Stoddard). In retrospect, he believed that because of his grandfather's influence, he had been unwilling to rely on his own judgment and had lacked the resolve to "testify boldly against some glaring false appearances and counterfeits of religion, till it was too late." He lamented to his Scots friend: "If I had had more experience and ripeness of judgment and courage, I should have guided my people in a better manner, and should have guarded them better from Satan's devices, and prevented the great spiritual calamity of many souls."[7]

Here Edwards had in mind his counsel to awakened sinners, later described at length in *A Faithful Narrative of the Surprising Work of God*, a virtual blueprint for contemporary evangelism. Despite his errors in judgment, however, he continued to champion a psychological notion of religious experience that was participatory, so that his self-criticism applied as well to the full series of texts central to the revival's dynamic, from *Faithful Narrative* through his *Life of David Brainerd*. What Edwards had privileged, first through his interactions with those going through "the work" and, later, in his writings about the awakenings, was nothing less than the final, unassailable significance of an individual's emotions— his or her *feelings*—to genuine religious experience. Concomitantly, while Edwards urged his countrymen to conceive of the self as the locus of truth, he also insisted that this belief bear tangible fruit within the Christian community and not lead to mere self-indulgence or solipsism.

In 1734 and again in 1740 Edwards believed that he understood true religious experience, for the newly awakened undeniably had been changed for the better. People laughed and cried, felt fear and loneliness as well as ecstatic joy and community. They yearned for more saintliness, assiduously studied the Scriptures, and eagerly heard sermons, often several times a week. As they experienced a transformation that brought them from the jaws of hell to the gates of heaven, they sought out ministers like Edwards to learn more about what had happened to them. He dutifully recorded their multiform stories, using them to buttress what he himself had experienced and then understood theologically of the "New Birth."

But in the excitement of such heightened religious experience he had not sufficiently distinguished the truly spiritual from that which was initiated by self-interest. Subsequently, of course, Edwards cast a perceptive backward glance; therein lies the greatness of a work like *Religious Affections*. But in the heat of the revivals, in such Pietistic works as *Faithful Narrative* and *Some Thoughts Concerning the Revival*, he had insisted on the central role of the emotions in one's spiritual life. The stories of Phebe Bartlett and Abigail Hutchinson, as well as of Sarah Edwards, offer the most striking examples of the consequences. His accounts, replete with episodes whose details he later questioned, circulated among thousands of other people to do what cultural work they might. Indeed, in this light his great treatises of the mid-1750s can be regarded as attempts to cage the monsters that he had created prior to 1743. In the headiness of the awakenings, however, he had welcomed the exhilaration of individuals who thought about themselves in wholly new ways as they discovered the peace and glory for which they so long had searched.

As much as anything else, the "New Birth" engendered human agency in people who hitherto had not known it.[8] No more would parishioners be held to artificial or dogmatic standards as they struggled with their religion. Rather, Edwards had told them that spiritual knowledge was available to any, the lowest as well as the wealthiest, and was verified internally, not by some autocratic clergyman. Edwards eventually learned that such centripetal notions could spin society into chaos. Yearning to be with God, individuals became godlier and so sought closer relations to the larger body of awakened souls to whom they felt linked in bonds of love. In Edwards's works about the revivals they found the freedom to develop a more Christian life in ways they *felt* were proper. Edwards came to fear the effects of such self-confidence and condemned it as a fruit of mere "enthusiasm," but his caution came too late to prevent the transformation of the awakened.

Edwards's readers also learned that as much as religion consists in a matter of the heart, it takes external form in one's Christian calling. To put it another way, genuine religion had to be made visible in one's behavior and activities, as it had, for example, in David Brainerd's life (and in Edwards's too). Hence the significance of Edwards's *The Life of David Brainerd* and the American Tract Society's redaction of his own spiritual autobiography, the *Conversion of President Edwards*, from the

"Personal Narrative." Reading of such lives, Americans learned that responsibility came with self-reliance and the effectual agency it bestowed. Edwards insisted on this in his twelfth sign of truly religious affections; they have their exercise and fruit in Christian practice. This is also why he devoted such intellectual rigor to *The End for Which God Created the World*, with its unsettling conclusion that because humans are bound in time, the day will never come when one can say that *now* he is with the eternal God. By insisting on the eternally progressive nature of the Christian life, Edwards gave people an existential thrust. He also insisted that as one validates his goodness through the heart, so he is also moved to respect a similar validation among others, thus spinning bands of sympathy among all humans.

A century before Edwards assumed his first pastorate, his illustrious New England predecessor John Cotton had observed that if "you tether a Beast at night, he knows the length of his tether before morning."[9] By the mid-1740s a whole generation of Americans who had measured their spiritual lives on the tethers to which Edwards and other revivalists had tied them now strained at their confinement. This frightened Edwards and others who condemned the religious radicalism, particularly the separatism, that many of the awakened embraced. But these liberated and awakened souls were exhilarated at what the power of God within allowed them to dream and accomplish. Some of them became the men and women of 1776; others, members of the abolitionist ranks in the 1850s; and still others, soldiers on the ramparts at Gettysburg, Shiloh, and the other battlefields where their religion of the heart demanded that they act for what they felt was right. Such behavior, such acts of will, flowed naturally from one's disposition. Implicitly, Edwards had codified a religious sensibility that inspired nothing less than such sacrifice for the good of the larger community.

EDWARDS AND THE CULTURE OF SENTIMENT

There was, however, no direct route by which Edwards's thought traveled from his day to the nineteenth century or from its enculturation in the antebellum period to our own. To claim such influence would beg the same opprobrium that fell on Perry Miller after he published his famous essay "From Edwards to Emerson." But as Miller pointed out when he reissued the essay (without embarrassment or apology), he had never intended to claim an uninterrupted line of influence from one thinker to another but rather to illuminate how these two individuals, separated as they were by a century, similarly came to understand the divine's relation to the human.[10]

Miller went even further in his influential biography *Jonathan Edwards*, claiming that Edwards's reworking of Calvinism presaged the mid-twentieth century's apocalyptical vision.[11] Regardless of one's accepting this argument, it is fair to state that too many of Edwards's chroniclers and interpreters have underestimated how his writings introduced powerful ways to imagine the relation between man and the universe. Absent this understanding, Edwards will too readily continue to be thought culturally irrelevant, left to acolytes and apologists for whom he remains primarily a Protestant theologian. Later generations will lose sight of the fact that he was a thinker whose central insights relate to our very humanity.

Edwards's controversial legacy derived from what, at the height of the colonial revivals, he had discerned of his own religious experience. Indeed, the more one ponders the shape and emphases of his work, the more it seems as though his metaphysics flowed inexorably from that one miraculous moment when he experienced grace, when he was "convinced, and fully satisfied" of the utter sovereignty of God, transformed as it were by "a new simple idea" and so evermore disposed to act in accordance with it. Edwards did not recognize any extraordinary influence of God's spirit in what had occurred, but only knew that he "saw further," his reason apprehending "the justice and reasonableness" of God's emanation into the world.[12] His life was irrevocably changed, and his days were filled with extraordinary joy and sweetness. He lived with a "sort of inward, sweet delight in God and divine things," feelings of a kind that he had not known before, ones that made him yearn to share them with others, to have others experience such things too.

It did not remain this way, of course. Edwards had his share of trials and tribulations. But when he grasped the new simple idea of man's utter insufficiency without the divine, he also apprehended the whole of God's dispensation. This was powerful knowledge, and he lived the rest of his life trying to explain and share it. The great treatises on free will, sin, true virtue, and the end for which God created the world are elaborations of his original insight into how a new simple idea irrevocably transforms behavior.

At any given time, few have grasped the entirety of Edwards's scheme. The nineteenth century adopted the Edwards found primarily in his theorization of a religion of the heart. To understand this claim involves consideration of what a recent historian, in a book on Nathaniel William Taylor (one of Edwards's intellectual descendants), has described as the "Edwardsian enculturation of Calvinist New England during the first third of the nineteenth century." As Douglas Sweeney explains, nineteenth-century Edwardseanism included "not only those approved by self-appointed Edwardsian gatekeepers, but all who participated in and took their primary religious identification from the expanding social and institutional network that supported and promoted Edwardsian thought," a network that included such organizations as the American Tract Society and others who similarly promulgated Edwards's understanding of religious experience.[13]

Given Edwards's immense cultural presence in antebellum America, his true legacy in that period resides in his contribution to the extensive discourse of sentimentalism, which appears most vibrantly in such varied writers as Harriet Beecher Stowe, Maria Cummins, and Susan Warner as well as Nathaniel Hawthorne, Herman Melville, and Walt Whitman.[14] In particular, Edwards's emphases on the necessity for an individual experience of conversion, emotion as a central component to this experience and thus to the religious life, and disinterested benevolence as the sign of true spirituality indelibly marked antebellum culture. Moreover, because as Adam's descendants all men and women, no matter of what station or race, are "*companions* in a miserable helpless condition," among humanity there is engendered a "mutual *compassion*," the basis for the profound sentiment of sympathy.[15]

Antebellum writers return over and over again to Edwards's in-sight that "if the great things of religion are rightly understood, they will affect the heart." It is not far from this sentiment to the mid-nineteenth-century novelist Maria Cummins's notion, expressed in her immensely popular *The Lamplighter* (1854), "I know of no religion but that of the heart."[16] The vibration of one heart to the stir-rings of another, the sympathy that flows among souls, is what more than anything else defined sentimentalism and derived in large measure from the increasing circulation of Edwardsean principles and language. In the nineteenth century, Edwards's ideas about goodness and virtue had become so internalized that they were inescapable. Influence is exerted in myriad ways and is not always immediately discernible. When he "saw further," he set into motion a series of waves that would wash against Hawthorne's and Stowe's doorsteps even as it had against Hopkins's and Bellamy's and as it still washes against our own.

SEEING FURTHER

Edwards saw humanity deficient in the principle of godliness that makes someone more interested in others than in himself. The only remedy for this deficiency is a personal transformation through the "new simple idea" of grace that restores a disposition to selflessness. No one knows precisely how and when such a change occurs; it can happen as one reads a book, is in the midst of a battle, volunteers in the Peace Corps, or climbs Mount Rainier. The new simple idea, however, results in the willing of goodness, an alignment with the end for which God created the world. To do good is thus to partici-pate in that which defines God, to consent to his exfoliation into all parts of the universe, and thus to holiness or that of which divinity fi-nally consists.

What has given Edwards's system its beauty is his profound sense of how interconnected all its parts are, how each of his ideas flows from others and how all, in the end, issue from one source. Speaking of God's dispensation to the world in his *History of the Work of Redemption*, Edwards talked metaphorically of such unity. "God's providence," he wrote, "may not be unfitly compared to a large and long river, having innumerable branches beginning in different regions, and at a great distance from one another, and all conspiring to one common issue." The different streams of this river, he went on, "are ready to look like mere jumble and confusion to us because of the limitedness of our sight, whereby we can't see from one branch to another and can't see the whole at once." But if we trace them, they all "unite at last and all come to the same issue, disgorging themselves in one into the same great ocean."[17] The limitedness of our sight is all that keeps us from giving Edwards a fair reading.

Finally, in its totality Edwards's vision is not dark and pessimistic but rather, as Perry Miller himself recognized, honest and realistic. Return, for a moment, to Edwards's treatise on sin. His strongest argument for sin's omnipresence in our lives lies in the book of experience. Think too of how he wanted people to understand grace as experiential and, as such, something that might happen naturally to any of us. Those who find in Edwards's principles the legacy of an era whose thinkers woefully underestimated mankind's nobility may, given the history since his time, be putting their heads in the sand. To believe, as he did, in the power of an idea to change one's life so that ever afterward she/he acts from its effect in ways that link her/him to the fount of all virtue, seems optimistic to its core. Our general failure to see further is no excuse for not appreciating the final beauty and value of Edwards's moral vision.

Critics who judge Edwards only by *Sinners in the Hands of an Angry God* and label him misanthropic, unsympathetic to the vagaries of life, ignore another and much more prevalent dimension to his thought. Consider his remarkable "Heaven Is a World of Love," the final sermon in his series *Charity and Its Fruits*, delivered just after the first Northampton awakenings as Edwards sought to consolidate their effects. After describing heaven as the place where perfect love exists between God and all his creation—a love "altogether holy and divine," not proceeding from corrupt principles, "not from selfish motives, and to mean and vile purpose," but a "pure flame"—he exhorts people to live "a life of love to God and love to all men" while still on earth. "This is the way to be like the inhabitants of heaven," he counseled, and this is the way "to have a sense of the glory of heavenly things."[18]

This is the end for which man was created: quite simply, to love, to have charity for all things, and in so doing to live in heaven on earth. All the rest—the envy, the selfishness, the contention that roils one's life—disappears when one exercises this Christian charity. To illustrate this profundity, Edwards constructed his remarkable theological system, an interpretation of the human condition that was not the fruit of a distempered brain but of a heart transformed by the new, simple idea of virtue.

Of course we have difficulty in facing Edwards. Reading him, we are forced to consider the immeasurable difference between sin and virtue and how far short we shall fall when we attempt to bridge that gap without the insight that Edwards termed grace. If, finally, we believe that someone such as Benjamin Franklin has more to offer us, we add only more proof to Edwards's sense of the infinite distance between saint and sinner.

A Note on Sources

The chief primary source for this biography is *The Works of Jonathan Edwards*, 23 vols. to date (New Haven: Yale University Press, 1957–), Perry Miller, John E. Smith, Harry S. Stout, general editors. I cite this as *Works*, followed by the volume and page. To date the volumes in this series are:

Vol. 1. *Freedom of the Will*. Ed. Paul Ramsey. 1957.
Vol. 2. *The Religious Affections*. Ed. John E. Smith. 1959.
Vol. 3. *Original Sin*. Ed. Clyde A. Holbrook. 1970.
Vol. 4. *The Great Awakening*. Ed. C. C. Goen. 1972.
Vol. 5. *Apocalyptical Writings*. Ed. Stephen J. Stein. 1977.
Vol. 6. *Scientific and Philosophical Writings*. Ed. Wallace E. Anderson. 1980.
Vol. 7. *The Life of David Brainerd*. Ed. Norman Petit. 1985.
Vol. 8. *Ethical Writings*. Ed. Paul Ramsey. 1989.
Vol. 9. *A History of the Work of Redemption*. Ed. John F. Wilson. 1989.
Vol. 10. *Sermons and Discourses, 1720–1723*. Ed. Wilson H. Kimnach. 1992.
Vol. 11. *Typological Writings*. Ed. Wallace E. Anderson and Mason I. Lowance, Jr., with David Watters. 1993.
Vol. 12. *Ecclesiastical Writings*. Ed. David D. Hall. 1994.
Vol. 13. *The "Miscellanies," A–500*. Ed. Thomas A. Schafer. 1994.
Vol. 14. *Sermons and Discourses, 1723–1729*. Ed. Kenneth P. Minkema. 1997.
Vol. 15. *Notes on Scripture*. Ed. Stephen J. Stein. 1998.
Vol. 16. *Letters and Personal Writings*. Ed. George S. Claghorn. 1998.
Vol. 17. *Sermons and Discourses, 1730–1733*. Ed. Mark Valeri. 1999.
Vol. 18. *The "Miscellanies," 501–832*. Ed. Ava Chamberlain. 2000.
Vol. 19. *Sermons and Discourses, 1734–1738*. Ed. M. X. Lesser. 2001.

Vol. 20. *The "Miscellanies," 833–1152*. Ed. Amy Plantinga Pauw. 2002.
Vol. 21. *Writings on the Trinity, Grace, and Faith*. Ed. Sang Hyun Lee. 2003.
Vol. 22. *Sermons and Discourses, 1739–1742*. Ed. Harry S. Stout and Nathan O. Hatch, with Kyle P. Farley. 2003.
Vol. 23. *The "Miscellanies," 1153–1360*. Ed. Douglas A. Sweeney. 2004.

The chief nineteenth-century biography of Edwards is Sereno Edwards Dwight, *Life of President Edwards*, vol. 1 of *The Works of President Edwards, with a Memoir of His Life*, 10 vols., ed. Sereno Edwards Dwight (New York: Converse, 1829–1830), also published separately in 1830. I cite this as Dwight, *Life*.

Edwards's chief disciple, Samuel Hopkins, prepared *The Life and Character of the Late Reverend Mr. Jonathan Edwards* (Boston: 1765). I use the edition found in David Levin, ed., *Jonathan Edwards: A Profile* (New York: Hill & Wang, 1969), 1–86, and cite it as Hopkins, *Life*. This edition does not, however, contain Hopkins's appendices. Still useful and eminently readable is Ola Elizabeth Winslow, *Jonathan Edwards, 1702–1758* (New York: Macmillan, 1940). The now-standard biography is George Marsden, *Jonathan Edwards: A Life* (New Haven: Yale University Press, 2003), cited as Marsden, *Life*.

Notes

PREFACE

1. Ezra Stiles, *The Literary Diary of Ezra Stiles, D.D., LL.D.*, ed. Franklin B. Dexter, 3 vols. (New York: Charles Scribner's Sons, 1901), 3:275.
2. Samuel Miller, *Jonathan Edwards* (1854; New York: Harper and Brothers, 1902), 4.
3. Ibid.
4. D[avid] Sherman, *Sketches of New England Divines* (New York: Carlton & Porter, 1860), 176, 178; Perry Miller, *Jonathan Edwards* (New York: William Sloane Associates, 1949), xii.
5. Sherman, *Sketches*, 176; Moses Coit Tyler, *A History of American Literature*, 2 vols. (New York: G. P. Putnam's Sons, 1879), 2:177.
6. Arthur V. G. Allen, *Jonathan Edwards* (1889; Boston: Houghton, Mifflin and Company, 1894), vi. For a series of essays that probe Franklin's and Edwards's centrality to American culture see Barbara B. Oberg and Harry S. Stout, eds., *Benjamin Franklin, Jonathan Edwards, and the Representation of American Culture* (New York: Oxford University Press, 1993).
7. Harriet Beecher Stowe, *Oldtown Folks* (1869; Cambridge: Harvard University Press, 1966), 387.

1. A PLACE IN TIME: THE CONNECTICUT VALLEY (1703)

1. Although there are many biographies of Edwards, the definitive work now is George Marsden's *Jonathan Edwards: A Life* (New Haven: Yale University Press, 2003). Throughout this work I am indebted to Marsden's painstaking labors to establish the facts of Edwards's life and career. See also Iain Murray, *Jonathan Edwards: A New Biography* (Edinburgh: Banner of Truth Trust, 1987). Still useful is Ola Elizabeth Winslow, *Jonathan Edwards, 1703–1758* (New York: Macmillan, 1940). Throughout, however, I

have been guided by the narratives that Edwards's first two biographers established; see Hopkins and Dwight.

2. The standard history of the region during the colonial period remains Charles M. Andrews, *The Colonial Period of American History*, 4 vols. (New Haven: Yale University Press, 1934–1938), 2:67–143.

3. Timothy Dwight, *Travels in New England and New York*, ed. Barbara Miller Solomon, 4 vols. (Cambridge: Harvard University Press, 1969), 2:224.

4. On the rise of Puritanism in England, see Diarmaid MacCulloch, *The Later Reformation in England, 1547–1603* (New York: St. Martin's, 1990); Patrick Collinson, *The Elizabethan Puritan Movement* (Berkeley: University of California Press, 1967), and *The Religion of Protestants: The Church in English Society, 1559–1625* (Oxford, UK: Oxford University Press, 1983); Peter Lake, *Moderate Puritans and the Elizabethan Church* (Cambridge, UK: Cambridge University Press, 1983); and, still valuable, M. M. Knappen, *Tudor Puritanism: A Chapter in the History of Idealism* (Chicago: University of Chicago Press, 1939).

5. On the attempts to reform the Church of England theologically, see R. T. Kendall, *Calvin and the English Calvinists* (Oxford, UK: Oxford University Press, 1979); John Coolidge, *The Pauline Renaissance in England* (Oxford, UK: Oxford University Press, 1970); Charles H. George and Katherine George, *The Protestant Mind in the English Reformation, 1570–1640* (Princeton: Princeton University Press, 1961); John F. New, *Anglican and Puritan, 1558–1640* (Stanford: Stanford University Press, 1964); and Nicholas Tyack, *Anti-Calvinists: The Rise of English Arminianism, c. 1590–1640* (Oxford, UK: Oxford University Press, 1987).

6. The best study of Puritan theology remains Perry Miller, *The New England Mind: The Seventeenth Century* (New York: Macmillan, 1939). Also see Dewey Wallace, *Puritans and Predestination: Grace in English Protestant Theology, 1525–1695* (Chapel Hill: University of North Carolina Press, 1982).

7. The best study of the Puritan notion of church membership remains Edmund S. Morgan, *Visible Saints: The History of a Puritan Idea* (1963; Ithaca, NY: Cornell University Press, 1965).

8. The best account of the early ecclesiastical history of the valley is Paul Lucas, *Valley of Discord: Church and Society Along the Connecticut River, 1636–1725* (Hanover, NH: University Press of New England, 1976), esp. 23–59 for my discussion here.

9. Ibid., 50–51, 83–85.

10. Lucas, *Valley of Discord*, discusses the background to these controversies, but see also Robert G. Pope, *The Half-Way Covenant: Church Membership in Puritan New England* (Princeton: Princeton University Press, 1969), 13–42.

11. See Pope, *Half-Way Covenant*, esp. 43–74. My account, below, is indebted to this work. Also see, however, E. Brooks Holifield, *The Covenant Sealed:*

The Development of Puritan Sacramental Theology in Old and New England, 1570–1720 (New Haven: Yale University Press, 1974), 139–96.

12. See Philip F. Gura, "Preparing the Way for Stoddard: Eleazer Mather's *Serious Exhortation* to Northampton," *New England Quarterly*, 53:2 (June 1984), 240–50; reprint in *The Crossroads of American History and Literature* (University Park: Pennsylvania State University Press, 1996), 55–63. On Northampton in general, see James R. Trumbull, *History of Northampton, Massachusetts, from Its Settlement in 1654*, 2 vols. (Northampton: Gazette Printing Company, 1898, 1902), vol. 1, passim.

13. John Russell to Increase Mather, March 28, 1681, *The Mather Papers*, in Massachusetts Historical Society, *Collections*, 4th ser., 8 (Boston: 1868), 82–84.

14. Standard treatments of Stoddard are Perry Miller, "Solomon Stoddard, 1643–1729," *Harvard Theological Review*, 34 (1941), 277–320; Thomas A. Schafer, "Solomon Stoddard and the Theology of the Revival," in Stuart C. Henry, ed., *A Miscellany of American Christianity: Essays in Honor of H. Shelton Smith* (Durham, NC: Duke University Press, 1963), 328–61; Paul R. Lucas, "'An Appeal to the Learned': The Mind of Solomon Stoddard," *William and Mary Quarterly*, 3rd ser., 30 (1973), 257–97; *Valley of Discord*, chaps. 9 and 10; "'The Death of the Prophet Lamented': The Legacy of Solomon Stoddard," in *Jonathan Edwards's Writings: Text: Context, Interpretation*, ed. Stephen J. Stein (Bloomington: Indiana University Press, 1996), 69–84; and Holifield, *Covenant Sealed*, 197–224. Less useful, though the only book-length treatment, is Ralph J. Coffman, *Solomon Stoddard* (New York: Twayne Publishers, 1978). Part of my discussion below derives from my "Solomon Stoddard's Irreverent Way," *Early American Literature*, 21:1 (Spring 1986), 29–43; reprint in *Crossroads*, 79–94.

15. Solomon Stoddard, *The Doctrine of Instituted Churches Explained and Proved from the Word of God* (London: 1700), 1, 3.

16. Ibid., 1, 6–8.

17. Solomon Stoddard, *The Inexcusableness of Neglecting the Worship of God* (Boston: 1708), ii.

18. Ibid., ii–iii.

19. Solomon Stoddard, *The Defects of Preachers Reproved* (Boston: 1724), 9.

20. For background to Timothy Edwards and his career in East Windsor, see Dwight, *Life*, 19–40; and Marsden, *Life*, 17–21, 23–27, 33–34; Patricia Tracy, *Jonathan Edwards, Pastor: Religion and Society in Eighteenth-Century Massachusetts* (New York: Hill & Wang, 1980), 51–58; Kenneth Pieter Minkema, "The Edwardses: A Ministerial Family in Eighteenth-Century New England" (Ph.D. dissertation, University of Connecticut, 1988); and "The East Windsor Conversion Narratives, 1700–1725," *Connecticut Historical Society Bulletin*, 51 (Winter 1986), 7–63; and, in general, John A.

Stoughton, *"Windsor Farmes": A Glimpse of an Old Parish* (Hartford, CT: Clark & Smith, 1883). Also see John L. Sibley and Clifford K. Shipton, *Biographical Sketches of Those Who Attended Harvard College*, 18 vols. to date (Boston: 1873–), 1:558–59.

21. See Henry R. Stiles, *The History and Genealogies of Ancient Windsor, Connecticut*, 2 vols. (Hartford, CT: 1891–1892), 1:556; and Winslow, *Jonathan Edwards*, 31–33.

22. For Edwards's early education, see William Sparkes Morris, *The Young Jonathan Edwards: A Reconstruction* (Brooklyn, NY: Carlson Publishing Co., 1991), chap. 1.

23. Dwight, *Life*, 16–18.

24. One contemporary even considered him a "greater man" than Stoddard; see Charles Chauncy, cited in William Sprague, *Annals of the American Pulpit*, 9 vols. (New York: Robert Carter and Brothers, 1857–1869), 1:209. For an account of Williams's career, see Philip F. Gura, "Sowing for the Harvest: The Reverend William Williams and the Great Awakening," *Journal of Presbyterian History*, 56:4 (Winter 1978), 326–41; reprint *Crossroads*, 95–113.

25. On the Deerfield raid and its effects on the Williams family, see John Demos, *The Unredeemed Captive: A Family Story from Early America* (New York: Knopf, 1994). Also see Evan Haefeli and Kevin Sweeney, *Captors and Captives: The 1704 French and Indian Raid on Deerfield* (Amherst: University of Massachusetts Press, 2003), and "Revisiting the Redeemed Captive: New Perspectives on the 1704 Attack on Deerfield," *William and Mary Quarterly*, 3rd ser., 52:1 (January 1995), 3–46; and Richard Melvoin, *New England Outpost: War and Society in Colonial Frontier Deerfield, Massachusetts* (New York: W. W. Norton, 1989).

2. SEASON OF YOUTH (1716–1727)

1. See *Works*, 6:163–69. For many years scholars assumed that Edwards had written his piece on spiders at an earlier age, but George Claghorn discovered the original letter about the phenomenon, dated October 31, 1723, after Edwards had received his M.A. from Yale.

2. This letter of August 7, 1711, is reproduced in Ola Elizabeth Winslow, *Jonathan Edwards, 1703–1758* (New York: Macmillan, 1940), 40–41.

3. George Claghorn, in his introduction to the "Personal Narrative," speculates that the narrative may have been written for Edwards's future son-in-law Aaron Burr, who may have inquired about Edwards's spiritual experiences. See *Works*, 16:747.

4. "Personal Narrative," in *Works*, 16:790–91.

5. Edwards to Mary Edwards, May 10, 1716, in *Works*, 16:29–30.

6. On Yale's founding and early history, see Richard Warch, *School of the*

Prophets: Yale College, 1701–1740 (New Haven: Yale University Press, 1973); and Franklin Bowditch Dexter, ed., *Documentary History of Yale University: Under the Original Charter of the Collegiate School of Connecticut, 1701–1745* (New Haven: Yale University Press, 1916).

7. On Timothy Edwards's difficulties with his congregation, see Patricia J. Tracy, *Jonathan Edwards, Pastor: Religion and Society in Eighteenth-Century Northampton* (New York: Hill and Wang, 1980), 54–57.

8. Edwards to Timothy Edwards, July 24, 1719, in *Works*, 16:33.

9. Warch, *School of the Prophets*, 187. I draw my description of the school's daily regimen and curriculum from this work.

10. Ibid., 195. Also see William Sparkes Morris, *The Young Jonathan Edwards: A Reconstruction* (Brooklyn, NY: Carlson Publishing Company, 1991), chap. 2.

11. On Edwards and Arminianism, see Gerald R. McDermott, *Jonathan Edwards Confronts the Gods: Christian Theology, Enlightenment Religion, and Non-Christian Faiths* (New York: Oxford University Press, 2000), 18–19, 46–50; and C. C. Goen's introduction to *Works*, 4, esp. 4–19.

12. Dexter, *Documentary History*, 225.

13. See Warch, *School of the Prophets*, 96–126, for an account of the apostasy. Also, John Corrigan, *The Prism of Piety: Catholick Congregational Clergy at the Beginning of the Enlightenment* (New York: Oxford University Press, 1991), for a good overview of the influence of Enlightenment thought in eighteenth-century New England.

14. Increase Mather cited in *The Diary of Samuel Sewall, 1674–1729*, ed. M. Halsey Thomas, 2 vols. (New York: Farrar, Straus and Giroux, 1973), 2:995. Also see Warch, *School of the Prophets*, 110.

15. "Personal Narrative," in *Works*, 16:797.

16. For a good description of the city in this period, see William Smith, Jr., *The History of the Province of New-York*, 2 vols., ed. Michael Kammen (1752: Cambridge: Harvard University Press, 1972), 1:202–27.

17. "Diary," in *Works*, 16:783.

18. *Works*, 14:132.

19. "Diary," in *Works*, 16:759, 779. On the steps of conversion considered normative, see Norman Pettit, *The Heart Prepared: Grace and Conversion in Puritan Spiritual Life* (New Haven: Yale University Press, 1966), 86–124.

20. *Works*, 16:760–61.

21. On such covenant renewals, see Charles Hambrick-Stowe, *The Practice of Piety: Puritan Devotional Disciplines in Seventeenth-Century New England* (Chapel Hill: University of North Carolina Press, 1982), 130–32, 248–53.

22. "Diary," in *Works*, 16:762, and "Personal Narrative," 792.

23. "Diary," in *Works*, 16:765.

24. Ibid., 756.

25. Ibid., 770, 774, 779.
26. Ibid., 791.
27. Ibid., 791–92.
28. Ibid., 793–95.
29. Ibid., 797–98.
30. Ibid., 797, 793.
31. Many of these works came as the gift of the colony's London agent, Jeremiah Dummer. On the Dummer gift, see Warch, *School of the Prophets*, 63–66, and Perry Miller, *The New England Mind: From Colony to Province* (Cambridge: Harvard University Press, 1953), 419–20. The books are listed in Louise May Bryant and Mary Patterson, eds., "The List of Books Sent by Jeremiah Dummer," in *Papers in Honor of Andrew Keogh, Librarian of Yale University*, ed. Staff of the [Yale University] Library (New Haven: 1938), 423–92. On the challenge of these radical ideas to Edwards, see McDermott, *Jonathan Edwards Confronts the Gods*, passim; and Leon Chai, *Jonathan Edwards and the Limits of Enlightenment Philosophy* (New York: Oxford University Press, 1998).
32. Cotton Mather, *The Christian Philosopher*, ed. Winton U. Solberg (1721; Urbana: University of Illinois Press, 1994). In his lengthy introduction, Solberg places the book in contemporary debates over the new science.
33. On Edwards's immersion in these authors, see Norman Fiering, *Jonathan Edwards's Moral Thought in Its British Context* (Chapel Hill: University of North Carolina Press, 1981). On deism, see McDermott, *Jonathan Edwards Confronts the Gods*, esp. 17–86.
34. *Works*, 6:202–07.
35. Ibid., 204–05.
36. Ibid., 334–35.
37. See, for example, *Works*, 6:337–38. Wallace E. Anderson's introduction to vol. 6 of the *Works* is essential to understanding Edwards's engagement with the new science.
38. *Works*, 11:53.
39. On the Cambridge Platonists, see Daniel Walker Howe, "The Cambridge Platonists of Old England and the Cambridge Platonists of New England," *Church History*, 57 (December 1988), 470–85. Also see Gerald Cragg, *The Cambridge Platonists* (New York: Oxford University Press, 1968); and C. A. Patrides, ed., *The Cambridge Platonists* (Cambridge: Harvard University Press, 1970).
40. "Personal Narrative," in *Works*, 16:796.
41. *Works*, 14:22.
42. *Works*, 6:193–94.
43. On Edwards's notions of love, with particular reference to Sarah, see Ruth Bloch, *Gender and Morality in Anglo-American Culture, 1650–1800* (Berkeley and Los Angeles: University of California Press, 2003), 102–11; and on

affection and sentiment in general in this period, Bloch's "Changing Conceptions of Sexuality and Romance in Eighteenth-Century America," *William and Mary Quarterly*, 3rd ser., 60 (January 2003), 13–42.

44. Dwight, *Life*, 114, citing Hopkins.

45. *Works*, 13:331–32.

46. "On Sarah Pierpont," in *Works*, 16:789–90.

47. See Tracy, *Jonathan Edwards, Pastor*, 1–11.

48. Winslow, *Jonathan Edwards*, 109.

49. Dwight, *Life*, 127–28, citing Hopkins.

50. "Diary," in *Works*, 16:788.

51. Increase Mather, in his preface to John Quick's *The Young Man's Claim unto the Sacrament of the Lord's Supper* (Boston: 1700), 28–29, gave Stoddard this appellation. For its aptness, see Marsden, *Life*, 515, n. 2.

3. SOWING FOR THE HARVEST: NORTHAMPTON (1727–1734)

1. Douglas C. Stenerson, "An Anglican Critique of the Early Phase of the Great Awakening in New England: A Letter by Timothy Cutler," *William and Mary Quarterly*, 3rd ser., 30 (1973), 480.

2. *Boston Weekly News-Letter*, February 20, 1729, reprinted as an appendix to Benjamin Colman's *The Faithful Ministers of Christ Mindful of Their Own Death* (Boston: 1729), 27–28.

3. Colman, *Faithful Ministers*, 2.

4. Ibid., "Appendix," 27–28.

5. Ibid., "Appendix," 27.

6. Solomon Stoddard, *The Efficacy of the Fear of Hell, to Restrain Men from Sin* (Boston: 1713), 185–86, 189. The contours of Stoddard's career are limned convincingly by Paul R. Lucas, "'An Appeal to the Learned': The Mind of Solomon Stoddard," *William and Mary Quarterly*, 3rd ser., 30 (1973), 257–97; and "'The Death of the Prophet Lamented': The Legacy of Solomon Stoddard," in *Jonathan Edwards's Writings: Text: Context, Interpretation*, ed. Stephen J. Stein (Bloomington: Indiana University Press, 1996), 69–84; but see also Patricia Tracy, *Jonathan Edwards, Pastor: Religion and Society in Eighteenth-Century Northampton* (New York: Hill and Wang, 1980), 13–37.

7. Stoddard, *Efficacy*, 189.

8. Solomon Stoddard, *The Inexcusableness of Neglecting the Worship of God* (Boston: 1708), 26.

9. Ibid., 20.

10. On the formation of the Hampshire Association, see Gregory H. Nobles, *Divisions Throughout the Whole: Politics and Society in Hampshire County,*

Massachusetts, 1740–1775 (New York: Cambridge University Press, 1983), 27–28.

11. William Sprague, *Annals of the American Pulpit*, 9 vols. (New York: Robert Carter and Brothers, 1857–1869), 1:207. For an account of Williams's career, on which the following is based, see Philip F. Gura, "Sowing for the Harvest: The Reverend William Williams and the Great Awakening," *Journal of Presbyterian History*, 56:4 (Winter 1978), 326–41; reprinted in *The Crossroads of American History and Literature* (University Park: Pennsylvania State University Press, 1996), 95–113.

12. See Philip F. Gura, "Going Mr. Stoddard's Way: William Williams on Church Privileges, 1693," *William and Mary Quarterly*, 45:3 (July 1988), 489–98. This treatise (like several anti-Stoddard pieces from Westfield's minister Edward Taylor) was never published but circulated throughout the valley in manuscript. See, for example, Thomas M. and Virginia L. Davis, eds., *Edward Taylor vs. Solomon Stoddard: The Nature of the Lord's Supper* (Boston: Twayne Publishers, 1981).

13. William Williams, *The Danger of Not Reforming Known Evils* (Boston: 1707), 4, 7, 13, 17ff.

14. William Williams, *A Painful Ministry, the Peculiar Gift of the Lord* (Boston: 1717), 10, 12.

15. Ibid., 21; *The Great Concern of Christians* (Boston: 1723), 20.

16. Williams, *Painful Ministry*, 12; and *Great Concern of Christians*, 27.

17. William Williams, *The Great Salvation Revealed and Offered in the Gospel* (Boston: 1717), 115, 118, 122, 144, 70, 167.

18. See Tracy, *Jonathan Edwards, Pastor*, 37–49.

19. Ibid., 148–53, and John L. Sibley and Clifford K. Shipton, *Biographical Sketches of Those Who Attended Harvard College*, 18 vols. to date (Boston: 1873–), 5:96–119.

20. *Works*, 4:146.

21. Edwards to Thomas Gillespie, July 1, 1751, in *Works*, 16:380–81.

22. See Tracy, *Jonathan Edwards, Pastor*, 38–39.

23. Edwards to Thomas Gillespie, July 1, 1751, in *Works*, 16:382–83.

24. For a good overview of early-eighteenth-century economic development in this region, see Allan Kulikoff, *From British Peasants to Colonial Farmers* (Chapel Hill: University of North Carolina Press, 2000), 203–54.

25. William Williams, *The Death of a Prophet Lamented and Improved, in a Sermon Preached at Northampton, Feb. 13, 1729* (Boston: 1729), 23, 28. Colman's sermon was *The Faithful Ministers of Christ Mindful of Their Own Death* (Boston: 1729).

26. *Works*, 14:365, 366–67, 369.

27. Timothy Edwards to Anne Edwards, September 12, 1729, cited in *Works*, 14:14–15.

28. Hopkins, *Life*, 40, 42–43.

29. Ibid., 42–43.

30. Ibid., 47–48.

31. Hopkins went so far as to suggest that Edwards's difficulties with some of Stoddard's ideas even dated from an earlier period, claiming that at first Edwards had been hesitant to accept the Northampton pulpit because of scruples regarding Stoddard's lax standards of admission to the Lord's Supper (Hopkins, *Life*, 56). This seems entirely likely, inasmuch as Timothy Edwards had always resisted Stoddard's innovations and would not have held back such opinions from the son he had trained for the ministry, no matter how great Stoddard's reputation.

32. Edwards particularly questioned his grandfather's belief that evangelical humiliation was only a matter of a sinner's preparation and had no saving grace in it. "A Principal thing that made Mr. Stoddard think there was no grace in humiliation," he observed, "was because he looked upon an explicit act of faith in Jesus Christ as evermore the first gracious act that ever was exerted," but he did not give enough thought to what that faith entailed. Edwards argued, "[T]he graces of the Spirit [that is, what constituted saving faith], especially those that more directly respect God and another world, are so nearly allied that they include one another." Thus "where there is the exercise of one, there is something of the other exercised with it; like strings in consort, if one is struck, others sound with it; or like links of a chain, if one is drawn, others follow." Because faith worked in this complex way and affected the totality of one's being, someone could be in a justified state "before a distinct and express act of faith in the sufficiency and suitableness of Christ as a Savior." *Works*, 13:457–58.

33. Ibid., 460.

34. *Works*, 14:254, 259–60.

35. Ibid., 346, 355.

36. *Works*, 17:96, 91, 92.

37. Ibid., 106, 111.

38. Ibid., 114, 120.

39. *Works*, 4:113.

40. On the Breck controversy, see David Hall's introduction to *Works*, 12, and Nobles, *Divisions Throughout the Whole*, 38–44. Also Charles Edwin Jones, "The Impolitic Mr. Edwards: The Personal Dimension of the Robert Breck Affair," *New England Quarterly*, 51:1 (March 1978), 64–79; and E. H. Byington, "Rev. Robert Breck Controversy," *Papers and Proceedings of the Connecticut Valley Historical Society, 1882–1903*, 2 (1904), 1–19.

41. On Thomas Clap's part in the Breck affair, see Louis Leonard Tucker, *Puritan Protagonist: President Thomas Clap of Yale College* (Chapel Hill: University of North Carolina Press, 1962), 47–58.

42. "The very thing I now want, to give me a clearer and more immediate view of the perfections and glory of God," Edwards wrote in his diary, "is as clear a knowledge of the manner of God's exerting himself, with respects to spirits and mind, as I have, of his operations concerning matter and bodies," a reference to his ongoing interest in science. "Diary," in *Works*, 16:787.

43. "Personal Narrative," in *Works*, 16:792.

44. The classic account of Locke's influence on Edwards is Perry Miller, "The Rhetoric of Sensation," in *Errand into the Wilderness* (Cambridge: Harvard University Press, 1956), 167–83, but also see Norman Fiering, *Jonathan Edwards's Moral Thought and Its British Context* (Chapel Hill: University of North Carolina Press, 1981); William Sparkes Morris, *The Young Jonathan Edwards: A Reconstruction* (Brooklyn, NY: Carlson Publishing Company, 1991); and Paul Ramsey's introduction to Edwards's *Works*, 1.

45. *Works*, 6:342.

46. *Works*, 14:72, 74, 75, 79.

47. *Works*, 13:533.

48. *Works*, 18:88–89.

49. *Works*, 17:202.

50. Ibid., 405–07, for editor Mark Valeri's discussion of the sermon.

51. Ibid., 410–12.

52. Ibid., 413–24.

4. THE CHIEF SCENE OF THESE WONDERS: HAMPSHIRE COUNTY (1734–1739)

1. Timothy Cutler to Zachary Grey, June 5, 1735, in John Nichols, *Illustrations of the Literary History of the Eighteenth Century*, 8 vols. (London: For the Author, 1817–1858), 4:298.

2. On the intermittent revivals in New England before 1735, see Edwin S. Gaustad, *The Great Awakening in New England* (New York: Harper & Row, 1957), 16–18. On the 1727 earthquake and its influence on revivals, see Erik R. Seeman, *Laity and Clergy in Eighteenth-Century New England* (Baltimore: Johns Hopkins University Press, 1999), 149–54.

3. Isaac Watts and John Guyse, in the preface to the London edition of Edwards's *Faithful Narrative of the Surprising Conversions*, in *Works*, 4:133.

4. *Works*, 19:52.

5. On Northampton's social structure, see Patricia Tracy, *Jonathan Edwards, Pastor: Religion and Society in Eighteenth-Century Northampton* (New York: Hill and Wang, 1980), 93–103.

6. *Faithful Narrative*, in *Works*, 4:147–48.

7. One biographer described his preaching as "not loud, but distinct and penetrating." See Alexander V. G. Allen, *Jonathan Edwards* (1889; Boston: Houghton, Mifflin and Company, 1894), 41.

8. Stephen Williams, "Diary," November 18, 1734, cited in *Works*, 4:17–18.

9. Edwards to Benjamin Colman, May 30, 1735, in *Works*, 4:103.

10. William Williams to Benjamin Colman, April 28, 1735, cited in ibid., 18.

11. *Faithful Narrative*, in *Works*, 4:148. The sermon is in *Works*, 19:143–242.

12. *Faithful Narrative*, in *Works*, 4:149.

13. *Works*, 19:797, 794, 795.

14. Edwards to Colman, May 30, 1735, in *Works*, 4:108.

15. Benjamin Colman's "Abridgment," in *Works*, 4:116.

16. Edwards letter to Colman, May 30, 1735, in *Works*, 4:103.

17. *Faithful Narrative*, in *Works*, 4:152.

18. Colman's "Abridgment," in *Works*, 4:120, and *Faithful Narrative*, ibid., 158.

19. Ibid., 150.

20. Ibid., 109–10, 206, 206–07.

21. "Our Weakness, God's Strength," in *Works*, 19:388.

22. *Works*, 4:209.

23. David D. Hall, introduction to *Works*, 12:5; and *Faithful Narrative*, in *Works*, 4:208, for the other affairs that took people's minds from religion.

24. "The Many Mansions," in *Works*, 19:743.

25. Edwards alluded to his trip to New Jersey in *Faithful Narrative*, in *Works*, 4:155–56.

26. Cutler to Grey, June 5, 1735, in Nichols, *Illustrations*, 4:297–99; Eliphalet Adams, "To the Reader," in Eleazer Williams, *Sensible Sinners Invited to Come to Christ* (New London, CT: 1735); Elisha Williams to Isaac Watts, May 24, 1736, in Thomas Milner, *The Life, Times, and Correspondence of the Rev. Isaac Watts, D.D.* (London: Simpkin and Marshall, 1834), 546.

27. See, for example, Charles E. Clark, *The Public Prints: The Newspaper in Anglo-American Culture, 1665–1740* (New York: Oxford University Press, 1994), 193–267; and Frank Lambert, *Inventing the "Great Awakening"* (Princeton: Princeton University Press, 1999), passim.

28. *New-England Weekly Journal*, May 12, 1735.

29. *Faithful Narrative*, in *Works*, 4:130. The publication history of the *Faithful Narrative* is detailed in C. C. Goen's introduction to *Works*, 4, but also see Lambert, *The "Great Awakening,"* 69–81.

30. The letter to Colman is printed in *Works*, 4:99–110.

31. William Williams, *The Duty and Interest of a People, Among Whom Religion Has Been Planted . . . with Directions for Such as Are Concerned to Obtain a True Repentance* (Boston: 1736). Benjamin Colman, preface to Williams, *Duty and Interest*, in *Works*, 4:112.

32. Colman's letter to Watts is quoted in Milner, *Life, Times, and Correspondence of Watts*, 553–54.

33. Isaac Watts to Edwards, February 28, 1737, in Massachusetts Historical Society, *Proceedings*, 2nd ser., 9 (1894–1895), 353.

34. Edwards to Colman, May 19, 1737, in *Works*, 16:69–70.

35. Douglas C. Stenerson, "An Anglican Critique of the Early Phase of the Great Awakening in New England: A Letter by Timothy Cutler," *William and Mary Quarterly*, 3rd ser., 30 (1973), 486.

36. Edwards to Colman, May 19, 1737, in *Works*, 16:70.

37. Watts to Colman, May 31, 1738, in Massachusetts Historical Society, *Proceedings*, 2nd ser., 9 (1894–1895), 360–61.

38. Ibid., 360.

39. Watts and Guyse, preface to the London (1737) edition of *A Faithful Narrative*, in *Works*, 4:130, and ibid., n. 2.

40. Watts to Colman, October 13, 1757, in Massachusetts Historical Society, *Proceedings*, 2nd ser., 9 (1894–1895), 357; and May 31, 1738, ibid., 360–61.

41. See Thomas H. Johnson, *The Printed Writings of Jonathan Edwards, 1703–1758: A Bibliography* (Princeton: Princeton University Press, 1940), 4–7.

42. Watts and Guyse, preface to the London (1737) edition of *A Faithful Narrative*, in *Works*, 4:133.

43. Ibid., 132.

44. Ibid., 136.

45. Ibid.

46. Abigail Hutchinson's narrative is in *Faithful Narrative*, in *Works*, 4:191–99.

47. Phebe Bartlett's narrative is also in *Faithful Narrative*, 199–205.

48. See *Faithful Narrative*, 160–87, for Edwards's account of the morphology of the Awakening, from which the above quotations are taken.

49. Ibid., 188–89.

50. Ibid., 189–90.

51. Ibid., 159–60.

52. *Works*, 19:16, n. 6.

53. *Faithful Narrative*, in *Works*, 4:207–08.

54. Edwards to Colman, May 19, 1737, in *Works*, 16:67.

55. *Works*, 19:463, 472.

56. *The Boston Gazette*, no. 899 (March 28–April 4, 1737), 2–3, reprinted in Watts and Guyse, preface to the London (1737) edition of *A Faithful Narrative*, in *Works*, 4:134–36.

57. *Works*, 19:549–51.

58. Ibid., 552.

59. Ibid., 674.

60. Ibid., 670.

61. Ibid., 671–77.

62. Edwards, preface to *Discourses on Various Important Subjects* (1738), in *Works*, 19:794–98.

63. The series on charity is in *Works*, 8:125–397; and that on the history of redemption is in *Works*, 9. On Edwards's sermon series on the ten virgins, still

unpublished, see Ava Chamberlain, "Brides of Christ and Signs of Grace: Edwards's Sermon Series on the Parable of the Wise and Foolish Virgins," in *Jonathan Edwards's Writing: Text, Context, Interpretation*, ed. Stephen J. Stein (Bloomington: Indiana University Press, 1996), 3–18.

64. *Works*, 19:677.

5. A GREAT DEAL OF NOISE ABOUT RELIGION (1740–1743)

1. *Faithful Narrative*, in *Works*, 4:156.
2. *Works*, 19:555–56. On revival activity in this area, see Marilyn J. Westerkamp, *Triumph of the Laity: Scots-Irish Piety and the Great Awakening, 1625–1760* (New York: Oxford University Press, 1988), chaps. 6 and 7.
3. Gilbert Tennent, *The Necessity of Religious Violence* (New York: 1735), 43.
4. On the emergence of these evangelical strains in England, see Horton Davies, *Worship and Theology in England: From Watts and Wesley to Maurice, 1690–1850* (Princeton: Princeton University Press, 1961), 143–83; W. R. Ward, *The Protestant Evangelical Awakening* (Cambridge, UK: Cambridge University Press, 1992), 296–352; and Michael J. Crawford, *Seasons of Grace: Colonial New England's Revival Tradition in Its British Context* (New York: Oxford University Press, 1991), passim.
5. On John Wesley and Methodism, see H. D. Rack, *Reasonable Enthusiast: John Wesley and the Rise of Methodism* (London: Epworth Press, 1989); Frank Baker, *John Wesley and the Church of England* (Nashville: Abingdon Press, 1970); and John Walsh, "The Cambridge Methodists," in Peter Brooks, ed., *Christian Spirituality: Essays in Honour of Gordon Rupp* (London: SCM Press, 1975), 251–83.
6. Nehemiah Curnock, ed. *The Journal of the Rev. John Wesley, A.M.*, 8 vols. (London: Epworth Press, 1911), 2:83–84.
7. On Whitefield see Harry S. Stout, *The Divine Dramatist: George Whitefield and the Rise of Modern Evangelicalism* (Grand Rapids, MI: Eerdman's, 1991); Frank Lambert, *"Pedlar in Divinity": George Whitefield and the Transatlantic Revivals, 1737–1770* (Princeton: Princeton University Press, 1991); and Arnold A. Dallimore, *George Whitefield: The Life and Times of the Great Evangelist of the Eighteenth-Century Revivals*, 2 vols. (Westchester, IL: Cornerstone Books, 1979).
8. *Boston Evening-Post*, August 13, 1744.
9. The author heard Alan Heimert relate this anecdote in lecture at Harvard University, c. 1971, and Harry S. Stout reports a similar version (e-mail to the author, October 11, 2003).
10. Cited in Frank Lambert, *Inventing the "Great Awakening"* (Princeton: Princeton University Press, 1999), 92.
11. On Zinzendorf, see Ward, *Protestant Evangelical Awakening*, chap. 4.

12. See Lambert, *"Pedlar in Divinity,"* passim, and The *"Great Awakening,"* 92–102, for discussions of Whitefield's rise to fame through his use of emergent print media.

13. Lambert, The *"Great Awakening,"* is the most sophisticated scholar of this phenomenon, but also see Crawford, *Seasons of Grace*; and Alan C. Guelzo, "God's Designs: The Literature of the Colonial Revivals of Religion," in *New Directions in American Religious History*, ed. Harry S. Stout and D. G. Hart (New York: Oxford University Press, 1997), 141–72.

14. Parsons's account is in Thomas Prince, ed., *The Christian History, Containing Accounts of the Revival and Propagation of Religion in Great-Britain and America* (March 1743–February 1745), 2 vols. (Boston, 1744–1745), 2:118–62, 125–26 for quotations. On the role of letter writing in the transmission of news (how someone like Parsons "heard" about revival activities), see John Fea, "Wheelock's World: Letters and the Communication of Revival in Great Awakening New England," *Proceedings of the American Antiquarian Society*, 109, part 1 (1999), 99–144.

15. Michael J. Crawford, "The Spiritual Travels of Nathan Cole," *William and Mary Quarterly*, 3rd ser., 33 (1976), 89–126.

16. Edwards to Benjamin Colman, May 27, 1738, in *Works*, 16:78.

17. Timothy Cutler to Edmund Gibson, May 28, 1739, in Douglas C. Stenerson, "An Anglican Critique of the Early Phase of the Great Awakening in New England: A Letter by Timothy Cutler," *William and Mary Quarterly*, 3rd ser., 30 (1973), 482.

18. Edwards to Moses Lyman, August 31, 1741, in *Works*, 16:97.

19. Edwards to George Whitefield, February 12, 1740, ibid., 80–81.

20. Edwards to Josiah Willard, June 1, 1740, ibid., 83–84. On Francke's labors, see Ward, *Protestant Evangelical Awakening*, especially 72–77.

21. Edwards to Eleazer Wheelock, October 9, 1740, in *Works*, 16:85–86.

22. *George Whitefield's Journals* (London: Banner of Truth Press, 1960), 476–79.

23. Edwards to Thomas Prince, December 12, 1743, in *Works*, 16:116.

24. Ibid., 115–27.

25. Edwards to Whitefield, December 14, 1740, ibid., and Edwards to Prince, December 12, 1743, ibid., 119.

26. Edwards to Prince, December 12, 1743, ibid., 117.

27. Ibid., 118–20.

28. On Buell, see Franklin B. Dexter, *Biographical Sketches of the Graduates of Yale College*, 6 vols. (New York: Holt, and New Haven: Yale University Press, 1885–1912), 1:664–69; and William Sprague, *Annals of the American Pulpit*, 9 vols. (New York: Robert Carter and Brothers, 1857–1869), 3:102–13. On Sarah Edwards's spirituality, see Sandra Gustafson, *Eloquence Is Power: Oratory and Performance in Early America* (Chapel Hill:

University of North Carolina Press, 2000), 51–74; Julie Ellison, "The Sociology of 'Holy Indifference': Sarah Edwards' Narrative," *American Literature*, 56:4 (December 1984), 479–95; and Amanda Porterfield, *Feminine Spirituality in America: From Sarah Edwards to Martha Graham* (Philadelphia: Temple University Press, 1980), 20–23, 39–48.

29. Edwards to Thomas Prince, December 12, 1743, in *Works*, 16:120–21.

30. Sarah Edwards's narrative of this period is in Dwight, *Life*, 171–86; the passages cited are from 171–72, 174–75. Significantly, when Edwards described Sarah's conversion (albeit without naming her) in his *Seasonable Thoughts on the State of Religion* (1742), he omitted those of her experiences that, in light of his growing dissatisfaction with some converts' behavior, he thought might give more ammunition to the revival's detractors. Compare Sarah's account in Dwight, *Life*, 171–86, with Edwards's account in *Works*, 4:331–41.

31. Dwight, *Life*, 178.

32. Edwards to Lyman, August 31, 1741, in *Works*, 16:97–98.

33. Edwards to Prince, December 12, 1743, ibid., 121.

34. The ceremony is described in ibid., 121–25.

35. Ibid., 125.

36. The literature on whether or not the awakenings deserve the appellation of "great" is extensive. The revivals were first so termed by Joseph Tracy on their centennial; see his *The Great Awakening: A History of the Revival of Religion in the Time of Edwards and Whitefield* (Boston: Tappan and Dennett, 1842). Jon Butler debunked the extent and continuity of the revivals in his seminal "Enthusiasm Described and Decried: The Great Awakening as Interpretive Fiction," *Journal of American History*, 69 (September 1982), 305–25; also see *Becoming America: The Revolution Before 1776* (Cambridge: Harvard University Press, 2000), 196–204. He has been challenged by Patricia Bonomi, *Under the Cope of Heaven: Religion, Society, and Politics in Colonial America* (New York: Oxford University Press, 1986) and Frank Lambert, *The "Great Awakening."*

37. Edwards to Eleazer Wheelock, June 9, 1741, in *Works*, 16:90.

38. Israel Loring, *The Duty of an Apostasizing People* (Boston: 1737), 45.

39. William Kidder, ed., "The Diary of Nicholas Gilman" (M.A. thesis, University of New Hampshire, 1972), entries for November 20, 1741, and September 21 and November 17, 1741: 230, 221–22, and 229.

40. John Cotton, in *The Christian History*, 1 (1743), 261; and William Williams, "Discourse on Saving Faith," in John Cotton et al., *Four Sermons* (Boston: 1741), 59.

41. Henry Messinger, in *The Christian History*, 1 (1743), 243.

42. John White, in *The Christian History*, 2 (1744), 42.

43. *Whitefield's Journals*, 352, 486; cited in Lambert, *The "Great Awakening,"* 147.

44. Stenerson, "Anglican Critique," 485.

45. On itinerancy during this period, see Timothy D. Hall, *Contested Boundaries: Itinerancy and the Reshaping of the Colonial American Religious World* (Durham, NC: Duke University Press, 1994); and J. William T. Youngs, Jr., *God's Messengers: Religious Leadership in Colonial New England, 1700–1750* (Baltimore: Johns Hopkins University Press, 1976), 121–30.

46. "Diary of Nicholas Gilman," January 15, 1743, 306.

47. Cutler to Grey, September 24, 1743, in John Nichols, *Illustrations of the Literary History of the Eighteenth Century*, 8 vols. (London: For the Author, 1817–1858), 4:304.

48. On Tennent's career as an evangelist, see Milton J. Coalter, *Gilbert Tennent, Son of Thunder: A Case Study of Continental Pietism's Impact on the First Great Awakening in the Middle Colonies* (Westport, CT: Greenwood Press, 1986). *The Danger of an Unconverted Ministry* is reprinted in Alan Heimert and Perry Miller, eds., *The Great Awakening: Documents Illustrating the Crisis and Its Consequences* (Indianapolis: Bobbs, Merrill, 1967), 71–99.

49. "Extracts from the Interleaved Almanacs of Nathan Bowen, Marblehead, 1742–1755," *Essex Institute Historical Collections*, 91 (1955), 167–68 (entry for May 4, 1742).

50. *Boston Evening-Post*, July 12, 1742.

51. On Davenport's flamboyant career, see Harry S. Stout and Peter S. Onuf, "James Davenport and the Great Awakening in New London," *Journal of American History*, 70 (December 1983), 556–78; and Richard Warch, "The Shepherd's Tent: Education and Enthusiasm in the Great Awakening," *American Quarterly*, 30 (Summer 1978), 177–98. Recently Douglas L. Winiarski has reexamined radical religious behavior in the revivals in his "Souls Filled with Ravishing Transport: Heavenly Visions and the Radical Awakening in New England," *William and Mary Quarterly*, 3rd ser., 61 (2004), 3–46.

52. The literature on Anne Hutchinson and the Antinomians is voluminous, but see especially Michael P. Winship, *Making Heretics: Militant Protestantism and Free Grace in Massachusetts, 1636–1641* (Princeton: Princeton University Press, 2002); and Philip F. Gura, *A Glimpse of Sion's Glory: Puritan Radicalism in New England, 1620–1660* (Middletown, CT: Wesleyan University Press, 1984), 237–75.

53. Alexander Garden, *Take Heed How Ye Hear* (Charleston, SC: 1741), 25.

54. Charles Chauncy, *Seasonable Thoughts on the State of Religion* (Boston: 1743), xxv–vi.

55. Samuel Johnson to the Secretary for the Society for the Propagation of the Gospel in Foreign Parts (SPGFP), September 30, 1743, in Francis L. Hawks and William S. Perry, eds., *Documentary History of the Protestant Episcopal Church in the United States of America*, 2 vols. (New York: J. Pott, 1863), 1:197.

56. Cutler to Gibson, May 28, 1739, in Stenerson, "Anglican Critique," 487.

57. Charles Brockwell to Secretary of the SPGFP, February 18, 1742, in William Stevens Perry, ed., *Historical Collections Relating to the American Colonial Church*, 5 vols. (Hartford, CT: For the Subscribers, 1870–1878), 3:353.

58. "Diary of Nicholas Gilman," January 31, 1742, 241.

59. Brockwell to the Secretary of the SPGFP, June 15, 1741, in Perry, *Historical Collections*, 3:356–57.

60. *Boston Weekly Post-Boy*, August 17, 1741.

61. Nathan Bowen, February 28 and August 2, 1742, in "Interleaved Almanacs," 165, 171.

62. Samuel Philips Savage, "Extract of a Letter," July 6, 1741, Samuel P. Savage Papers II, Massachusetts Historical Society, Boston. Permission courtesy of Massachusetts Historical Society. The author of the letter may have been one of Benjamin Colman's many correspondents, for the extracts are in the handwriting of Savage, a prominent merchant and member of Colman's Brattle Street Church who eagerly followed news of the revivals. Professor Douglas Winiarski generously brought to my attention this hitherto unnoticed account of Edwards's preaching.

63. Stephen Williams, Diary, July 8, 1741, quoted in Marsden, *Life*, 219–22; also see *Works*, 22:400; Patricia Tracy, *Jonathan Edwards, Pastor: Religion and Society in Eighteenth-Century Northampton* (New York: Hill & Wang, 1980), 133; and Benjamin Trumbull, *A Complete History of Connecticut, Civil and Ecclesiastical*, 2 vols. (New Haven: Maltby, Goldsmith and Company, and Samuel Wadsworth, 1818), 145.

64. *Works*, 22:404–5, 411.

65. Ibid., 411–12.

66. *Distinguishing Marks* is reprinted in *Works*, 4:215–88.

67. Ibid., 276, 223.

68. Ibid., 219–21.

69. Ibid., 234–35.

70. Ibid., 241–42.

71. Ibid., 254; also see 257.

72. Ibid., 255.

73. Ibid., 268.

74. Ibid., 277, 282, 288.

75. "Diary of Nicholas Gilman," February 8, 1742, 249; and Jonathan Dickinson, *A Display of God's Special Grace* (Boston, 1742), ii.

76. John Caldwell, *An Impartial Trial of the Spirit* (Boston: 1742), 23.

77. On Chauncy, see Edward M. Griffin, *Old Brick, Charles Chauncy of Boston, 1705–1787* (Minneapolis: University of Minnesota Press, 1980); and Charles Lippy, *Seasonable Revolutionary: The Mind of Charles Chauncy* (Chicago: Nelson-Hall, 1981). *Enthusiasm Described and Cautioned Against* is reprinted in Heimert and Miller, *The Great Awakening*, 228–56.

78. In "A Sketch of Eminent Men in New-England," Massachusetts Historical Society, *Collections*, 1st ser., 10 (1809), 162.

79. See Charles Chauncy, *A Letter from a Gentleman in Boston, to Mr. George Wishart* (Edinburgh, 1742). For the Scottish revivals, see Arthur Fawcett, *The Cambuslang Revival: The Scottish Evangelical Revival of the Eighteenth Century* (London: Banner of Truth Trust, 1971); D. MacFarlan, *The Revivals of the Eighteenth Century, Particularly at Cambuslang* (1847; Wheaton, IL: Richard Owen Publishers, 1980); and Ned Landsman, "Evangelists and Their Hearers: Popular Interpretation of Revivalist Preaching in Eighteenth-Century Scotland," *Journal of British Studies*, 28 (1989), 120–49.

80. *Some Thoughts* is reprinted in *Works*, 4:291–530.

81. Jonathan Ashley, *The Great Gift of Charity Considered and Applied* (Boston: 1742); and Gregory H. Nobles, *Divisions Throughout the Whole: Politics and Society in Hampshire County, Massachusetts, 1740–1775* (New York: Cambridge University Press, 1983), 50–52. William Rand, *Answer to Edwards* (Boston: 1742); Benjamin Doolittle, *An Inquiry into Enthusiasm* (Boston: 1743).

82. *Works*, 4:296–97.

83. Ibid., 479.

84. Ibid.

85. Edwards's account of Sarah's conversion: ibid., 331–42; quotation on 341.

86. Ibid., 353.

87. Isaac Watts to Benjamin Colman, September 14, 1743, in Massachusetts Historical Society, *Proceedings*, 2nd ser., 9 (1895), 402.

88. Charles Chauncy, *Seasonable Thoughts*, 372 n.

89. Ibid., 323–27.

90. On the assembly of ministers and its aftermath, see Gaustad, *Great Awakening in New England*, 61–66; and Tracy, *The Great Awakening*, 286–302.

91. Edwards to William McCullough, May 12, 1743, in *Works*, 16:106–07.

92. Edwards to James Robe, May 12, 1743, ibid., 108–10.

93. Edwards to Benjamin Colman, December 12, 1743, ibid., 126.

94. *Religious Affections* is in *Works*, 2; the quotation here is at 95.

95. Ibid., 97.

96. Ibid., 96–97.

97. Ibid., 99, 120.

98. Ibid., 184–85.

99. Ibid., 197, 205–06.

100. Ibid., 206.

101. Ibid., 240, 339, 365.

102. Ibid., 379, 383.

6. NORTHAMPTON IN TURMOIL (1744–1750)

1. On the connections between the Scots and American ministers and their revivals, see Susan O'Brien, "A Study of the First Evangelical Magazines, 1740–1748," *Journal of Ecclesiastical History*, 27 (July 1976), 255–75; and "Eighteenth-Century Publishing Networks in the First Years of Transatlantic Evangelism," in Mark Noll et al., eds., *Evangelicalism: Comparative Studies of Popular Protestantism in North America, the British Isles, and Beyond, 1700–1900* (New York: Oxford University Press, 1994), 38–57.

2. See Patricia Tracy, *Jonathan Edwards, Pastor: Religion and Society in Eighteenth-Century Northampton* (New York: Hill and Wang, 1980), 157–59.

3. See, for example, Edwards's will, printed in *Bibliotheca Sacra*, 33 (1876), 438–46, which lists some luxury goods. Like many other New England gentry, the Edwardses also kept at least one family slave; see Marsden, *Life*, 255–56.

4. Edwards to the First Precinct, Northampton, November 8, 1744, in *Works*, 16:150–51.

5. Tracy, *Jonathan Edwards, Pastor*, 160–64; Hopkins, *Life*, 53–54; Dwight, *Life*, 299–300. Also see Ava Chamberlain, "Bad Books and Bad Boys: The Transformation of Gender in Eighteenth-Century Northampton, Massachusetts," *New England Quarterly*, 75:2 (June 2002), 179–203.

6. Northampton church covenant, in a letter from Edwards to Thomas Prince, December 12, 1743, in *Works*, 16:123–24.

7. Here, as elsewhere, when I invoke the term *agency*, I follow James E. Block, *A Nation of Agents: The American Path to a Modern Self and Society* (Cambridge: Harvard University Press, 2003), esp. 183–233, where the author treats the importance of the revivals to his argument.

8. See Chamberlain, "Bad Books, Bad Boys," 187–90, for a discussion of these books, and Mary Fissell, "Hairy Women and Naked Truths: Gender and the Politics of Knowledge in *Aristotle's Masterpiece*," *William and Mary Quarterly*, 3rd ser., 61:1 (January 2003), 43–74.

9. Some of the relevant documents from this case are reprinted in John E. Smith, Harry S. Stout, and Kenneth P. Minkema, eds., *A Jonathan Edwards Reader* (New Haven: Yale University Press), 174, for quotation here.

10. Ibid. Oliver Warner thought the texts so desirable that he would only share *Aristotle's Masterpiece* for a fee of ten shillings.

11. Ibid., 173.

12. Ibid., 173–74.

13. Edwards to Eleazer Hannam's wife, March 26, 1744, in *Works*, 16:143.

14. *Jonathan Edwards Reader*, 176–78. The emergence of such populist challenges to clerical authority is discussed in James F. Cooper, *Tenacious of Their Liberties: The Congregationalists in Colonial Massachusetts* (New York: Oxford University Press, 1999), 197–217.

15. Hopkins, *Life*, 54.

16. See Chamberlain, "Bad Books, Bad Boys," passim.

17. Northampton church records, cited in Tracy, *Jonathan Edwards, Pastor*, 161.

18. On these conflicts, see Douglas Edwards Leach, *Arms for Empire: A Military History of the British Colonies in America, 1607–1763* (New York: Macmillan, 1973), chap. 6; and Fred Anderson's magisterial *The Crucible of War: The Seven Years' War and the Fate of Empire in British North America, 1754–1766* (New York: Knopf, 2000).

19. On such "concerts of prayer," see Stephen J. Stein, "Introduction" to *Works*, 5:29–48, where he also does a good job of setting the scene of international conflict; Arthur Fawcett, *The Cambuslang Revival: The Scottish Evangelical Revival of the Eighteenth Century* (London: Banner of Truth Trust, 1971), 210–35; and Leigh E. Schmidt, *Holy Fairs: Scotland and the Making of American Revivalism*, 2nd ed. (1989; Grand Rapids, MI: Williams Eerdman's, 2001), 50–59.

20. *Some Thoughts*, in *Works*, 4:516.

21. Edwards to Prince, December 12, 1743, in *Works*, 16:116.

22. Edwards to "A Correspondent in Scotland," ibid., 181.

23. This is reprinted in *Works*, 5:309–436.

24. Ibid., 360, 364.

25. Ibid., 364–66.

26. Edwards to William McCulloch, May 23, 1749, in *Works*, 16:272.

27. Joseph Bellamy to Thomas Foxcroft, May 6, 1749, cited in Donald Weber, "The Recovery of Jonathan Edwards," in *Jonathan Edwards and the American Experience*, ed. Nathan O. Hatch and Harry S. Stout (New York: Oxford University Press,1988), 52.

28. See Norman Pettit's Introduction to *Works*, 7, for a good account of Brainerd's career. The best source of course is Edwards's own book about him, from which my narrative is taken.

29. *Works*, 7:500.

30. See Joseph A. Conforti, *Jonathan Edwards, Religious Tradition, and American Culture* (Chapel Hill: University of North Carolina Press, 1995), 62–86; and *Works*, 16:250, where the editor notes that the subscription list for the *Life of Brainerd* was an astonishing 1,953.

31. *Works*, 7:155.

32. On Horton, see Franklin B. Dexter, *Biographical Sketches of the Graduates of Yale College*, 6 vols. (New York: Holt, and New Haven: Yale University Press, 1885–1912), 1:536–37.

33. Edwards to John McLaurin, May 12, 1746, in *Works*, 16:206. For Brainerd's career among the Native Americans, see Richard Pointer, "'Poor Indians' and the 'Poor in Spirit': The Indian Impact on David Brainerd," *New England Quarterly*, 67 (1994), 403–26.

34. Edwards to Eleazer Wheelock, September 14, 1748, *Works*, 16:251.

35. Edwards to Joseph Bellamy, January 15, 1747, ibid., 217; and Edwards to John Erskine, August 31, 1748, ibid., 249.

36. *Works*, 7:523.

37. Ibid., 525–26.

38. See ibid., 80–83, for examples of Edwards's excisions.

39. Ibid., 96.

40. See Gail Thain Parker, "Jonathan Edwards and Melancholy," *New England Quarterly*, 41:2 (June 1968), 193–212.

41. *Works*, 7:95, 500.

42. Ibid., 502, 505, 510, 501.

43. For a narrative of the events relating to the communion controversy, see Hall, introduction to *Works*, 12; and Dwight, *Life*, 288–448; quotations here from Edwards's "Narrative of Communion Controversy," *Works*, 12:507–08.

44. "Narrative of the Communion Controversy," *Works*, 12:509.

45. Ibid., 283.

46. Solomon Stoddard, *An Examination of the Power of the Fraternity*, in *The Presence of Christ* (Boston: 1718), 1.

47. Ibid., 10–11, 16.

48. *Works*, 12:167, 169.

49. Ibid., 169–70.

50. Ibid., 174, 176.

51. Ibid., 205, 207.

52. Ibid., 308–09.

53. Ibid., 213.

54. Edwards to Thomas Foxcroft, May 24, 1749, in *Works*, 16:283–84.

55. "Narrative of Communion Controversy," in *Works*, 12:511–12.

56. Ibid., 524.

57. Edwards to Foxcroft, November 21, 1749, in *Works*, 16:301.

58. Edwards to Bellamy, December 6, 1749, ibid., 308–09.

59. Ibid.

60. Edwards to Erskine, July 5, 1750, ibid., 347.

61. Edwards to Thomas Foxcroft, November 21, 1749, ibid., 301.

62. "Narrative of Communion Controversy," in *Works*, 12:565.

63. Hopkins, *Life*, 54.

64. Ibid., 65.

65. Edwards to Foxcroft, May 24, 1759, in *Works*, 16:284–85.

66. Edwards revealed these facts later, in a letter to Isaac Hollis, July 17, 1752, ibid., 504–05.

67. *Misrepresentations* is reprinted in *Works*, 12:349–504.

68. Edwards to Foxcroft, May 24, 1749, in *Works*, 16:284.

69. Edwards to Erskine, July 5, 1750, ibid., 355.
70. The sermon is reprinted in Wilson H. Kimnach, Kenneth P. Minkema, and Douglas A. Sweeney, eds., *The Sermons of Jonathan Edwards: A Reader* (New Haven: Yale University Press, 1999).
71. Ibid., 213–14, 217.
72. Ibid., 218–19.
73. Ibid., 227–28.
74. Ibid., 241.

7. STOCKBRIDGE AND THE HOUSATONICS (1750–1757)

1. John McLaurin to William Hogg, November 8, 1751, cited in Rachel Wheeler, "'Friends to Your Souls': Jonathan Edwards' Indian Pastorate and the Doctrine of Original Sin," *Church History*, 72 (2003), 743, n. 26. Edwards to John Erskine, July 7, 1752, in *Works*, 16:492. On the Great Awakening in Virginia, see Wesley Gewehr, *The Great Awakening in Virginia* (Durham, NC: Duke University Press, 1930); and Rodger M. Payne, "New Light in Hanover County: Evangelical Dissent in Piedmont, Virginia, 1740–1755," *Journal of Southern History*, 61 (November 1995), 665–94.
2. See Edwards to John Erskine, July 5, 1750, *Works*, 16:355–56, for Edwards's mention of the Scots' efforts. He worried about "moving with my numerous family over the Atlantic."
3. As Edwards put it to his Scots correspondent William Hogg, "a door seems to be opened for my further ministry in this place." Edwards to William Hogg, July 13, 1751, in *Works*, 16:392.
4. For the history of Stockbridge, see Electa Fidelia Jones, *Stockbridge, Past and Present* (Springfield, MA: S. Bowles and Co., 1854); and Sarah C. Sedgwick and Christina S. Marquand, *Stockbridge, 1739–1939: A Chronicle* (Great Barrington, MA: Berkshire Courier, 1939). See Dwight, *Life*, 449–541, for an account of Edwards's Stockbridge years, with 449–54 for background to the mission. My narrative follows his and that of Patrick Frazier, whose *The Mohicans of Stockbridge* (Lincoln: University of Nebraska Press, 1992) offers a good history of the tribe and missionary efforts among them. For a description of the Mahican tribe, see T. J. Brasser, "Mahican," in Bruce G. Trigger, ed., *Handbook of North American Indians*, vol. 15 (Washington: Smithsonian Institution, 1978), 198–212. On the mission school, see Margaret Connell Szasz, *Indian Schooling in the American Colonies, 1607–1783* (Albuquerque: University of New Mexico Press, 1988), 206–13. On the New England Company's activities, see William Kellaway, *The New England Company, 1649–1776* (London: Longmans, Green, 1961).
5. On Sergeant, see Franklin B. Dexter, *Biographical Sketches of the Graduates of*

Yale College, 6 vols. (New York: Holt, and New Haven: Yale University Press, 1885–1912), 1:394–97.

6. Samuel Hopkins, *Historical Memoirs Relating to the Housatonic Indians* (1753; New York: Johnson Reprint Corp., 1972), 53.

7. Edwards to Thomas Foxcroft, November 21, 1749, in *Works*, 16:301–02.

8. On Stiles, see Edmund S. Morgan, *The Gentle Puritan: A Life of Ezra Stiles, 1727–1795* (New Haven: Yale University Press, 1962).

9. Wheeler, "'Friends to Your Souls,'" 744, provides the population statistics.

10. Gideon Hawley, "A Letter from Rev. Gideon Hawley of Marshpee, Containing an Account of His Services Among the Indians of Massachusetts and New-York, and a Narrative of His Journey to Onohoghgwage," Massachusetts Historical Society, *Collections*, 1st ser., 4 (1795), 51.

11. For my understanding of Edwards's sermons from the Stockbridge years, I am indebted to Wheeler's analysis in "'Friends to Your Souls,'" particularly 748–61. She mentions the professions of faith on 759.

12. Edwards to Timothy Edwards, January 27, 1752, in *Works*, 16:420.

13. Wyllis Eaton Wright, ed., *Colonel Ephraim Williams: A Documentary Life* (Pittsfield, MA: Berkshire County Historical Society, 1970), 61. Interestingly, Edwards never learned the Housatonics' language and thus preached to them in English. On Edwards's attitudes toward Native Americans, see Gerald McDermott, "Jonathan Edwards and American Indians: The Devil Sucks Their Blood," *New England Quarterly*, 72:4 (December 1999), 539–97.

14. Wright, *Williams,* 61–62.

15. Edwards to Thomas Hubbard, March 30, 1752, in *Works*, 16:469–70.

16. Edwards to Isaac Hollis, July 17, 1752, ibid., 504–05.

17. Ibid., 505–06. Writing in November to William Hogg, Edwards reiterated what he had told Hollis: that the source of his present difficulties had to do with "a number of gentlemen belonging to other towns, of a certain family of considerable note in New England, which had long manifested a jealous and unfriendly spirit" toward him, particularly in "the late great controversy in Northampton." Edwards to William Hogg, November 27, 1752, ibid., 550.

18. Edwards to Hollis, July 17, 1752, ibid., 505.

19. Wright, *Williams*, 61.

20. For a good overview of the Williams family's self-serving plans, see Lion G. Miles, "The Red Man Dispossessed: The Williams Family and the Alienation of Indian Land in Stockbridge, Massachusetts, 1736–1818," *New England Quarterly*, 67:1 (March 1994), 46–76. Also, for the inordinate influence the family wielded, see Kevin Michael Sweeney, "River Gods and Related Minor Deities: The Williams Family and the Connecticut River Valley, 1637–1900" (Ph.D. dissertation, Yale University, 1986).

21. Edwards to Andrew Oliver, February 18, 1752, in *Works*, 16:424–25, 429.

22. Edwards to Jasper Maudit, March 10, 1752, ibid., 458; and Edwards to Hubbard, March 30, 1752, ibid., 466, 467.

23. Edwards to Joseph Willard, July 17, 1752, ibid., 511.

24. Edwards to Oliver, October 1752, ibid., 534.

25. Ibid., 536; and Edwards to Sir William Pepperell, January 30, 1753, ibid., 553–63.

26. Edwards to Hubbard, March 19, 1753, ibid., 564.

27. Edwards to Thomas Prince, May 10, 1754, ibid., 642.

28. Edwards to John Erskine, July 5, 1750, ibid., 353.

29. Edwards to Joseph Hawley, November 18, 1754, ibid., 646–47, 650.

30. Ibid., 650, 652, 654.

31. Joseph Hawley to David Hall, May 5, 1760, in Hopkins, *Life*, 65–72, and in Dwight, *Life*, 421–27. Edwards to Gideon Hawley, October 9, 1756, *Works*, 16:690.

32. Dwight, *Life*, 542.

33. Edwards to Erskine, August 31, 1748, *Works*, 16:249, and July 5, 1750, ibid., 348.

34. Edwards to Erskine, July 7, 1752, ibid., 491.

35. Edwards to Erskine, November 23, 1752, ibid., 541.

36. Edwards to Foxcroft, May 24, 1753, ibid., 596.

37. Edwards to Foxcroft, February 5, 1754, ibid., 619, and March 6, 1754, ibid., 624–25.

38. Paul Ramsey, introduction to *Works*, 8:10.

39. George Claghorn, headnote to letter no. 198, in *Works*, 16:656.

40. Edwards to Foxcroft, February 11, 1757, ibid., 696.

41. Edwards to Erskine, August 31, 1748, ibid., 248.

42. *Works*, 12:449, 501.

43. Edwards to Foxcroft, February 11, 1757, in *Works*, 16:696. During this period Edwards refined some of his notions about original sin in his Stockbridge sermons, those to both the Native Americans and the English settlers. In particular, he stressed how all humans, regardless of race, were universally depraved, a point of doctrine that suggests his belief in the equality of all peoples, regardless of whether they had yet become Christians; see Wheeler, "'Friends to Your Souls,'" 736–65, esp. 761–65.

44. Edwards to Bellamy, August 6, 1757, *Works*, 16:724.

8. TRANSATLANTIC DEBATE (1754–1758)

1. Dwight, *Life*, 603.

2. *Works*, 13:238.

3. Ibid., 239–40, 282.

4. Ibid., 435.

5. Edwards to John Erskine, July 5, 1750, in *Works*, 16:353.
6. On Chubb, see Paul Ramsey, introduction to *Works*, 1:66–81; Alan C. Guelzo, *Edwards on the Will: A Century of American Theological Debate* (Middletown, CT: Wesleyan University Press), 54–59; and T. H. Bushell, *The Sage of Salisbury: Thomas Chubb, 1679–1747* (London: Vision, 1968). Edwards knew of Chubb's ideas from his *Collection of Tracts on Various Subjects* (1730).
7. On Whitby, see Ramsay in *Works*, 1:81–89; and Guelzo, *Edwards on the Will*, 60–64.
8. On Watts, see Ramsay in *Works*, 1:89–118; Guelzo, *Edwards on the Will*, 64–71; and Arthur P. Davis, *Isaac Watts: His Life and Works* (New York: Dryden Press, 1941). Edwards knew Whitby's *Discourse on the Five Points* (1710) in its second, expanded edition of 1735, to which Whitby had added one of John Edwards's replies to him as well as other new material.
9. See Ramsay, introduction to *Works*, 1:65; 32, and 70; and 218 n. On Turnbull, see James McCosh, *The Scottish Philosophy* (New York: Robert Carter and Brothers, 1875), 95–105.
10. Guelzo, *Edwards on the Will*, 71–72.
11. In *Edwards on the Will*, Guelzo traces in meticulous detail the various attempts to rebut Edwards's work.
12. *Works*, 1:353–54, 137–39.
13. Ibid., 140, 142, 147, 148.
14. Ibid., 156.
15. See Guelzo, *Edwards on the Will*, passim.
16. Edwards to Erskine, July 25, 1757, in *Works*, 16:706. Also see *Works*, 1:443–52, for Paul Ramsay's discussion of Kames's use of Edwards, and McCosh, *Scottish Philosophy*, 173–82.
17. *Works*, 1:364.
18. *Works*, 8:420, 424.
19. Ibid., 434–35. Roland Delattre, in *Beauty and Sensibility in the Thought of Jonathan Edwards: An Essay in Aesthetics and Theological Ethics* (New Haven: Yale University Press, 1968), speaks to Edwards's sense of the beauty of creation.
20. *Works*, 8:442, 447.
21. Ibid., 461–62.
22. Ibid., 462–63, 527.
23. Ibid., 528, 531, 533.
24. Ibid., 533–35.
25. Ibid., 536.
26. On Hutcheson, see Paul Ramsay, introduction to *Works*, 8:40, n. 4.; and McCosh, *Scottish Philosophy*, 49–85. On Wollaston, Ramsay in *Works*, 8:570, n.1.
27. *Works*, 8:339, 540.

28. Ibid., 544, 540–41, 552, 558.

29. Ibid., 570.

30. *Works*, 18:73–76.

31. *Works*, 8:575, 577.

32. Ibid., 591, 592–93.

33. Ibid., 596, 597, 599.

34. On Hume, ibid., 604, n. 1, and 603–04 for the quotations here.

35. Ibid., 605.

36. Ibid., 610–11, 619, 621.

37. Edwards to Erskine, in *Works*, 16:248–49.

38. Taylor's *Scripture-Doctrine* was first published in 1740, but Erskine sent Edwards its third, a Belfast, Ireland, edition. On Taylor, see Clyde A. Holbrook, introduction to *Works*, 3:68–70.

39. On Briant, Mayhew, and Arminian thought in general in early America, see Conrad Wright, *The Beginnings of Unitarianism in America* (Boston: Beacon Press, 1955).

40. Edwards to Thomas Gillespie, November 24, 1752, in *Works*, 16:546.

41. On this acrimonious debate, see Joseph Haroutunian, *Piety Versus Moralism: The Passing of the New England Theology* (New York: Henry Holt, 1932), 15–42.

42. Edwards to Foxcroft, February 11, 1757, in *Works*, 16:696, and 3:102.

43. On Turnbull and Edwards, see Holbrook, introduction to *Works*, 3:70–74.

44. Ibid., 107.

45. Ibid., 121, 120, 129.

46. Ibid., 158.

47. Ibid., 353, 357.

48. Ibid., 381.

49. Ibid., 382.

50. Ibid., 397.

51. Ibid., 397–99.

52. Ibid., 401–04.

53. For a provocative reading of the immediate social context of *Original Sin* — that is, Edwards's Stockbridge pastorate — see Wheeler, "'Friends to Your Souls,'" 736–65. Wheeler notes that the egalitarian implications of this treatise may have derived in part from his experience with the Native Americans.

9. PRINCETON (1757–1758)

1. On Burr and his presidency, see Thomas J. Wertenbaker, *Princeton, 1746–1896* (Princeton: Princeton University Press, 1946), 3–47; and John Maclean, *History of the College of New Jersey, from Its Origin in 1746 to the Commencement of 1854*, 2 vols. (Philadelphia: Lippincott & Co., 1877), 1:127–68.

2. Carol F. Karlsen and Laurie Crumpacker, eds., *The Journal of Esther Edwards Burr, 1747–1757* (New Haven: Yale University Press, 1984), 289.

3. Edwards to William McCullough, November 24, 1752, in *Works*, 16:544.

4. The center of this circle was the remarkable poet Annis Boudinot Stockton, who kept a literary salon at her Princeton home. See Carla Mulford's introduction to *Only for the Eye of a Friend: The Poems of Annis Boudinot Stockton* (Charlottesville: University Press of Virginia, 1995).

5. Edwards to Esther Edwards Burr, March 28, 1753, in *Works*, 16:577, and Edwards to Thomas Foxcroft, May 4, 1753, ibid., 595.

6. Edwards to Aaron Burr, May 6, 1752, ibid., 478.

7. Burr, cited in a letter from Edwards to John Erskine, April 12, 1757, ibid., 703–04.

8. Ibid., 704.

9. Edwards to Esther Edwards Burr, November 20, 1757, ibid., 730.

10. Ibid., 731.

11. Edwards to the trustees of the College of New Jersey, October 19, 1757, ibid., 725–26.

12. Ibid., 726.

13. Ibid., 726–27.

14. Ibid., 727–28.

15. Ibid., 729.

16. Ibid.

17. Hopkins, *Life*, 78.

18. Edwards to Gideon Hawley, January 14, 1758, in *Works*, 16:737.

19. Hopkins, *Life*, 79. On Edwards's career at Princeton, see Maclean, *History of the College of New Jersey*, 169–91.

20. Hopkins, *Life*, 80–81.

21. Clyde A. Holbrook, introduction to *Works*, 3:19.

22. See John F. Wilson, introduction to *Works*, 9:17. Wilson cites a letter from Samuel Hopkins to Joseph Bellamy, January 19, 1758, in which he told of Edwards's having left his papers in Great Barrington.

23. On Hopkins, see Joseph A. Conforti, *Samuel Hopkins and the New Divinity Movement: Calvinism, the Congregational Ministry, and Reform in New England Between the Great Awakenings* (Grand Rapids, MI: Christian University Press, 1981).

24. On Bellamy, see Mark Valeri, *Law and Providence in Joseph Bellamy's New England: The Origins of the New Divinity in Revolutionary America* (New York: Oxford University Press, 1994).

25. Paul Ramsey, introduction to *Works*, 8:3–5.

26. Samuel Hopkins to Joseph Bellamy, April 4, 1768, cited by Ramsey, ibid., 114, n. 7.

27. John Erskine to Joseph Bellamy, June 8, 1759, cited in Wilson, introduction to *Works*, 9:18.

28. N. Hazard to Joseph Bellamy, October 31, 1759, cited in ibid., 18–19.

29. Jonathan Edwards, Jr., preface to Jonathan Edwards, *A History of the Work of Redemption* (Edinburgh: W. Gray, 1774), iii, cited in Wilson, introduction to *Works*, 9:21.

30. Ezra Stiles, *The Literary Diary of Ezra Stiles, D.D., LL.D.*, ed. Franklin B. Dexter, 3 vols. (New York: Charles Scribner's Sons, 1901), 3:275.

31. For my understanding of Edwards's recuperation in the nineteenth century, I am indebted to Joseph A. Conforti, *Jonathan Edwards, Religious Tradition, and American Culture* (Chapel Hill: University of North Carolina Press, 1995), esp. 11–86.

32. Douglas A. Sweeney, *Nathaniel William Taylor, New Haven Theology, and the Legacy of Jonathan Edwards* (New York: Oxford University Press, 2003), 141–42, speaks of such an "enculturation" of Edwards's thought.

33. On these revivals, see David W. Kling, *A Field of Divine Wonders: The New Divinity and Village Revivals in Northwest Connecticut, 1792–1822* (University Park: Pennsylvania State University Press, 1993).

34. On Edwards's publication in this period, see Thomas H. Johnson, *The Printed Writings of Jonathan Edwards, 1703–1758: A Bibliography* (Princeton: Princeton University Press, 1940).

35. See Conforti, *Jonathan Edwards*, 18–21; "Life and Character of Rev. Jonathan Edwards," *Connecticut Evangelical Magazine and Religious Intelligencer*, 1 (1808); *The Works of President Edwards, in Eight Volumes* (Worcester, MA: Isaiah Thomas, Jr., 1808); Benjamin Trumbull, *A Complete History of Connecticut, Civil and Ecclesiastical*, 2 vols. (New London: Maltsby, Goldsmith and Company, 1818), 2:134–264.

36. See Conforti, *Jonathan Edwards*, 33–34, 46.

37. The literature on sentiment in the antebellum period is legion, but see especially Ann Douglas, *The Feminization of American Culture* (New York: Knopf, 1977); Julie Ellison, *Cato's Tears and the Making of Anglo-American Emotion* (Chicago: University of Chicago Press, 1999); Mary Louise Kete, *Sentimental Collaborations: Mourning and Middle-Class Identity in Nineteenth-Century America* (Durham, NC: Duke University Press, 2000); Lori Merish, *Sentimental Materialism: Gender, Commodity Culture, and Nineteenth-Century American Literature* (Durham, NC: Duke University Press, 2000); Glenn Hendler, *Public Sentiments: Structures of Feeling in Nineteenth-Century American Literature* (Chapel Hill: University of North Carolina Press, 2001); and Glenn Hendler and Mary Chapman, eds., *Sentimental Men: Masculinity and the Politics of Affect in American Culture* (Berkeley and Los Angeles: University of California Press, 1999).

38. Joseph Tracy, *The Great Awakening: A History of the Revival of Religion in the Time of Edwards and Whitefield* (Boston: Tappan and Dennet, 1842).

39. Conforti, *Jonathan Edwards*, 62–86.

10. CODA: THINKING THROUGH EDWARDS

1. D[avid] Sherman, *Sketches of New England Divines* (New York: Carlton & Porter, 1860), 138.

2. Joseph Bellamy to Thomas Foxcroft, May 6, 1749, cited in Donald Weber, "The Recovery of Jonathan Edwards," in *Jonathan Edwards and the American Experience*, ed. Nathan O. Hatch and Harry S. Stout (New York: Oxford University Press, 1988), 52.

3. Bellamy to Samuel Hopkins, January 30, 1756, cited in ibid., 53.

4. Benjamin Trumbull, *A Complete History of Connecticut, Civil and Ecclesiastical*, 2 vols. (New London: Maltsby, Goldsmith and Company, 1818), 2:145. On the persistence of interest in this sermon, see Edward J. Gallagher, "'Sinners in the Hands of an Angry God': Some Unfinished Business," *New England Quarterly*, 73:2 (June 2000), 202–21.

5. Sherman, *Sketches*, 149.

6. On the American Tract Society and its publications, see David Paul Nord, "The Evangelical Origins of Mass Media in America, 1815–1835," *Journalism Monographs*, 88 (May 1984), and "Free Books, Free Grace, Free Riders: The Economics of Religious Publishing in Early Nineteenth-Century America," *Proceedings of the American Antiquarian Society*, 106:2 (October 1996), 241–72.

7. Edwards to Thomas Gillespie, July 1, 1751, in *Works*, 16:384.

8. Here, as elsewhere in my invocation of the "agency" that the revivals made possible, I follow James A. Block's brilliant *A Nation of Agents: The American Path to a Modern Self and Society* (Cambridge: Harvard University Press, 2002), esp. part II. I have also profited from Allen C. Guelzo's "God's Designs: The Literature of the Colonial Revivals of Religion, 1735–1760," in *New Directions in American Religious History*, ed. Hary S. Stout and D. G. Hart (New York: Oxford University Press, 1997), 141–72. Underlying both these is Alan Heimert's magisterial *Religion and the American Mind, from the Great Awakening to the Revolution* (Cambridge: Harvard University Press, 1966).

9. John Cotton, *An Exposition on the Thirteenth Chapter of the Revelation* (London: 1655), 77.

10. Perry Miller, "From Edwards to Emerson, in *Errand into the Wilderness* (Cambridge: Harvard University Press, 1956), 184–203; see 184–85.

11. Perry Miller, *Jonathan Edwards* (New York: William Sloane Associates, 1949).

12. "Personal Narrative," in *Works*, 16:793.

13. See Douglas A. Sweeney, *Nathaniel William Taylor, New Haven Theology, and the Legacy of Jonathan Edwards* (New York: Oxford University Press, 2003), 141–42. Some have remarked such connections between eighteenth-century theology and Romanticism in England; see particularly Richard E. Brantley, *Locke, Wesley, and the Method of English Romanticism* (Gainesville:

University Press of Florida, 1984) and *Coordinates of Anglo-American Romanticism: Wesley, Edwards, Carlyle and Emerson* (Gainesville: University Press of Florida, 1993).

14. See, for example, such recent work on the culture of sentiment as Julia Sterne, *The Plight of Feeling: Sympathy and Dissent in the Early American Novel* (Chicago: University of Chicago Press, 1997); Elizabeth Barnes, *States of Sympathy: Seduction and Democracy in the American Novel* (New York: Columbia University Press, 1997); Julie Ellison, *Cato's Tears and the Making of Anglo-American Emotion* (Chicago: University of Chicago Press, 1999); Mary Louise Kete, *Sentimental Collaborations: Mourning and Middle-Class Identity in Nineteenth-Century America* (Durham, NC: Duke University Press, 2000); Lori Merish, *Sentimental Materialism: Gender, Commodity Culture, and Nineteenth-Century American Literature* (Durham, NC: Duke University Press, 2000); Glenn Hendler, *Public Sentiments: Structures of Feeling in Nineteenth-Century American Literature* (Chapel Hill: University of North Carolina Press, 2001); and Glenn Hendler and Mary Chapman, eds., *Sentimental Men: Masculinity and the Politics of Affect in American Culture* (Berkeley and Los Angeles: University of California Press, 1999).

15. *Works*, 3:424.

16. Maria Cummins, *The Lamplighter*, ed. Nina Baym (1854; New Brunswick, NJ: Rutgers University Press, 1988), 305.

17. *Works*, 9:520.

18. *Works*, 8:374, 396.

Acknowledgments

I do not presume that herein there is somehow a "new" Edwards, for other scholars (most recently, George Marsden, whose *Jonathan Edwards* [2003] now stands as the definitive life) have established the general contours of his biography as well as its discrete facts. Indeed, as I considered this project, I admit to a bit of relief when I learned that Professor Marsden was completing his. His biography liberated me to concentrate on what I call a *consideration* of Edwards, as I range selectively through his life and works to locate those moments that suggest his largest significance to the twenty-first-century reader.

Like any contemporary scholar of Edwards, I also am immensely indebted to the editors of *The Works of Jonathan Edwards*, which, as I write, extends to twenty-three magnificent volumes and whose introductions constitute the primary scholarship in the field. The heroic labor that has gone into *The Works*, particularly in the transcription and dating of thousands of Edwards's manuscript pages, has brought to light whole new aspects of his habits of reading and composition. Only the recently completed edition of the *Journals and Miscellaneous Notebooks of Ralph Waldo Emerson* has comparable importance for American cultural history.

As I stand on the shoulders of these scholars, as well as on those of all the others who, from Samuel Hopkins on, have grappled with the complexity of Edwards and his legacy, I must single out the individuals most instrumental to my own introduction to this thinker. First is Richard Rabinowitz, founder and director of the American History Workshop, who in the spring of 1969 admitted me to Harvard College's concentration in American history and literature. Shortly thereafter Richard left graduate school for Old Sturbridge Village, where he began a revolution in the ways that outdoor history museums represented and interpreted the past. At the same time, he lived in and was caretaker of Roseland Cottage in historic Woodstock, Connecticut, where he hosted undergraduate interns whom he had lured to work at the Village (as employees affectionately call it). There at the Pink House, usually after arcane games of Botticelli, he shared his enthusiasm for his two great loves in American culture, Herman Melville and Jonathan Edwards. There too Richard let me browse in his magnificent collection of primary sources in American church history, including Isaiah Thomas's 1808–1809 edition of Edwards's *Works*, which formed the basis for Richard's pathbreaking *The Spiritual Self in Everyday Life* (1989).

In the late 1960s others who studied (as Richard had) under the aegis of Perry Miller extended my introduction to Edwards. Among these were Gail Thain Parker, soon to become the youngest president of Bennington College (and who published "Jonathan Edwards and Melancholy"), and Barry O'Connell, who worked as Alan Heimert's research assistant as he wrote *Religion and the American Mind, from Awakening to Revolution* (1966), a magisterial treatment of the influence of Edwardsean thought on the revolutionary generation. And there is the late Heimert himself, who lived and breathed Edwards's thought, having learned it at the feet of Perry Miller. If in 1972, when I completed a senior thesis under Heimert's direction, someone had told me that someday I too would write a book on Edwards, I would have laughed, Heimert's erudition on the subject (and, indeed, on all American history and literature) so intimidated me. Having arrived at a degree of intellectual maturity, if not at the level of sophistication he represented, I am saddened that he cannot cast his eagle eye over what I have done. This book is, in large measure, written in homage to him, with respect for what he taught about how in the late twentieth century one could take Edwards seriously.

Ernestine Rathborne, a year behind me in Harvard's History and Literature program, knew me well enough to give me, from her exuberant generosity, a copy of the Yale edition of Edwards's *Treatise Concerning the Religious Affections*, accompanied by a poem written for the occasion.

At the same time as Ernestine gave me the *Treatise*, I began to take an interest in books as physical artifacts with their own intrinsic interest, a path that led me eventually to the new field of the history of the book and of print culture. Thus, as I pursued my interest in Edwards, I found my way to secondhand bookshops. On a frosty morning in October 1969 Richard Rabinowitz brought me to a bookstore along the Connecticut River in Westmoreland, New Hampshire, where I bought an early edition, albeit "crippled," of Edwards's *Farewell Sermon*. Closer to home, in Sturbridge, Massachusetts, I acquired a copy of the American Tract Society's edition of Edwards's *Religious Affections*. In bookstores in Connecticut I found a copy not only of the true first edition (London: 1737) of *A Faithful Narrative of the Surprising Conversions* but, even more rare, of William Williams's *Duty and Interest of a People* (1736), which carries as a brief appendix (in tiny type) Edwards's original letter to Benjamin Colman describing the Northampton, Massachusetts, revivals. Finally, on an early visit to Chapel Hill, when it was not yet my home, I purchased a first edition of *Freedom of the Will*. Sad to say, over the years as the exigencies of family life demanded, I parted with these books. Thus I wish to thank Dr. Ted Steinbock for kindly sending me a handful of Edwards's volumes from his magnificent collection of American imprints to serve as talismans as I wrote this book.

At the University of North Carolina my colleagues Darryl Gless and James Thompson expedited my work in various ways; I heartily thank them for their long-standing support (and indulgence) of my scholarship. Ruel Tyson graciously extended an invitation to the Institute for the Arts and Humanities, where I enjoyed much good fellowship. I thank my students Anne Bruder, Maura McKee, Karah Rempe, Bryan Sinche, and Elizabeth Stockton, who spent a semester reading early American religious thought with me while I was writing this book. Their questions and comments helped focus my work.

As always, I thank my wife, Leslie, and children, David, Katherine, and Daniel, for tolerating my idiosyncrasies and overlooking my foibles.

Index

AMERICAN PORTRAITS

Edited by Louis P. Masur and Thomas P. Slaughter

Published and Forthcoming Titles

Eric Arnesen on A. Philip Randolph

Mia Bay on Ida B. Wells

Philip Gura on Jonathan Edwards

Steven W. Hackel on Father Junipero Serra

Charles Ponce de Leon on Elvis Presley

Darren Staloff on Alexander Hamilton,
John Adams, and Thomas Jefferson

Camilla Townsend on Pocahontas